Steve McQueen

Steve McQueen

LIVING ON THE EDGE

Michael Munn

BOOKS

First published in Great Britain in 2010 by
JR Books, 10 Greenland Street, London NW1 0ND
www.jrbooks.com

First published in paperback, 2011

A catalogue record for this book is available from the British Library.

ISBN 978-1-907532-35-1

1 3 5 7 9 10 8 6 4 2

Printed by CPI Bookmarque, Croydon

Contents

This book is especially for Betty

Introduction

Steve McQueen was the last person in the world I expected to find in Cornwall – England's southernmost county; the foot of Great Britain – in September 1970. But there he was, at a house director Sam Peckinpah was renting in Penzance while scouting locations for *Straw Dogs*, which he would shoot there in early 1971. McQueen was eating breakfast, drinking coffee and smoking a cigarette.

Steve McQueen was the most depressed person I'd ever seen in my 17 years and 11 months, and for some reason he had chosen to take refuge from his personal and private crises in the reluctant arms of Sam Peckinpah, who, it turned out, didn't want him there at all. But he had turned up some time in the night, probably not many hours after I'd staggered off to my B&B after an evening in which Peckinpah did his best to get me as drunk as him – an impossibility – and, although I didn't know it, he was trying to figure out how to get rid of McQueen.

A few years later, on location in Yugoslavia, where I went to watch him filming *Cross of Iron*, Peckinpah admitted to me that he had no idea why McQueen came to him in his time of crisis because they were hardly friends, especially since McQueen had not intervened when Peckinpah was fired from Steve's hit movie *The Cincinnati Kid*.

McQueen had simply turned up out of the blue, having fled from France, where his dream project *Le Mans* had turned into a nightmare, generally of Steve's own making, and from his marriage, which had also turned into a living hell, again of his own making. His wife, Neile, had fled France a week or so earlier back to California with their children, Chad and Terry.

McQueen, it seemed, had escaped France too, for a few days, arriving in England but finding no one to call a friend – until he heard that Sam Peckinpah was in Cornwall.

As it turned out, I wasn't really wanted either by Peckinpah. I was there purely as a learning experience. I worked in the publicity department of the Cinerama film company in London, had met Peckinpah a few months before in London and had persuaded him to allow me to come down and observe him at work. He was adamant I couldn't be there for the actual filming, but he allowed me to visit during pre-production. By the time I arrived, overflowing with youthful enthusiasm, he had come to regret his decision.

It was mid-morning when I walked bleary-eyed into Peckinpah's kitchen to find McQueen sitting at the breakfast table.

'This is the young fella I was telling you about,' said Peckinpah.

I was, of course, shocked but also delighted to come face to face with Steve McQueen. I was a movie maniac, and I loved meeting movie-stars. I never got over the thrill of it. I wanted to be a film director, which is why I wanted to spend time with Peckinpah and, for a long period of my life, spending time with some of the greatest names in movie history – at least, the ones in my lifetime – was what I did. That was my life.

Steve was polite, quiet and curiously interested in me. I didn't know it but Peckinpah had told him I was a juvenile delinquent, and I was even able to relate to Steve a few embellished tales of my teenage escapades which I'd told to Sam the night before under the influence of alcohol.

I was to discover over the next few days that Steve had a sincere passion about helping young people, especially those who were in trouble with the law. Steve was himself a reformed juvenile delinquent, or as he put it, 'I was the most delinquentist kid you ever saw.'

For the next four days he was to become my counsellor, my teacher and my mentor. Now, I have to point out that I never was an actual juvenile delinquent, but I did get into a bit of trouble with a few gangsters when I was 14, out of which I was helped by none other than Frank Sinatra at the behest of George Raft, who, for reason I'm not going into at this time, felt responsible for my seemingly imminent criminal career. And I wouldn't have even mentioned Sinatra but for the fact that he was to also play a part in my mentor–delinquent relationship with McQueen, as I'll explain later.

So there we were, a depressed movie-star with a mission, and a young man thrilled suddenly to have the attention of one of the greatest movie-stars on the planet – neither of whom was wanted by Sam Peckinpah.

It helped that I sort of looked the part of a youth in need of guidance. I liked to wear jeans and a denim jacket and, for reasons too embarrassing to explain, I wore a bandana. I was dark-haired, Italian-looking, lean and looking like I was ready to jump on a motorbike. Appearances are often deceiving. Motorbikes scared me – still do.

Steve was dirty, unshaven, in jeans and a T-shirt, and he looked every bit the motorcycle-riding escaping POW I'll never forget from *The Great Escape*. And my questions to him about that movie, and the famous motorcycle jump over the barbed-wire fence, led him to invite me to take a ride with him.

I didn't want to admit I was scared of motorbikes, or anything that went fast, or didn't have sides to it, but Peckinpah murmured to me, 'If you do this he'll be your friend for life. If you don't, you'll lose face.'

Not realising I could cope with not being his friend for life and not wanting to lose face, I accepted the invitation. He said he'd be back soon, disappeared from the house, and returned an hour later with the biggest motorbike I have ever seen.

He told me to get on behind him. I said, 'Where are the helmets?'

He said, 'We don't need helmets.'

So with Sam Peckinpah quietly urging me on and standing there to wave goodbye to us, I got on, trying not to look afraid, and off we roared – Steve McQueen and I – on a road trip that would last not just the few hours I expected but four days, leaving on Tuesday and returning on Friday.

Down winding country lanes, overtaking traffic, reaching God knows what speed. We didn't stick to roads. We tore across fields we probably had no business being in, sending one herd of cattle stampeding.

We circled a lake and sent ducks, geese and swans that had been dozing on the bank flapping and quacking and hooting into the river. We roared through a wood, missing trees by inches, Steve somehow finding a track almost as if by instinct; he certainly didn't know the area and had no planned route to follow. I have no idea how he did it.

We rode like that for about half an hour – it seemed like a day to me, hanging on terrified but never complaining. Steve was loving it. My ordeal seemed to be over when we pulled up outside an old country pub. 'Let's get a few beers and some food,' said Steve.

The pub landlord didn't realise at first that he had Steve McQueen walking into his pub. The landlord was a genial, fat man, delighted to be of service, and it was only after we had ordered food and he had brought it to our table that he said, 'Pardon me, but you are Steve McQueen, aren't you?'

'Yeah, but keep it to yourself, will ya?'

The landlord put a finger to his lips. 'Mum's the word.'

'Yeah, well, that'd be good.'

Steve told the landlord to put the beers and food on his tab. There was no question about whether he could have one; the landlord wasn't going to deny Steve McQueen a tab.

Over lunch, Steve began telling me about his early life by way of encouraging me to talk about mine. I felt I needed to think of something to tell him, so I told him a little about the time I was friends with George Raft and had hooked up with a Mafia friend of his who got me into a spot of trouble. This delighted Steve, who wanted to know more. So I told him. He got especially interested when the name of Frank Sinatra came into the story.

It seemed as though what I told Steve made him decide something. He asked the landlord if he had a couple of rooms we could have until tomorrow, which he did, and so we settled in.

That night, after we had a long talk, he put in a call to Frank Sinatra. I know this because Steve told me what he did the next morning. 'Frank said you're okay.' That seemed to matter. I didn't know then that Steve had an inbuilt distrust of people, but his passion to help young offenders and Sinatra's recommendation allowed me to earn his trust, and I wasn't even trying. I just thought I was having a great time with Steve McQueen, still thinking we'd be going back to Peckinpah's house some time soon.

The second day we rode for hours, stopping briefly now and then, but mostly it just seemed that Steve liked riding endlessly. He told me it made 'a big difference' riding through the English countryside to riding into the desert. I think he meant it made a pleasant change.

We stopped at another country inn for the night, and again we sat up for hours as he told me about his life. He wasn't listening to me quite so much now but delving deeply into his own misspent youth. This, I was to discover over the ensuing years, was a practice of his with people he came to like and trust. I think it was his way of trying to exorcise his past and the demons which followed him through life, but it was also something else. Steve was a competitor.

I came to realise that what he was doing with me was saying, 'You think you had a bad time. Wait till you hear what happened to *me*.' And, 'You think you were a bad kid –' which I didn't – 'wait till you hear what *I* got up to.' And sure enough, a lot of what he told me had the hairs on my neck standing to attention.

'Steve has to prove he had a worse childhood than anybody else,' James Coburn told me. 'Only one other person I know can compete with him and that's Charlie Bronson.'

McQueen always felt *nobody* had it worse than him. And, as it happened, it was just about the most deprived and troubled childhood I have ever heard first-hand. (Mind you, Charlie Bronson also had harrowing tales to tell.)

From the day I started at Cinerama, almost a year before this, I had learned a lesson from the company's managing director: write down everything anyone famous says to me so I will always remember it. And that's what I did. I had great recall back then, able to remember almost verbatim what anyone ever told me, if I found it interesting, and each evening I would write it down. I wrote maybe two dozen pages during my road trip with Steve McQueen.

He was, perhaps, the most inarticulate actor I ever knew. He often had trouble finding the right words to express himself. He also had a very 'hip' vocabulary and used a lot of four-letter words. In transcribing his words for the purpose of this book, I have at times filled in words which I believed he was searching for and often couldn't find, but I have also tried to maintain his simple style of delivery because there was something of the essence of the man in his inarticulation. (I have also removed much of his swearing.)

During those late evenings and nights, he relaxed by smoking dope. I didn't. I never touched it. But I was used to people around me using it. He said he needed it to relax. (Well, a lot of people in entertainment use it – always have, always will.) In the mornings, he tended to wake up surprisingly early considering we had talked much of the night, and he was unbelievably active. He wasn't so much energetic as hyperactive. He simply had trouble staying still.

He had, I think, the kind of hyperactive behaviour that one usually associates with a child. In fact, he was, in many ways, like a child. He had a childlike attitude to life, as though he never completely grew up. He lost his temper when he couldn't get his own way. He played practical jokes on people and laughed with glee. Like a child, he had a contradictory nature, going from being your best friend to suddenly being your worst enemy. Happily I never became his enemy, but then, I didn't see him often enough. And also, I was never what I could claim to be a really close friend of his.

But for four days in September 1970 I was his best and only friend. In that time Steve went from being a paternal mentor to seeing me as his confessor, as though he had to unburden himself. He talked to me about how his career rose and fell – virtually sliding off the track with *Le Mans* – and how he came to find himself on the brink of divorce from a woman he had loved from the start, and whom I think he loved to the very end.

This book is based largely on the things he told me in 1970. We met again in 1974, then in early 1977, when he came to England and actually sought me out. I didn't see him again, but did speak to him on the telephone from Yul Brynner's house (when Brynner was in London for *The King and I*) in 1980, just weeks before Steve died. He hadn't yet publicly announced he was suffering from mesothelioma, a rare form of cancer, and even many of his closest friends were kept from the truth. But I had heard the rumours that inevitably sweep through the film industry, about his illness and his new-found Christianity (I was a journalist at *Photoplay* then). I had a special link with Steve because in 1977, the last time we met, we talked about how we both sought some kind of spirituality in our lives, and then in 1980, having both thought we had found answers to what we sought, we talked openly on the telephone about all that. We understood each other. He was forthright and didn't find it hard to admit to me that he was dying, or rather that he was *fighting* death, yet at the same time preparing for it.

Surprisingly, one of the few people he had told was Yul Brynner, who, many told me, he hated so much that nobody was ever to mention his name. In 1970 I hadn't known that golden rule, and broke it over and over without retribution. The fact was, in the end, he not only didn't hate Brynner, but actually felt beholden to him. So Brynner knew, and I knew, maybe because he thought I was a former juvenile delinquent he had helped rehabilitate (a fact I discovered in 1976, when Sam Peckinpah finally told me what he'd told Steve about my so-called misspent youth).

I never interviewed Steve. Everything he told me came out of our conversations.

I've drawn on interviews and conversations I've had over the years with many of Steve's friends and co-workers. This book is about their perceptions of him as much as it is about mine, and they do not always coincide with each other. He could be a kind, caring friend to some, and a troublemaking pain in the ass to others. Almost everyone agreed he was full of contradictions.

Virtually without exception, all the quotes in this book come from either formal interviews or casual conversations I had with people I was lucky enough to meet, or talk to over the telephone – I did a number of telephone interviews in November 1980 for a tribute I planned to write about Steve.

In no particular order, those people were James Coburn – I had known him as a friend since 1970, and interviewed him in 1979 in London, over the telephone in 1980, and in 1986 in London; Don Gordon – I interviewed him in London in 1980 when he was filming *Omen III: The Final Conflict* and then a few months later by telephone after Steve died; Suzanne Pleshette – I interviewed her by telephone in 1980 for my tribute, and again in 1984 in London; John Sturges – I worked with Sturges for a short time as a volunteering dogsbody when he was in London in 1976 doing pre-production on *The Eagle Has Landed*, and he shared many memories of Steve and other things; Don Siegel – I interviewed him at length when he was at Pinewood Studios doing pre-production in 1979 on *Rough Cut*; James Garner – I persuaded him to do an interview when I saw him in a London hotel in 1978 while I waited to interview another actor; Richard Attenborough – I interviewed him in London in 1977, 1978 and 1982, also over the telephone in 1980, and talked casually with him on the set of *Brannigan* in 1974; Gordon Jackson – I interviewed him in London on the set of *The Professionals* in 1978; Buzz Kulik – interviewed in England in 1988 when he directed *Around the World in 80 Days*; Eli Wallach – interviewed in Norfolk in 1981 when he was making *Tales of the Unexpected*; Ben Johnson – interviewed by telephone in 1980; William Wiard – interviewed in London in 1982; Charles Durning – interviewed in 1977 when he was in England making *The Greek Tycoon*, and by telephone in 1980; George Schaefer – interviewed in London,

1981; John Guillermin – interviewed at Pinewood Studios in 1977 when he was directing *Death on the Nile*; Franklin J. Schaffner – interviewed at Shepperton Studios in 1978 when he was directing *The Boys from Brazil*; Dustin Hoffman – interviewed in London in 1979 promoting *Kramer vs. Kramer*; Sam Peckinpah – interviewed in 1976 in Yugoslavia on location for *Cross of Iron*; Sally Struthers – interviewed in London in 1984; Peter Yates – interviewed over the telephone in 1980, and at Pinewood Studios in 1982 when he was directing *Krull*; Robert Wise – interviewed in 1979 in London promoting *Star Trek the Motion Picture*, and by telephone in 1980; Henry Hathaway – interviewed by telephone in 1974 and 1980; Rod Steiger – interviewed in London in 1984; Robert Culp – by telephone in 1980; Robert Mulligan – interviewed in London in 1982; Natalie Wood – a friend since 1971, I interviewed her in Manchester in 1976 when she was recording *Cat on a Hot Tin Roof*, and in London in 1980; Martin Landau – interviewed in 1979 at Elstree Studios where he was making *Space 1999*; Paul Newman – when I worked with Newman on some of his dialogue for *The Mackintosh Man* in 1972 there was lots of chat but no formal interview; Irvin S. Yeaworth Jr – I interviewed him in London in 1976, long after he had retired from making mainstream movies, and he was happy to talk about Steve McQueen and *The Blob*; Charles Bronson – interviewed in London in 1984 when he was making *Death Wish III*; Walter Mirisch – interviewed in 1978 at Shepperton Studios when producing *Dracula*, and by telephone in 1980; Mike Frankovich Jr – someone I came across a number of times in my life as a publicist when I was at Columbia between 1974 and 1975; Norman Jewison – interviewed by telephone in 1980; Robert Vaughn interviewed in London in 1982; Walter Hill – interviewed in London in 1975 when he was promoting *The Streetfighter* aka *Hard Times*).

And there was the conversations I had with Steve himself. Only now, 40 years on from my first experience of Steve McQueen in person, can I look back and realise what a fantastic time and a unique experience it was to have had that road trip with him, riding through Cornwall, Devon and Somerset, stopping to stay the night at country pubs, and talking into the late hours. During those four days on the road, and three nights in country inns, Steve opened his heart and soul, and I opened mine to him. Taking a road trip with Steve wasn't just a scary ride on a motorcycle. It was a window to his life, and a light into his darkest experiences and thoughts.

CHAPTER 1

—

Dumped

'I wasn't born. I was dumped.'

That's how Steve, 40 years after that event, described his arrival into the world. To say he was morose, as we sat in his room in a Devonshire inn that September of 1970 where he began to outline the highlights of his life, is to overstate it slightly, but he wasn't exactly celebrating his existence.

Steve was certainly making sure I knew that my working-class upbringing in post-war London, which I had nothing to complain about and didn't even consider deprived in any way, couldn't compare to what he went through. He didn't hold back his thoughts and memories, which didn't surprise Jim Coburn when I told him about it. 'Steve can usually sum up his life in three words. "It was *shit*!" But when he has someone's ears, he can really lay it on.'

I assume I was just the right pair of ears in the right place at the right time when he was, by his own admission, in a suicidal state of mind. He said he had actually tried to kill himself in a staged accident while shooting *Le Mans* in 1970, but had 'chickened out' at the last minute and turned away from the pile-up.

He knew his marriage to Neile was all but over, and his career was on the skids. He didn't know where to go from here. So he talked. A lot. Seven years later, when I reminded him about it, he said, 'Taking a bike trip will do that.' I assumed he meant that it would do that to *him*. Steve was sometimes so laconic that he made economy with words almost an art form. He did that on screen too. 'Just say what you have to say and move on,' he told me, talking about acting . . . and life.

He was dumped into the world on 24 March 1930 in a small hospital in Beech Grove, a suburb of Indianapolis. His mother was a woman he hated from the moment he discovered he had emotions. 'She was a whore,' he said.

Her name was Julia Ann Crawford. She was called Julie-Anne as a child, and it became Julian by the time Steve was born. She'd left her family's farm in 1927 and went on to make a meagre existence by dancing in bars with men who paid for the privilege. They paid for sex too. 'I guess she did what she thought she had to do,' was Steve's comment on her lifestyle.

Steve's father was a former navy pilot, Bill McQueen. Julian had met him in 1929 and 'they shacked up'. Steve never knew his father properly. 'The only thing he gave me was his genes.'

Steve inherited Bill's addiction to danger; Bill loved aeroplanes and had worked in an aerobatic circus after leaving the navy. 'My dad didn't seem to mind that he could get killed.' It might seem that Steve sometimes thought that way too, but he dismissed that idea, despite a history of crashing speeding cars, saying, 'I don't speed to die, I speed to live.' I expect Bill McQueen thought that too, but Steve preferred to think of his dad as being irresponsibly reckless. I think Steve would have preferred to have been able to look up to his father with pride, but Steve was to become a child abandoned by his father, and so was never able to have anything other than negative feelings about his dad. Had things been different, Steve would undoubtedly have been able to boast he was 'a chip off the old block'. For the rest of his life, Steve searched for substitute father figures.

Before meeting Julian, and with a windfall of $2,000, Bill opened an illegal casino on Illinois Street in Indianapolis, but when it failed and closed, he drifted around, by then a hopeless alcoholic. He was only in his late 20s when he shacked up with Julian, but he was, said Steve, 'an old man'.

Still, Bill did look for work, but the Depression deprived him and many Americans of an honest living. He and Julian lived in a rooming house and were so poor that when Steve was born they were able to receive funds under the Poor Law.

I asked Steve if Bill married Julian, since Steve had his surname. 'Who knows? Who gives a shit? He dumped me and Mom when I was six months old.'

Julian and Bill might have married, but Steve always felt like he was illegitimate. 'I was born a bastard. I'll die a bastard.' Even if the first part of his mantra was true, the last part would prove to be false. While some would have considered him a bastard when he was at the peak of his career, he died a much changed man, a relatively decent man, and one who was humbled by terminal disease and a conversion to Christianity.

By 1977 he had begun to see his life differently, telling me, 'I'm not angry no more. It took me a long time to know it but I only got successful because of what I was – where I came from, so I can't complain.' He had, by then, spent most of his life complaining about his upbringing. But in 1980, when he was dying from cancer, he said, 'I was born in shit. I'll die in grace. I didn't do so bad.'

But 1970 was the year he went over the edge, having been living on the edge all his life, and he didn't hold back on unleashing his angst. Or his hatred for his mother. 'I couldn't love her. She never loved me.' He paraphrased Shakespeare. 'The sins of the mother are to be laid on the children. I got 'em all.' I was impressed he knew Shakespeare. He admitted, 'I read it somewhere. Haven't a clue what it's from.' (*The Merchant of Venice* is the answer to that.)

Six months after he deserted Julian and Steve, Bill returned, begging for forgiveness, but Julian turned him away. Steve hated his mother for turning away his dad, and he hated his dad for leaving him. That was a lot of hate for one small child to carry around. By the time Steve was an adult, he no longer hated his father. His emotions for him were mixed, but he insisted it wasn't hate. 'I couldn't hate him. I didn't *know* him.'

I asked Steve if he thought his life would have been better if

Julian had let Bill back in. 'Who knows? She couldn't keep a man. She always found the wrong kind.'

He couldn't remember how old he was, but he had a vivid memory of hearing Julian screaming from upstairs in some slum house where they lived for a while. 'She sounded like she was being killed. I ran up the stairs. Thought I'd find her being killed. She was in bed with a sailor. He was paying her so he could hurt her. I can't forget it. I figured women didn't mind being hurt.' He never used that as an excuse when he admitted that he hit his wife Neile. In 1970, their marriage had reached a crisis point in France when he discovered she had been having an affair (he ignored the fact that he had multiple affairs). He lashed out at her.

'I can't help myself when I get so fuckin' . . .' He didn't finish the sentence but I would guess he was going to say 'angry'. Anger was something that just came naturally to him. He was angry at his mom for letting a sailor hurt her for money. He never stopped being angry at her, right up until the day she died. He grew up with no respect for women. He believed they were servile creatures. A wife was someone who stayed home, took care of his kids, cooked his meals and was available for sex. That didn't mean he didn't love his wives – Neile Adams, Ali MacGraw and Barbara Minty – but he insisted they all sacrifice their careers for him. And they did. Which means that he wasn't as irredeemable as he thought himself to be. They loved him enough to do what it took to make him happy. But those marriages – or the first two, since the last was terminated by his death – were strained by his almost caveman attitude. The trouble was, he never had the chance to learn to respect women. He was never able to respect his mother. She drank heavily and had sex for money.

The neighbours also heard Julian screaming. 'The grown-ups and the bigger kids *knew* what she was doing. The kids laughed at me for not knowing.' He remembered the feeling of shame and humiliation he suffered. He was a small kid in britches. All the other kids his age were bigger, and they were poor too, but, said Steve, 'they were rich to what I had. They had parents.'

He was often teased mercilessly by the kids on the block. They shoved him around, stopping short of actually beating him. He'd go off on his own and cry, walking the streets where drunks were on every corner and rats ran in and out of buildings. 'I took it out on the rats,' he said. 'I beat them with sticks, though most were too fast for me. I hated going home coz I never knew if she was turning a trick. And when I knew she was, I stayed out. I had nowhere to go, and no kid to be my friend.'

Before he was five he was a loner, an outsider, pacing the streets and fending off unwanted advances from predatory old men. 'These old shits would come out of doorways and try to grab me. They'd speak nicely, but they scared me, so I always dodged them.'

He told Julian about these men and, for the first and only time he could remember, she hugged him tightly. 'Stay away from them,' she told him. When he recalled that moment to me, he said, 'It was the only time I knew she loved me. After that I never knew it again. I told her if only she'd let me be with her, if she'd stop taking men to our house, I'd be safer. I remember that. But she didn't stop what she did.'

Steve also remembered being five and telling his mother, 'I'm starving.' She drank away much of the money she made whoring. Not long after that they both moved in with Julian's uncle, Claude Thomson, who ran a 320-acre hog farm near Slater, a small faming community in Missouri. 'He was rich compared to everyone I ever knew,' said Steve.

Julian's parents were also living there; her mother, Lillian, a devout Catholic, was Claude's sister. Claude couldn't be described as a devout anything, except as a hard worker who imbibed moonshine. He was also the first man who showed kindness to Steve.

'I think he loved me, though he never showed it,' said Steve. 'He wasn't that kind of man. But he made me feel loved. That was the first time in my life I felt happy. I'd just been dead inside for the first five years.'

Not that Claude was a pushover. He had strict rules which Steve had to abide by, and he made Steve work for his keep. 'Milking cows, cutting wood, out in the cornfields,' recalled

Steve. 'If Claude caught me slacking, he whacked me with a hickory switch. It didn't harm me. I already had violence in me, just waiting to come out. When Claude beat me with a stick I learned quickly – do your work and you don't get hit. You don't work, you don't eat.'

'One day Claude said to me, "You know what your mother is?" I don't know if I really understood what she was. At five, when your mom is a whore, you don't know other moms aren't. Claude said, "She won't be no more." I took that to mean she wouldn't be making men hurt her. He said, "This is our family." I think I remember hugging him, and if I did it was the first and last time coz he was never a hugger. Or maybe I *wish* I'd hugged him, just that one time. I thought he was my new dad. He loved me a lot, and he disciplined me a lot, too. I needed it a lot. I mean, both love and discipline. But one time when I told him I thought of him as my dad, he said very gently, "I'm not your dad. I'm your Uncle Claude. That's all I need to be to you." He was right, but I wished he was my dad.'

It wasn't long before Steve had to make do without any kind of a true parent; Julian left without even saying goodbye to her son.

Steve recalled the farm as 'a big ol' rambling place where the paint was older than the earth. It was a new life for me. A lot of animals. I really dug animals. I even felt bad about the rats I killed.'

The rats on the farm, he recalled, were as big as cats. 'I'd bash 'em on the head with big sticks,' said Steve, 'over and over till they were dead. I hated doing that. I was just a kid and killing didn't come easy. But I'm glad I did it then coz it made me hate killing, and sometimes I think I might have grown up different. Maybe I could have been a killer, or liked killing, either in the army or on the streets. I can be a violent man when I get worked up to it, so I sometimes feel like there were times when I might have killed someone. But killing rats made me hate killing anything.'

Steve was killing rats when he was just five. He was also learning to be angry and to hate. A group of local boys in Slater used to taunt him as he passed them, always on his own, always lonely. They'd call out 'Bastard!' Steve remembered, 'I just kept on walking, my head down, ashamed, hating them. I wouldn't let them see me cry. I did my crying when I was out of sight of them.'

After a year or so of this taunting, Steve cracked. He might have been six or seven, but he had become so full of rage that he finally lashed out.

'I was walking through Main Street and this same group of kids were calling me names, and I just saw red. I mean, I literally *saw* red. I don't know where it came from. But I was so blinded by it that I don't even recall why I laid into this one boy. He was even older than me. I just began punching him until I broke his nose. I didn't stop. I think I could have gone on to kill him if two grown-ups hadn't yanked me off him. These two men grabbed me by the arms and hauled me off to the cops. I was crying and kicking and pulling.

'The sergeant was good though. He got me some soda and cleaned me up. He knew my Uncle Claude and so he drove me home and told Claude to go easy on me. Claude said he had to punish me, but he didn't use the birch that time. He just made me go to my room without supper. I'd been hungry before so it didn't hurt.'

Steve had no friends – except for a pig. 'I loved that pig,' he said. 'I swear it knew me when it saw me. It would run up to me and I'd stroke him and he ran round me, and it was like he would've jumped on me and hugged me and played if he'd been human. Claude told me, "Don't go loving that hog, we're gonna have to eat him one day." So I begged Uncle Claude to spare him, and he did.'

I asked Steve if he gave the pig a name. 'I just called him Pig. And he knew it was his name too. I'd call "Here, Pig!" and he'd come trotting over.'

Claude was a man who could overlook a lot of things a small boy got up to, but he didn't allow Steve to skip his chores, or be ill-mannered to his betters. When Steve needed punishing, Claude laid down the law. But it was rarely harsh or violent.

'Claude punished me the best way he knew how, and that was to keep me in my room when I should have been out playing with my pig, or riding the tractors. Jesus, I loved those tractors. It was something about those big wheels and just watching them turn. They were just so constant, no matter what. You always knew that any particular point of a wheel would come around again. That just seemed kind of comforting to me.'

He also loved riding in Uncle Claude's Jeep. 'Feeling the wind in my hair and on my face was like the most free feeling I ever had. And the faster we went, the better it was. That feeling of freedom, and the feeling that wherever you were going, you were leaving behind something – I've always loved leaving something behind.'

Escape seems to be a theme in Steve's life. He said to me once, 'I just gotta break out,' but he never seemed quite sure what he was trying to break out from. It was something that attracted him to two films, *The Great Escape* and *Papillon*. In both he played men who made escaping an art form. In *The Great Escape* he was a POW intent on breaking out, not as part of the mass escape the film is about, but on his own, and in *Papillon* he was a man trying to escape from Devil's Island.

'I *knew* those guys,' he told me in 1977. 'I dug those guys – Hilts [in *The Great Escape*] and Henri [Charrière in *Papillon*], couldn't be caged. Escape wasn't a game. It was a way of life.'

I don't think Steve ever stopped trying to escape, until, perhaps, he was in his last dying months, by which time he had escaped into religion, and that was the one thing, it seemed, which brought him peace. Perhaps that's what he was seeking all his life, but didn't really know it because, when I challenged him in 1970 to explain what he was trying to escape from, he couldn't be specific. He simply said, 'Just my life.'

I couldn't understand what he could still be wanting to get away from. He told me, 'We all have stuff we need to escape from now and then. That never changes.'

But there was more to it than just an episodic need to get away from what Steve called 'the shit of life', by which he meant just the occasional shit we all have from time to time. I think he was forever escaping *all* the shit of his life – in fact, his *whole* life – and so one day, in 1977, I asked him if this might be the case. He replied, 'That's what it is with me. It never goes away, no matter how fast I move. I can't shake it off. I can't *lose* it, man. But if I go fast enough for long enough, I'll find something that'll make it all go away.'

But in 1977 he didn't think he had much time to find that 'something', because, he said, 'I'm gonna be dead by 50.' That was a prediction he often made, but had nothing to back it up with other than the fact that both his parents would die at the age of 50.

He didn't seem bothered by his prediction. James Coburn said it was just 'Steve being Steve' when I saw him in 1979. 'Steve always has to have it worse than anyone else, rougher than anyone else, tougher than anyone else. If you've had it bad, he's had it badder. If you got a terminal illness, he's already dead.'

It seems that even when it came to the worst things life could throw at a person, Steve had to compete. It seems he spent his life competing, and escaping.

He was, by his own admission, a paranoid kid. 'I was sure they were all out to get me. Even my own mother. I felt everyone was trying to con me. I was suspicious of everyone except my Uncle Claude. I didn't have friends. I wasn't on the baseball team. I didn't believe in teamwork. I'm not sure I do now.'

He knew how to throw a baseball and to catch it. 'Not so good with a bat,' he said. What he liked to do was practise alone with the ball, throwing it, bouncing it against a wall and catching it. And when he made *The Great Escape* he made that a part of his character when Hilts is alone in the cooler cell . . . throwing a baseball against a wall. He told me, 'That's what I did as a kid. Throw the ball . . . it hits the ground . . . off the wall . . . into my hand . . . throw it again . . . over and over. It was like a hypnotic spell. I lost myself in it. And I could catch as well as anyone.'

He recalled playing at least one game of baseball. 'The kids had it in for me,' he said. 'I wasn't so hot with the bat. They knew they could get me on that. But when I was fielding I could catch the highest and the furthest ball. I wanted them to hit it further and higher. Then the other kids thought I was cool. But I was just showing them I was the best at what I could do. I didn't want to be one of the team. I wanted to be the star.'

Football was something he insisted he never played as a kid.

'Too much contact. I'd have wanted to bust somebody wide open.'

He conceded that he probably wasn't a kid who others would ever want to be friends with. 'I was a moody kid. I was mad at everyone. I wasn't even eight and I was a rebel.'

As well as experiencing his own violent moods, he was witness to extreme forms of violence that appalled him. He recalled walking down the main street in Slater with Claude – he was sure this was in 1937 – and seeing a group of protesters. I asked him what they were protesting about. He said, 'Being dirt poor.'

Suddenly cops charged at the protesters. The police were armed, the protesters were not. Steve heard a number of gunfire shots. When he and Claude went to investigate they saw one of Claude's farmhands being beaten by three policemen. 'His face and shirt were covered in blood. Claude said, "We better not get involved. Best to stay out of it." I couldn't understand why the police beat up people. It made no sense. These people just wanted to not be poor any more.'

Steve had another early memory which remained indelibly etched. 'I saw John Dillinger – you know, the gangster. There were a lot of gangsters around then. Some were folk heroes. I saw Dillinger being taken into court at Crown Point (in Indiana). And he looked at me and winked. Maybe he was being friendly, but I didn't sleep for nights, thinking of that killer's face looking at me. Scared the shit outta me!'

At age eight Steve began school. He rode his bike the three miles to the elementary school in Slater. 'Blacks were segregated. I didn't know why. It wasn't as though the school was all that big. But the black kids had their own lessons and we had ours. I didn't even feel a part of my own race.'

The teachers thought he was illiterate. He had trouble reading and writing, and that only singled him out all the more acutely from the rest of the class. (Years later he was diagnosed as dyslexic.) And if a kid dared to snigger at him, which was often, Steve laid into them in a dirt area behind the schoolyard. 'School wasn't an option for me,' he said. 'I either got into fights or just didn't go.'

When he did turn up at school, usually reeking of pig dung

because he cleaned out the pigs before class, he tried to keep his head down and ignore all the kids he knew were just dying to goad him into a fight. He said, 'It was about 50/50 whether I'd fight, and when I did I was whacked by the school principal. The more they whacked me, the more I faced up to it and wasn't afraid any more of the pain.'

Claude never tolerated Steve's truancy. 'Nothing hurt me more than being kept in my room. Claude knew it was pointless to whack me. That didn't work. Being locked in did. So I got better at hookey. I'd head off to school, get registered and then slip away.'

By the time he was nine it was obvious that Steve was never going to grow tall. He was shorter than most other kids of his age, but that didn't deter him from fighting bigger kids. He also slouched a lot and would grow round-shouldered. He had a quizzical look which had nothing to do with an inquisitive mind; it was because he had trouble hearing from what turned out to be an undiagnosed infection in his left ear, and so he would cock his head slightly to the right and frown. Much later, his left eardrum would become damaged, causing him further hearing loss. These imperfections in his health and posture, and his personality traits – the escapologist, the loner, the outcast and rebel – which developed within the first eight years of his life, all became aspects of his screen persona.

It was on Claude's farm that Steve really blossomed. By the age of 10 he could shoot and drive a truck. He loved to hunt and earned his uncle's admiration one time by taking down two birds with a single shot. 'It was crazy, like being two or three different people,' he said. 'I'd have to go to church because my grandma was a crazy religious woman, and I hated church, which meant nothing to me, but I sang the hymns, said the prayers. I'd have to go to school, which meant nothing to me, and when I didn't skip school I'd be bored to death. And then I'd be this other kid on the farm, shooting and hunting, driving, just feeling alive and wishing it was always like that.'

Inevitably, the rebel got into trouble with the law. 'I'd drive into town and get stopped by the cops. I was too young, and I'd usually have a gun with me. I never shot it in town. I shot it outside town, hunting rabbits and birds. I just wanted to be left alone to do what I wanted, but I got busted for it. Claude was okay about it. He said, "Stay out of town when you drive. Don't go hunting far from here. Folks don't understand you." I think he did.'

Life on the farm was idyllic, and if he couldn't be happy away from his home, then he could at least be happy when he was there. But as Steve said, 'My mom knew how to fuck up my life.' And she did, in September 1939, when she sent for him to live with her in Indianapolis as she now had a steady job waitressing.

It was an almost unbearable wrench for Steve to leave Claude, the farm and his favourite pig. Claude let him go because Julian was Steve's mother and had a legal right to custody of him. Steve, however, thought she had no moral right. 'She was wrong, just plain wrong,' he said to me about their unhappy reunion.

As a parting gift, Claude gave Steve a gold pocket watch. Steve said, 'The inscription read, "To Steve who has been like a son to me." When I read that, I wanted to stay, but I had to go. I felt like my heart was ripped out by my mom for doing that.'

Steve had to leave the only home – the only true parent, albeit a substitute parent – he had ever known.

CHAPTER 2

—

Scams, Sex and Violence

Steve travelled alone by bus to Indianapolis, where he was met by Julian and taken home to a boarding house where she lived with a man. There is confusion over whether this man was her wedded husband or just someone she shacked up with. Some have confused him with the man who later became her husband, who had the surname Berri. The man Steve was to meet and have to consider as his first stepfather was probably someone else. Steve told me he didn't remember the man's name, probably because Julian never took his surname and so neither did Steve.

When Julian later married Berri, Steve couldn't remember his first name. The confusion about which man was which, and whether or not Julian married them both, and even the suggestion that they were not two men but just the one – called Berri – seems to have come from the anecdotal evidence of Steve himself rather than any legal records. Steve told me, 'They became one and the same man. They were both psychos.'

It's clear that Steve blocked out much about his first 'psycho' stepdad. What he did remember was 'hearing him beat up on Julian'. He often referred to his mother by her name. 'She'd beg for mercy. Did no good.'

He also beat up on Steve. 'I thought Julian would protect me. She didn't.'

His impressions of his mother's weakness against a man obviously much stronger than her were clearly marred by his deep unhappiness, which he still felt in 1970. But he acknowledged that his 'stepfather' was a psychotic bully, regularly beating both mother and son. 'Half the time I didn't know what I was getting whopped for. Sometimes I think that's half the reason I can beat my own wife. I just got so much shit in me. I don't like who I am. I want to escape from it.'

Steve was running from himself all his life.

His schooling didn't improve, so he hardly bothered to go. He visited a lot of his old haunts, including a cinema, the Roxy. Unlike many other movie-stars who were turned on to movies as a child and inspired to become actors, Steve simply went for the sheer escapism. Although he had his screen heroes, in particular Humphrey Bogart and James Cagney, he had no thoughts of being an actor. Not yet.

He only thought of surviving. 'I went hungry a lot of times, so I got what I could find in dustbins. I'd find beer bottles with beer still in them. That got me liking beer.'

He finally made friends . . . the hard way. He recalled, 'I was too hungry to care what I did, and when I found an open window I climbed in the house to get some food and money, and when I climbed out again this tall boy, about 15 or 16, stood there and saw me with all this food and money, and I thought he was going to beat me up and take it all. So I said, "You might be bigger than me but you don't want to mess with me." I liked Jimmie Cagney coz he was a small tough guy and I wanted to be like him, so I thought of myself as a small tough guy like Cagney. I guess it worked, coz this big kid said, "Come with me," and I did, and he introduced me to a gang that was like those Dead End Street kids. I was suddenly like their kid brother. I shared some food with them but kept the money, and they said, "Yeah, you're all right, kid," and I was suddenly one of them.'

Being one of them, he learned how to steal hubcaps and get cash for them at a store in town where the store owner was happy to pay a small amount for stolen hubcaps and then sell them at a higher price. Steve was learning the art of the scam. 'It was like organised crime but on a small scale. Suddenly I was like Cagney and Humphrey Bogart in those gangster movies.'

Steve's description of the gang being like organised crime was no exaggeration. They printed fake government coupons; the real coupons were for poor people, who handed them over at stores for food, and then the stores were reimbursed by the government. The gang Steve was in sold their fake coupons to a particular store-keeper at a good price who then sought reimbursement from the government and made a profit.

'It was a pretty sophisticated set-up,' said Steve, and although he didn't feel proud of his criminal past, which got a lot worse in later years, he said that at the time he felt he was 'getting even with everyone'.

The gang regularly got drunk on beer. Steve was getting drunk from the age of 12. He rarely slept at home at nights but ran with the gang. And he had his first experience with girls.

'I'd just turned 13. The guys thought I should pop my cherry. So they took me to a local whore who was 15. Her name was Matilda. You didn't pay her with money. You bought her cakes. She was getting fat but at 15 it gave her big tits. The guys chipped in and bought a big iced cake, and she said for that they could all have a turn. I went first. We did it in a disused storeroom. She never got naked, just dropped her panties, sat on a table and . . . vavoom! I bought her a lot of cakes after that.'

Steve had no home life. He had just 'a shit life', as he was fond of reminding me. But on the streets he finally had friends who became a surrogate family. They looked out for each other. Steve impressed the older boys with his capability for petty crime. 'I was showing them I could do it,' he said. 'I was showing the rest of the world they couldn't shit on me.'

Perhaps that's the motivation of many who grow to be professional criminals. Steve couldn't say for sure if he ever thought that he was consciously heading for a life of crime because he didn't think ahead. 'I only thought of today. Who cared about tomorrow? My groove was not starving.'

He was rolling drunks when the opportunity came along. 'Some bum would be heading home after a skinful, and I'd push 'em into an alley. They'd fall over, I'd pick their pockets and run like hell.'

He said he only ever got picked up by the police once, when he was caught running from a fire which he had nothing to do with.

'A store was burning and we all watched. It was like the Fourth of July. But I had nothing to do with it. The cops came roaring in and every boy scattered. I don't know if any of them started it. I didn't. But I got caught. Four cops got around me and I had no chance.

'I was lucky because one of the schoolteachers had seen me in the street and began giving me shit about not coming to school. She was a nice lady. She was just trying to do the right thing. And it was while she was giving me all this shit that we saw the fire down the street. When she saw the cops take me, she came to the station and told them I was innocent. They had to release me, but they took me home and told Julian and my stepdad what had happened. I'd begged them not to do that because I knew that he would beat me. They didn't believe me. As soon as they'd gone, he punched me, and Julian just cried and ran out.'

Whether it was that incident that sparked an ultimatum from Julian to her 'husband', or whether it just happened to be around that time – Steve couldn't recall – the psycho stepfather cleared out for good. Unable to afford the rooms they had, Steve and Julian moved into a single room where they had to share the one and only bed. Not that Steve was home that often. To make ends meet, Julian turned to prostitution again, and Steve was usually out committing more petty crime. 'When I went home I tried to be sure she wasn't screwing.' When he returned home during the early hours, he usually slept in a large cupboard downstairs from their room where he'd made up a bed of cardboard boxes.

Saturday mornings, mother and son were reunited for a few hours when Julian, who could now afford to dress well while Steve wore only his usual faded dungarees, took him to the Roxy. 'Those were the best times with my mom,' Steve said. 'They were the *only* good times with her.'

But even those good times came to an end when, in late 1940, Julian decided she couldn't take care of Steve any longer – not that she had taken care of him at all – and sent him back to live with Claude in Slater.

At first, Steve was delighted to be going back to the farm. But it was a different place to the one he had been so happy in about a year earlier. Claude had got engaged to a burlesque dancer from St Louis called Eva, who was half Claude's age and was spending his money at an alarming rate. Steve's grandparents were still there, living in a small building across the field, but his grandfather was dying from cancer, and his grandmother had become senile, lost in a religious haze, to be found at times wandering naked and praising God. 'Most times she didn't know me,' Steve said. 'Grandpa was dying. Claude was drunk most of the time and his fiancée was driving around making a fool of herself. Everyone was fighting or shouting at each other. It was a madhouse. And Claude took the strap to me. So I ran away. I just took some things in a knapsack and my dog Cagney, and Bogie my cat, and I lit out.'

When Steve told me this, I asked him if he really had a dog and a cat called Cagney and Bogie. He gave a small laugh and said, 'You bet. My pig got eat, so I took to a mongrel I called Cagney and a cat I called Bogie. They slept in my room and went everywhere with me, so when I ran away, they just followed.'

He didn't get very far, just to the train depot, where he hid out in one of the buildings. 'In the morning I realised I had no idea where I was going. So I went back. Nobody missed me.'

There were other attempts to run away over the next two years. Steve couldn't recall just how many. But he never got far. Often, after only a single night, he'd be found by someone who knew him and they would kindly lead him home. 'They always said I'd be better off at home. I told them they had no idea.'

One day he managed to get further than the train depot and spent three or four nights sleeping rough, still accompanied by Cagney and Bogie. He'd also taken one of Claude's guns to shoot rabbits. A patrol car heard the shots and came to investigate. 'As soon as I saw the cop coming through the brush, I ducked down and hoped he wouldn't see me. Cagney and the Bogie were tearing about. You didn't usually see cats unless they were wild cats, but Bogie was a stupid thing who took a liking to the cop and was round his ankles and purring. And then Cagney padded up to him and this cop suddenly had a cat and a dog wanting to be patted and stroked. Then the cop yelled out, "Come on out, Steve. Your animals gave you away." Turned out Claude had missed me after all and had gone to the cops with a description that included a cat and dog, and those stupid animals gave me away.'

So back Steve went to the farm, and Claude took the strap to him, saying, 'This is for your own good.' But after just a few strokes, Claude stopped.

'There were tears in his eyes. I think he was ashamed. Like he really didn't want to be doing it. And then he told me my granddaddy was dead and grandma was insane, and his fiancée had left him.' (Though she would come back.) 'I was all he had left.'

It might have been a more happy existence after that, but, as Steve put it, 'Julian fucked it up again.'

She hadn't even bothered to visit Steve in the two years he had been with Claude. Suddenly, in the summer of 1942, she sent for him to come and live with her and her new husband in Los Angeles, California. Cagney and Bogie were not invited, so Steve had to leave all he loved once more and return to the mother he hated.

Julian had by now married the man with the surname of Berri. And after they were thrown out of the last boarding house in Beech Grove, they decided, for reasons Steve never was able to explain, to move to Los Angeles, where Berri was able to find steady manual work. 'I think he worked in some of the film studios, building sets,' said Steve.

Only just turned 13, Steve arrived, with his spirit badly fractured, in Los Angeles and moved in with his mother and new stepfather in a run-down apartment in a run-down part of town. To his horror, when he stepped off the bus to be met by Julian, he saw that she had become a peroxide blonde. She told him to behave around his stepfather. 'Our name is now Berri.'

Steve decided his name would never be anything other than McQueen.

'We lived in a dump,' he recalled. 'That was okay, I was used to dumps. But I thought being close to Hollywood and movie-stars things would be different. The rats were bigger than the ones in Beech Grove and Slater. And there were snakes. You'd see prairie wolves. None of that really mattered either. Especially when I realised my stepdad was another psycho. That mattered.'

Steve was subjected to regular beatings by Berri. 'He'd just rip off and punch and kick me. I wrote to Claude to come and get me, but Berri found the letter and tore it up, and then laid into me again. He even took out my light bulb in my room, and after beating me left me in the dark. I lay on my bed, all tightly curled up, crying coz of fear and pain and hate, and I thought about how I would kill the son of a bitch.'

It didn't take Steve long to find another gang to run with, and he was back to committing petty crimes. Things were as bad, if not worse, than they had been in Beech Grove.

Ironically, it was Julian who saved him by writing to Claude and letting him know that Steve was running wild and getting into so much trouble that she and her husband were considering sending him to a reformatory. Within a few weeks, Claude wired money to Julian to pay for Steve's bus fair back to Slater.

'I didn't know if this was for the good or the bad,' Steve said. By this time he was feeling totally confused. 'Yeah, I think I was a little insane,' he said.

Claude had married Eva, who welcomed the dirty urchin Steve, washed and fed him and made him take a bath. 'She was more a mom than Julian ever was,' said Steve.

Before Steve's return to the farm, Eva had sent for an illegitimate daughter she had, Jackie, so suddenly Steve found himself with a sort of surrogate stepsister who was a year older than he. 'That wasn't so bad,' he said, 'but she didn't have to do hardly any chores, and I got them all.'

There was compensation though. 'I peeked at her through a crack in the bedroom door and saw her naked. First time I ever saw a snatch.' When he told me this, I said, 'What about the cake-eating whore in Beech Grove?'

He said, 'Nope. Never saw hers. I just knew where to find it.'

I could see from the faint smile that this was one of the very few precious and welcome memories he had from his childhood. But the smile vanished when he told me, 'Claude seemed almighty interested in his stepdaughter. That caused a lot of trouble with him and Eva.

'And then they finally took away Grandma. Off to an asylum. I watched her being taken in a straitjacket. She was screaming and kicking as they dragged her off to the ambulance, and she was so frail that they dislocated her shoulder. Then she somehow got free and was screaming stuff from the Bible. They had to gag her and just dragged her into the ambulance, and I never saw her again.'

There was little of the happiness Steve had known when he had first lived with Claude. 'There wasn't much to do other than my chores and go to school, which I didn't do too much, and the only friend I had was my old dog Cagney and a mouse. Bogie the cat had run away or been killed or something.'

By this time Steve had become quite fanatical about the films of James Cagney and especially Humphrey Bogart. 'I liked the way those guys handled themselves. I imagined they were just like that in life. I emulated them, and I started to get it into my head that if I were in pictures, I'd be like those two actors, but mostly Bogie. He had a fuck-you way about him.'

Steve had a lot of that too, even when he was just 13. It was an attitude that grew as he did, and got bigger as his ego got bigger when he became a star. And yet it was clear – at least it was in 1970 when I got to know him – that he needed you to *know* that he was saying 'Fuck you!' to the world. That seemed very important to him. Somebody who really tells the world 'Fuck you' doesn't care if you know or not. He *cared*. And I think it's because he really didn't want to be that guy. He wanted something more. And he looked for it all his life.

By now Steve's obsession with Bogart and Cagney had led to ideas of becoming a movie-star, and he told his teacher this. 'She didn't think I had much chance,' he said. 'So I went off and stood on a street, put my cap on the ground and began doing impressions of Cagney and Bogart, and people threw quite a few coins in the cap. That made me think I could actually do it, and when I got home I told Claude and his wife, and all Claude did was give a drunken belch. I'd hoped he'd approve, but he just didn't give a shit any more.'

Rejected by the man he most admired in the world, Steve began to feel more isolated than ever. By the time he was 14 he was getting into trouble with the law. 'I ran wild. I got back into stealing. I'd roll drunks. Break into houses. I was a punk. I had a BB rifle. Not usually lethal but they can hurt. And they can kill rats.' Even the rats didn't get Steve's sympathy any more.

'I started carrying that gun with me. I must've thought I was a gangster or a cowboy. I started wishing I had a real gun. I really dug the idea of the loner on the road, packing a gun. So one day I carried it to town, went to a coffee house, and while I was there I accidentally fired it.

'That evening the cops turned up at the farm saying I'd been firing the gun in the cafe, and although I swore to Claude I hadn't, he yelled at me and told me I was no good, and I told him if I was no good I'd better leave, and he said to get the hell out then. We'd never argued like that before, and so I lit out that night.'

Steve left the farm, his uncle, his dog Cagney, his mouse, his surrogate stepsister, and his uncle's wife who was more a mother than Julian had ever been, and embarked on making a new life for himself. He thought he could become the next Humphrey Bogart, so he set out for Hollywood. He thought he might finally escape his background. But it was always right there, on his heels. As fast as he ran, he could never run fast enough.

There had been a travelling circus in Slater and Steve had been among the crowd of excited onlookers. 'The guy in the circus spotted me and said, "Son, join the circus and see the world." So that's what I did when I ran away. I thought I was going to do something glamorous and dangerous. All I did was sell pencils.'

Only years later, in 1957, when Steve returned to Claude for the first time since running away with the circus, did he learn that Claude, his heart broken at the mysterious disappearance of his nephew, spent days searching for him.

Steve's plan was to head back to California to reunite with Julian, not because he yearned for his mother, but because he figured Los Angeles was the place where he might become the next Bogart. When the circus went off in a different direction, Steve left it and began hitchhiking and riding freight trains.

'I met a lot of hobos. They scared me at first but then I realised they were like me. I was like them. They'd all run away from life. I came across a whole camp of them. They seemed to look out for each other, and they made me welcome and gave me food and water. They told me every now and then the cops came and ran them in, and then they'd get released and go back to the camp. For kicks they rode the freight trains, or sometimes they'd simply do that just coz they wanted to go somewhere. They never stayed around in one place too long. The camp was somewhere they could stop off at or return to, but mostly they were on the road. A lot of them had lost their jobs and homes and families in the Depression. Now they just liked to live that way. I could have been a hobo too, but I still had dreams. So I stayed a little time with them, and moved on.'

When he arrived in Los Angeles, Steve made his way to the place where Julian and Berri lived, but he was not greeted like the prodigal son. 'They let me stay but swore if I got out of line they'd send me to reform school.'

Having been warned, Steve being Steve, he started getting into trouble. 'There wasn't anything else to do. It was either stay home and get slugged by Berri or be out on the streets with a gang I joined. I had to prove myself. Now they weren't all older than me, but I was just a small kid, smaller than all the rest. I had to prove I was the baddest ass of all of 'em. I stole more hubcaps than any of 'em. I rolled more drunks.'

He enrolled at school but hardly ever went to start with. Then he stopped going altogether.

He had been made to take on the name of Berri – he was now Steven Berri. He hated the name because it was the name of a man he hated. Berri was worse than he had been before, laying into Steve drunk or sober – although by Steve's account more drunk than sober – and Steve often turned up to meet the gang with black eyes and cut and swollen lips. One day he left the house in tears, tasting blood on his lips, swearing that he was going to kill both Berri and Julian.

'I broke into a butcher's store that night, smashing the window – I didn't even care if anyone heard me. I stole the biggest sharpest meat knife I could find. Nothing else. No meat. Just something to kill 'em with. By the time the butcher had come down I'd gone. He probably never even knew it was just a knife that went. I guess all he saw was a broken window.

'I went home. Got to the door. I was ready to go in there and kill 'em both. I saw it in my head. The knife, blood, their faces as they saw it was me. I thought it would turn me on. That I'd just *do* it. But I just couldn't. I wanted to kill 'em, but I had been turned off killing years before. Sometimes I figure that it was too . . .' He struggled to find the right word, then said, 'personal to use a knife and that's why I couldn't do it. But if I'd had a gun! Well, I might just be a killer.'

As well as possessing a rage that was close to driving him to murder, Steve was also dealing with raging hormones. 'I was so damn horny all the time,' he said.

So I went looking for a girl who'd do it for money, or cakes, or free. One of the guys in the gang said we could easily find a girl and make her do whatever we wanted. I knew what he had in mind, and I didn't like it at all. I said a girl had to be willing, and he called me a fag, and that implied something which I didn't like, and we got into a fight. He was bigger than me, but I beat the shit out of him. I had him on the ground and I was laying into him, and I know I could have killed him, but I stopped myself. I *had* to stop or I'd have killed him.

I got off of him, but I had this pure rage. White hot rage. I thought the only way I could get rid of it was if I had sex. It just seemed to be a compulsion or whatever – something I knew would get this violence out of me.

There was a girl at school. She wasn't pretty. She had buck teeth. She always smiled at me, made eyes, mainly when she saw me in the street coz I wasn't at school that much. And when I was, she'd keep getting in my way, giving me those looks. So I thought, what the hell? Maybe she'd give me what I want.

I knew where she lived, and it was late, so I threw small stones at her window, and she looked out. She was in her nightgown. I told her to come down. She didn't even ask why. She came out the back door and I met her, and we went into an outhouse. There was just a cold stone floor in there – nothing to lay on. She was the same age as me, not pretty but not really ugly – just plain. She took off her nightgown, and she had a real nice pair of tits. Not big. But nice. And I just dove in. Down on the cold floor. She was better than Matilda the whore who never really cared. This girl, like, *cared*. She wanted it. She made so much noise I had to put my hand over her mouth. It didn't last long, if you know what I mean.

She put on her nightgown and said, 'Any time.' So I knew I'd go back again.

When I told a couple of the guys about her, they said, 'She did you for *free*?'

'Sure, why not?'

'She charges us five bucks.'

I thought, Jeez, she charges them and I get it free. Turned out she couldn't get enough but knew the guys would pay, so she was getting it a lot and getting paid. But then I started getting it every night, and the other guys didn't get a look in, which pissed them off. Or they'd have to wait, and then they'd have to pay.

And then that led to more trouble and I got into a fight with some guys, and some other guys came to help me. It was a huge fight we had, and the cops broke it up and we all went off to the station, and I was let go coz I was the smallest and they thought I was youngest.

The cops took Steve home and Julian told him to go and clean himself up. He went to bed, but when he woke in the morning he had pain all through his head.

I felt like I'd been run over in my sleep. Turns out Berri had come up drunk, and Julian told him what I'd done, so he came in and beat me while I was asleep, and hit me so hard so many times that I stopped sleeping and became unconscious. He actually knocked me out while I was sleeping. Or maybe I had come to because I had a vague memory of looking up and seeing him, and then he knocked me out. The son of a bitch could've killed me.

It took me a while to get my senses, and I could just remember that moment of looking up and seeing him, and I knew from the fresh bruises and cuts and broken teeth what he'd done. I just went crazy. I wanted to kill him. I saw him and I just threw myself at him. I'd never done that before. I'd never fought back. But I rammed into him so hard he fell against the door and fell out, and I fell out after him, and we rolled down the hard concrete steps into the road. He just lay there, the wind knocked out of him, curled up – maybe he was in agony, maybe he was just a coward and suddenly scared shitless of me – but I stood over him and said, 'You ever lay hands on me again, I'll kill you, sure as hell.' He never laid hands on me again.

Steve's rage, his violence, was now unleashed. He said, 'I was gonna be hard to tame.' He got into more fights, and finally he got hauled off by the police and locked up for the night. 'I was put in the pen – a cage for drunks drying off and killers waiting for a vacant cell. I was shit scared. I felt like I was locked up and would maybe never come out alive.'

It might have been this incident, or some other – Steve didn't remember – but there was a final straw for Julian and Berri as far as Steve's violent behaviour was concerned, and on 6 February 1945 they filled in a court order to have Steve placed in the California Junior Boys Republic at Chino for 14 months. It wasn't a prison, but it wasn't freedom either. It was a school for wayward boys, and Steve would be marked by it for the rest of his life.

CHAPTER 3

—

Chino

It was evening when Steve arrived at the Boys Republic, a 200-acre campus set in the foothills of the Santa Anas in Chino, an eastern suburb of Los Angeles. 'The first thing I noticed was there were no fences,' he said. 'I figured this should be the easiest prison to escape from.'

But, as he found out, it was no prison but a modern experiment to reform boys with criminal tendencies. The idea was for the boys to dig in, settle down and work hard for the sake of character building and self-respect. It was thought that if the boys were not actually confined, they would not want to escape. They didn't count on the teenage Steve McQueen.

He lived in a cottage with several other boys. 'There were these cottages all over the place,' he recalled, and in retrospect said, 'It was real nice. I had a bed every night. They didn't lock you in.'

But when he first arrived Steve was full of attitude and anger. He didn't want to be there and didn't want to be tamed. The other boys took an instant dislike to him. 'I was determined to not conform like they did. We had to take care of ourselves, get our own meals, lay the table, wash up. I wasn't going to do any of that. So I didn't get fed, so I *had* to do my share.

'I took my turn in the kitchen. Washing up. Dishes, cups, knives, forks. I figured they wouldn't miss a knife so I put one in my pocket. One of the bigger boys saw me. He was a trustee. He said, "You take that and you'll have to use it." I said, "Supposing I do?" He said, "You'll hurt someone bad or you'll be hurt bad, and here there's no reason to do that. It's easy here, if you're up to it." That was like a challenge. I thought, "Sure, I'm up to it." So I put the knife back.'

Steve might have compromised his principles by helping with the chores, but he admitted he didn't do as much as the others, 'and they really hated me for it. That just made me worse. I thought, "Go ahead, hate me." But if you went too far they paid you for it. I got beaten a few times.'

'Every month we were allowed to go into town and see a movie. Each cottage had its turn. A bus would drive us there, bring us back. It was the treat of the month. Then I went and ruined it one time because I hadn't done my share, and when we got inspected, we were told there'd be no trip to town, no movie. And they beat me up. I didn't blame them. I missed going to the movies too. So I put in more effort. I never made any friends, but I tried not to make more enemies.'

There were classes in the morning, and this time there was no opportunity to skip class. He had work too, fulfilling the school's motto, 'Nothing without Labour.'

'In the afternoons I worked in the laundry building. Every afternoon. That was my job. The stench of that place got in my nose and never got out again. Like chemicals. It was in the walls. The stench of the laundry! A place that was supposed to smell clean. It never did.'

After three months of laundry, classes and learning to do his share of chores, Steve decided he'd had enough. 'I just walked out. There was no fence. Nothing to stop you.' He didn't get far. 'I didn't know where the hell I was.' It didn't take long for him to be found and taken back.

Then he discovered what happened to boys who tried to escape. 'You were put in solitary.' It was just for a night, but he didn't know that at the time and thought he might be left there for weeks, maybe even forever. 'I was in the dark, alone, scared. I laid awake all night. Just an old mattress to lie on. No bed, no nothing. The sound of other boys. Some talking low. Some crying. You'd hear some kid whisper, "Hey, buddy, what you done?" I didn't know if they meant me, so I stayed quiet. Just lay there smelling what smelt like cabbages.

'I used those memories when I was in the cooler in *The Great Escape*. When I went into that cooler for the second time [in the movie] I remembered going back into solitary the second time – and the third time.'

On his second escape from the Boys Republic, Steve made his way to the southern outskirts of town and headed towards the mountains. 'I was figuring they had to catch me soon. I didn't want to be heading into the mountains, so I sheltered in a stable and waited to be found. Turned out the principal had decided to give me a 24-hour start before he called the cops to go find me.'

There were five escapes in all, and each time he never got far. 'I never escaped to get free. I just did it because I could. But you knew if you walked out they'd come and find you and you'd end up in solitary again.'

Life at the Boys Republic was made harder for Steve with each escape. 'After solitary, I dug ditches and cleaned urinals. Dug out tree stumps. Painted walls, ceilings. Mixed cement. Seemed each time I came out of solitary there was a harder chore to do. It was punishment, but all it did was make me madder than I already was.'

Steve didn't make life easy for himself or the boys who watched over him. 'It isn't like prison where you got guards. You just got the other boys keeping an eye on you, and if you don't toe the line, they let you have it.

'There were adults there. Just regular guys in suits. They didn't come after you with dogs if you decided to walk on out. They just called the cops. But they were no pushovers. I think some of them had been cops or prison guards. They could deal with the tougher boys. I wanted to show them I was no pushover either. I wanted to show everyone. And that got me into fights.

'It wasn't always my fault. We'd get taken to the principal and he'd try to find out who started it. We never snitched on each other, and usually he let us go. I think he thought it was a good thing when we showed some kind of loyalty to each other.'

There was, however, one incident for which Steve felt shame the rest of his life – or certainly up until 1970, when he told me about it. 'There was a kid smaller than me. I didn't like his attitude. Maybe he reminded me of me. He just said the wrong thing to me once and I laid into him with my fists and my feet. I really tried hard not to let this rage I had control me, but sometimes I couldn't hold it down, and this was one time. This poor kid was on the floor, curled up and crying. I looked down and saw myself. That had been me once. Then I stopped. I cleaned him up, dried his eyes, told him how sorry I was. But he was hurting and I'd done that to him. I felt ashamed. I still do.'

With so much rage still simmering inside of him, it didn't take a great deal to ignite it. Nothing affected Steve more than what he saw as an act of betrayal by his mother for never coming to see him. 'I'd get so hot about that I'd suddenly lose it, but I usually took it out on stuff like furniture. Or doors. The boys usually tried to cover for me so I wouldn't get it in the neck.'

But it all got too much for him when Julian, now deserted by her husband, arranged to take Steve out of the Boys Republic for the weekend and then failed to turn up. 'I waited for her from when we finished breakfast till supper time. I sat in a chair all day, didn't speak, and in the evening I was trying not to cry. I just got madder. Then I just went crazy. I kicked in the door, punched everything – walls, windows, turned over the bed, broke stuff. I couldn't get control. It was more than I could bear – that betrayal by that fucking woman.'

Boys, too terrified to tackle him, called for adult reinforcements. The first to arrive was promptly hit by a chair Steve threw at him. 'Then I laid into him. Punching, kicking. I was out of my mind. I made his nose bleed – maybe broke it even. Others arrived, and I was jumped on. I was crying and . . . Jesus, I was just a crazy man. So they dragged me off to solitary, and I went screaming and kicking, like my grandma did when they took her. I thought they'd put me in one of those straitjackets. But they gave me a shot of something to calm me down. A tranquilliser or something. They just closed the door on me and left me there to cool down.'

The principal, Mr Panter, was coming to the conclusion that punishment wasn't working on Steve. 'He was a good guy,' said Steve of Mr Panter. 'Took me a long time to realise that. He started inviting me to his house to talk things over. He got me to tell him what was bothering me. I had a lot to tell him. He'd have me over some evenings, just to talk, sometimes about my problems, sometimes about movies and movie-stars. We talked about those movies with Bogart and Cagney. I liked a movie called *Each Dawn I Die* with Cagney and George Raft. It was a prison movie. So me and Mr Panter talked about prisons, and rehabilitation, which he was interested in. He didn't believe a man should be just locked away but rehabilitated, and that impressed me.

'He really listened to me, and he said, "You got to give life a real honest shot and you could be somebody special one day." I never heard anyone say that to me. I didn't expect it from someone like him. Someone in authority. No teacher had ever talked like that to me. And that was the turning point.'

Steve not only reformed, he became a role model and was even elected to the Boys Council, which made the rules for all the other boys.

'That place was the best thing to happen to me,' he told me. 'I owed it everything.' And he repaid it in later years by making frequent returns as a famous movie-star, sitting with the boys to tell them of his experience there and encouraging them to buckle down as he had learned to do.

'I just talk to them,' he told me. 'I don't know any other way than just talk. Most of them are very smart. But they have a hard time adjusting to any school, like me. And if they're loners from the street, like me, I can really relate to them, and they dig me. When you're from that kind of place, on the streets, running alone, you got a lot of insecurity, and insecurity is a lot of motivation, especially when you find yourself in the Boys Republic and you find the place is run by the boys. You learn to get on with it when you have a dozen other boys on your back, making you toe the line. Adults can't do that. They're the enemies of teenagers.

'I hope I've had a hand in saving a few boys, maybe a whole lot more,' Steve said to me. 'If it was only one it was worthwhile.' I get the feeling that to be a wayward boy at the Boys Republic having a face-to-face talk with one of the coolest of screen stars confessing his own wayward past and subsequent salvation because of the California Junior Boys Republic at Chino must have been an inspiration. I know *I* felt inspired by him, and I wasn't, as he still thought I was, a juvenile delinquent.

Just as Steve's 14-month term ended at the Boys Republic, Julian decided she wanted him back. She had become widowed before her divorce from Berri came through and now she had another man, in New York, where she was living, and she intended to marry him. Steve had no choice but to return to his mother, but, he said, 'I wasn't going to take any of the shit I got before.'

He arrived by bus in New York in April 1946. Julian was there to meet him at the depot. 'There was gin on her breath. Made me want to puke,' he recalled.

He followed her to his new home, an apartment in Greenwich Village, and there met his new stepfather-to-be, a man who worked 'doing something or other' called Victor Lukens. In later years, Greenwich Village would be a fashionable area to live, but then, as Steve pointed out, 'it was a place where people who were broke lived'.

Julian explained to Steve that he would be sharing a room with another man. 'I felt uneasy straight away,' he said. When he went to his room, he discovered his room-mate was lying on the bed with another man. 'I won't say what they were doing, but I knew I wasn't going to stay *there*. I ran upstairs and told Julian I wasn't staying. She said this was a rough city but if I left I wasn't to come back. So I told her I won't ever be back again. And I went.'

I have no idea how much Steve's memories of his mother, as bitter as they always were, were distorted by his hatred of her. If his recollection was accurate she certainly displayed no sensitivity at all, and could even be termed cruel. I never met anyone who actually knew Julian and might be able to give another version of events, but I think it's accepted by all who knew Steve later in life that Julian was every bit as bad as Steve says she was. 'She was the mother from hell,' is how James Coburn described her, based on everything Steve had told him.

I asked Steve why, if she didn't want him, she took him from his uncle twice. He said, 'I was just a possession.'

She certainly never had his best interests at heart, bringing men into his life who were violent thugs, driving him onto the streets and into petty crime, and ultimately into the Boys Republic at Chino, where, at last, he changed his ways. Yet she never once visited him there, and then, when he was a reformed teenager, she brought him to New York, where he was expected to share a bedroom with a lodger who was having sex with another man.

When Steve said he was leaving, she told him never to come back, and I think that's all Steve needed to hear. He was able to get her out of his life at her own command – although she would drift back into his life without welcome when he was famous.

But it meant that all the good work the Boys Republic had put into him, and all the good work he had put into himself, was wasted. Steve was on the run again.

CHAPTER 4

—

Like John Dillinger

S teve ran. He didn't know where he was running to, only what he was running from. Over the days and night I spent with him in 1970, he gave me slightly differing accounts of what happened to him when he finally ran out of Julian's life. At first he said he found a bar in Little Italy where he met two sailors who bought him a few drinks, talked about how wonderful the merchant navy was and, before he knew it, took him on board the SS *Alpha*.

But that tale was moved along in the timescale to make way for a few tales Steve wanted to relate as he competed – though there was no competition – to be the one who had 'had the worse shit', as he put it more than once.

'I needed money, and I could play pool, so I found a pool hall and played. I put all my money on the table, and I won. Game after game. I was hot. Suddenly I had all this bread. I got myself a room and for the first time I had a bed to sleep in, and a room with no one else, and no sound of my mom being beaten, or dreading her latest man coming in and beating me black and blue. There were no sounds of other boys breathing or snoring. Or smells. And all I could think of was what scams I could dream up.'

The next day he played pool again, and won again. As word

spread about the new hustler in town, quite a crowd gathered, among them a young woman who, Steve said, 'was making it obvious she was interested in me. Turned out to be a whore. I figured I needed something to make me feel good, so I took her back to my room. Turned out she liked it rough. I was kind of surprised. She said, "Come on, baby, hurt me a little." So I did. She wanted to be slapped around a bit. I slapped her. Harder than she wanted. I just got mad at her for making me do that. I didn't know where the line was – her liking it and not liking it. I was crying more than she was and I told her to get out. She yelled, "You'll be sorry," and she got dressed and got out of there, and I wondered what she meant. Later a guy came to my room and told me I ought to clear out coz someone would be coming for me. He said I'd get killed if I stayed there, so I took his word for it and split.'

When Steve told me this, he wasn't boasting, or trying to be entertaining. He was as confounded by his ability to hurt women as I was. He said, 'My mom made me that way.' He believed that, and he might even have been right. 'I heard her being hurt by men. I thought she liked it. I think she did.' Recalling the time he found Julian in bed and allowing a sailor to hurt her for money confounded him. I think he remained confused about the line between being a woman and being a whore – as though there had to be one. When it came to women, he was screwed up.

'I don't want to hurt women, or anyone,' he told me. 'But when I get mad, I mean really mad so that I can't control it, I strike out – men or women. I can hurt anyone.'

Afraid for his life, he escaped from his rented room, hit the streets and wandered aimlessly until he came to another bar, where he had several beers. 'I was 16 and a drunk,' he recalled.

When he left the bar he fell asleep in an alley. 'I don't even remember getting there. I just remember waking up.'

He had one more tale to relate before getting back to how he joined the merchant navy.

'I had some money left over. I went to a restaurant to eat and they threw me out coz I looked such a mess. I said, "Hey, I got money," but they wouldn't let me in. I got so mad I wanted to do something to them but I walked away, found a small place to eat, and then thought about that restaurant again, and got so mad I went back and put a brick through the window. Then I ran like hell. I wished I hadn't done it. I got scared. I thought I'd get arrested and put in prison. So I joined the navy.'

Steve told me how that came about. He hit a bar where two sailors called Tinker and Ford plied him with drink. He told them that he was being chased by the cops, although he didn't actually know for sure he was being hunted. He was just scared that he was. Tinker and Ford told him he'd be safe in the merchant navy, and suddenly running away to sea seemed like a good idea. They just happened to have some kind of contract on them and before long he was signing up to be a merchant mariner. 'They took me onto a ship, the SS *Alpha*, and we sailed for Trinidad. Those two sailors must have been paid to recruit young guys like me who they got drunk.'

In the bar he had been fed a vision of adventure on the high seas and visiting far-off exotic locations, but on board he fell to the deck with a bump. 'I was cleaning the urinals, which were just fucking unspeakable. I was clearing out the garbage, which stank, and made me stink so nobody would come near me.'

The vessel was barely shipshape. 'It was a death trap. We had only just got out of harbour when it caught fire. I thought we were all going to die. They got the fire out but we were slowly sinking and only just made it to the Dominican Republic.'

That was enough for Steve, and he jumped ship. 'I was underage anyway. They couldn't come after me.'

He needed a job and somewhere to get his head down. 'I went from bar to bar asking for any work. Some guy said he could offer me a nice job, so I took it. He took me to a brothel, where all I had to do was make sure all the rooms had clean towels, and fetch anything the ladies wanted. And I collected payment from the men.'

I thought it was interesting that in this instance Steve referred to the prostitutes as 'ladies' and not 'whores'. It seems he differentiated between the cheap whores, among whom he counted his mother, and the ladies of this bordello who treated him well and, apparently, gave him a few 'favours'.

He stayed for eight weeks. Why he left is not entirely clear, as Steve managed to provide two explanations. One was that the police raided the establishment. 'All hell broke lose. They came in, rounding up all the girls, and the men, and the guy running the place. Only they missed me, maybe coz they didn't think a small yellow-haired kid could really be *in* there.'

The other is that he simply wanted to get back to America. 'I didn't want to stay in that place coz I knew I needed to get back to the States, though what I was going to do when I got back . . . I had no idea.'

Maybe both stories are true – Steve just happened to tell them to me on different nights. I would suppose that after the raid and he was somehow overlooked by the police, he decided there was no point in hanging around as he wanted to get back to America as quickly as possible. He managed to earn his way back on a small ship, this time prepared to do any dirty job just so long as the ship managed to reach Port Arthur, Texas, which it did.

From there he travelled from state to state, taking any jobs he could get, including selling pens and pencils in a travelling carnival. 'I was an expert at selling pencils,' he said. 'I bought them in sets at 25 cents each and then sold them for a buck, but I told my boss I sold them at half a buck so I made a good profit. I figured he was screwing the public anyway. Then he found out and I got fired.'

He worked on oil rigs at Corpus Christi, although what he did exactly he didn't say. I doubt it was anything to do with being an engineer, although he was good at messing about with engines, which he'd learned to do on his uncle's farm, so maybe he was useful working as a mechanic.

He also resorted to petty crime again.

It took me no time at all to break into cars. Usually it was so I could steal something inside but sometimes is was just the car I wanted. I didn't need it for anything mostly, but one time I thought I'd try holding up a gas station. I'd seen it in the movies and it looked easy enough.

I picked one that was just outside a small town in Carolina, and no one else was there. I filled up the car, then stuck my hand inside my jacket pocket and made it look like I had a gun in there, went inside and told the guy to hand over all the cash. He looked at me, spat out some tobacco, and the next thing he was reaching for a shotgun. I never ran so fast. He would have shot a hole [in me] as big as a beach ball for sure. I heard the blast as I crashed through the door, fell on the ground, got up and got to the car. I got that sucker going and drove, and he fired again, which made me duck and swerve, and I came off the road and into a ditch.

I thought he'd come for me for sure, so I got out of there and looked back, and saw him just walking down the road like Gary Cooper, reloading his shotgun, and I ran like a jack rabbit till I was sure he wasn't coming for me any more.

I gave up trying to be John Dillinger after that.

He didn't give up petty crime though, and broke into stores and houses at night, when he felt it was safer to steal without getting shot at. 'I never made off with very much,' he said. 'I really took just what I needed to buy food. That's no excuse. I feel bad about those folks I stole from. That wasn't cool.'

Years later Steve felt so bad about what he had done that he made an effort to revisit the places he had broken into, 'though I couldn't remember half of them, and half of those I did remember had either been demolished or the people had gone away. Or died. I'd knock on doors and people looked very surprised to see me standing there, and I'd ask if they remembered someone breaking into the house around 20 years ago. Some said they couldn't recall, or that they were broken into more than once, but some said they did remember being broken into, and then I'd say, "I figured you had coz I have a friend who did it, and he asked me if I'd come and pay you back, so here's however much he owes you," and I'd pay them with whatever I figured I owed, and then I'd leave before they asked questions. That made me feel a little better, but I'll never feel good, which is partly why I make those visit to the boys' school at Chino.'

After retiring from his brief career as an armed robber, Steve got a job as a mechanic at a garage where he met a local girl called Sue Ann. She was his first love.

'Sue Ann was a babe. She came from money, but she was sweet to me. She didn't care that I was just a mechanic. She lived in Myrtle Beach, which was a town back then. It was a great place for a 16-year-old to be. There was the sea, the beach, girls. I met her when her daddy came to have his car fixed. She was with him. I swear, I looked at her green eyes and it was love at first sight for me.'

Somehow he found the courage and the opportunity to ask her on a date and, to his never-ending surprise, she said yes.

'Her parents were such nice folks. They had this big house, and I'd get invited there for dinner. I had to get slicked up, and they'd make me so welcome. I began to feel like part of the family, which was wonderful but strange, coz I'd never felt that before – being part of a family. They threw a party for me when I turned 17.'

Sue Ann declared her love for him, and he panicked. Although he felt welcome and loved, he felt the sudden need to escape. And when he saw a recruitment poster for the marines, he enlisted.

'I loved Sue Ann and I told her I'd be back,' he said. 'She cried a lot, and that made me feel bad. I wasn't used to anyone loving me. I told her we'd get married one day and then I went.'

By the time he became a private in the marines, in April 1947, he had stopped calling himself Steven Berri and was finally Steven McQueen again. He was stationed at the military training facility, Camp Lejuene near Jacksonville in North Carolina. After three months he was assigned to the tank division.

After earning a stripe, Steve was given a weekend pass and spent the time with Sue Ann, which suggests that he was serious about settling down with her. In fact he stayed for two weeks, going absent without leave. 'I was still trying to show 'em all I could do what I wanted,' he told me. 'That was stupid. You don't tell the marines what you can do. *They* tell you what you can do.'

He was found by the shore patrol and when they tried to arrest him he fought back, was overpowered and returned to base, where he was stripped of his stripe and thrown in the brig for 41 days – 20 of them for resisting arrest with violence. During his time as a marine, Steve was busted down to private seven times in all. 'The only thing I got out of it,' he said, 'was more experience of being in the cooler that I used in *The Great Escape*.'

He did try harder when he was released and proved to be a good worker. 'I found motivation in trying to see if I could soup up a tank to make it the fastest tank in the division. I never did crack that one, coz I realised you just can't soup up a tank.' But he had fun trying.

Although he was still undisciplined and prone to being busted down to private every time he managed to earn a single stripe – he never did make corporal during his three years in the marines – Steve proved his mettle when the chips were down. It happened when he was on a military exercise in the Arctic. A tank with five marines on board got stuck in ice that was breaking up beneath them, threatening to send the tank into the frozen depths. There was panic but Steve, proving he really was the king of cool (as he has been called many times since being a movie-star), kept a cool head as he jumped onto the tank and got the five terrified marines out. That's the story Steve told me, and I'm inclined to believe it because he hardly ever boasted about anything good he did but preferred to highlight his flaws.

There was another tale of heroism he told me about, but it was no boast. It was actually an example of how dangerous he could be when he was armed, and the violent rage that could explode within him. 'I saw these guys hassling a girl [one night]. Three of them. They had her and were dragging her down a side street, and I knew what was gonna happen. I had a small handgun on me – we were not supposed to carry weapons but I did sometimes in case of trouble.'

I think Steve grew up expecting trouble.

'I followed them and they had her on the ground and one was getting on top, and I just boiled up inside and pulled this gun and told them to leave her the hell alone. These guys just freaked when they saw me with this gun, and they cried for their lives – I mean really cried, man. Cowards! I wanted to shoot them then and there. I coulda shot them. I told them to run and don't stop. The girl was on the ground and crying. I put my gun away and went to her and held my hands up – showed her I wasn't going to hurt her. I shoulda spoke softly but I was like, "Stop crying already, okay? They're gone. You're okay." I didn't know how to deal with a crying girl.

'She looked up at me, and I saw these big brown eyes. Her hair was dark, all messed up. I figured she was 14, maybe 15. I took her to her home, and she said, "If I had a brother I'd want him to be like you." I made a joke, like, "You don't want me as a brother coz I'm kinda wild." She said, "I'd feel safe with a brother like you." I never saw her again, but I wondered about her a lot. I hope she was okay.'

In April 1950 Steve was honourably discharged, though still a private. He returned to Myrtle Beach and Sue Ann. Welcoming him home, her father took Steve aside and told him he had special plans for him. 'He was thinking of me as his son-in-law,' said Steve, 'and that scared the shit outta me. I loved Sue Ann and wanted to marry her, but there was her father saying he would give me a job and a great salary, but I just knew I didn't belong there. I was scared they'd one day discover who I really was and where I came from, maybe meet my mother – I couldn't let that happen. I couldn't pretend to be something I wasn't. And I realised I had a lot of living to do before settling. And I didn't know how to be a good husband, or even a good man to love. So I bummed out.'

When I asked him if it broke his heart to leave his first love, he said, 'More than I can say. But I *had* to do it, not just for me but for her.'

He jumped a freight train to Washington, DC, where he drove a cab, but he felt he needed to be 'where the action is', and that was in New York. So he returned to Greenwich Village, where he rented a cold-water flat for around $20 a month.

He took any spare-time job he could get, including repairing TV sets: 'I learned a lot of useful skills in the marines;' delivering newspapers: 'Any kid can do that;' boxing: 'I managed to deck a few guys, but I got knocked out myself too many times so I quit;'

and playing poker: 'I thought I could be a professional gambler but I lost more than I made.' He also worked in a garage recapping tyres, made sandals at a cobbler's shop, worked in a post office loading mail into bags, collected bets for a bookie, sold pens and artificial flowers, and even sold encyclopedias at the door. He also rolled drunks when the opportunity arose.

'I began slipping into my bad old ways,' he said. 'I was on the lookout for any scam. One time I was in a drugstore and just picked up a shower nozzle. I was just looking at it, but the clerk saw me and thought I was returning it, and asked if I'd like a refund, so I said, "Yes," and I made $20 – it was just an accident, but I did it a few more times.'

Then Steve started getting into more serious crime. 'This guy came up to me and said he'd been watching me. All I'd been doing that day was driving a car I'd fixed. I was turning it on its handbrake, and really just having a good time racing it up and down in a street. I was good at it. I'd even thought about becoming a stuntman in movies maybe, driving fast cars and crashing them.

'So he said he had a job for me and the next thing I knew I was driving a car for him and his [two] partners, who were robbing stores in the Bronx. I was their getaway driver. Now I really *did* feel like I was in a Bogart and Cagney movie.'

Steve was entering one of the darkest periods of his life. He was a petty thief on the brink of becoming a major criminal. 'Driving the [getaway] car was a groove but I didn't carry a gun,' he said. 'One of the guys wanted me to have one and I wanted one, but the other guys said they didn't think I was ready. I said to them, "What's to be ready about? I was a *marine*." But these guys were very democratic considering they were hoods. Unless they all agreed, they didn't do anything. So I didn't get a gun. I didn't care. I had the wheels. It was better than a gun.'

He was on track to becoming like John Dillinger again, and he began to realise that his first true friend was the gangster who had got him the job of wheelman. That was also the gangster who had been one of those to vote against Steve being given a gun. Steve always thought he did him a favour by doing that.

'My experience of friendship was limited to a dog, a pig and a cat. Now I had an actual human friend who was a gangster. And I believed what he told me. I trusted him . . . probably the first time I trusted anybody. He started telling me I was wrong for the game. I thought he didn't trust me or something, and I said, "What do you mean, wrong?" and he said, "Steve, you're no gangster. You just love driving fast." And I said, "Sure, I love driving fast. I love being on the edge, man." He said, "It ain't the same thing." I said, "Who cares? I'm in the game." He shook his head and said, "Steve, trust me, you're not into this the way I am. You wanna be like in a movie, like James Cagney. But this is real, man. You're just *playing* the part."

'That hurt my feelings, I can tell you. But he was right. He saw it. I was too stupid to see it.'

Steve stressed to me that he wasn't a 'full-time wheelman', but did the job when they needed him. 'I was just getting a payback now and then – good money, but not the kind of bread they were on.' He had even been able to buy himself a 1946 Indian Chief motorbike, which he kept in his apartment, usually by his bed. But he needed a regular income. 'I saw that getting a regular job didn't amount to much, so I figured I'd try something which seemed an okay thing but was illegal. I became a pimp.'

He knew a local prostitute. Her name was Lindy. He told me, 'You met those kinds of girls when you hung out with gangsters. They'd be around – like in bars, sometimes at a party, always looking to turn a trick.' Lindy told Steve her pimp had been arrested and gone to jail, and she had no one taking care of her. 'So I said, "I'll take of you." She laughed and said, "You're sweet, but you're no pimp." I said, "I can learn to be." Besides, I'd worked in a brothel, I'd seen what went on, and I collected the money. I figured it couldn't be so hard.'

I wondered if Steve felt some connection to Lindy because his mother had been a prostitute; he'd always had the lowest opinion of Julian's part-time occupation. I asked him about this and he got angry and said, 'Julian was my *mother*. Moms don't whore themselves.'

That was the difference between Lindy and Julian – one was

his friend, the other his mother. Otherwise, Steve had no moral objections to a woman whoring herself. Besides, as Steve noted, Lindy was a 'professional', and his mother just a 'part-timer'.

So Steve began pimping, although he didn't have very much to do. 'I just kept an eye on her. If a guy was interested, I stepped in, made sure he understood the rules, took his money and wished him well.' He never made personal use of Lindy's services. 'It kind of sickened me to think of it,' he said, talking about the idea of having sex with a prostitute. He still laughed when he recalled his early years paying a young teenage girl with cakes for a quickie: 'That was part of growing up. It was "You show me yours and . . ." But she only wanted cakes. Real hookers sell themselves, and while some of them were real nice ladies, they were also kind of dirty. I wouldn't go there.'

Lindy, he said, was one of those 'real nice ladies'. 'She was real okay, you know? Reminded me of Claire Trevor in *Stagecoach*. She was a whore but had a heart of gold.' Steve often equated nefarious activities and the people involved with situations and characters from movies. 'Movies were my education. But it was all images. Not real life. All the blood was in black and white so it never looked so bad. So you didn't learn the truth.'

Steve finally learned the truth – seeing blood red and gushing – during one of the hit-and-runs when one of the gangsters got shot by a storekeeper who fired back.

'I'd seen people injured but not like this. The blood was pumping out coz an artery had been hit. This tough guy was crying for his mother. I was panicking and saying, "We got to get him to a doctor," and one said, "Just keep driving," and all the time this guy was crying, "I'm gonna die, oh mother and Jesus don't let me die." After a couple of minutes he was very quiet. I just drove. We always had a different place to head for – never used the same location twice. And we got there, and he was dead. I thought this wasn't what I thought it would be. I felt sick. I would have quit, but the two guys made the decision for all of us – not that they quit; they just went their own ways, and I went mine. They were going to find other work doing what they did, and I had Lindy to take care of.'

Steve said he never made a lot of money from Lindy. 'I let her keep most of it. I just took a small cut. I didn't feel good about taking her money. I mean, *she* earned it. I just watched out for her. It was a piece of cake.'

Steve wasn't earning enough from Lindy to pay the rent for his Greenwich apartment and food and bills, but one of the two surviving gangsters from his wheelman days did put some extra work his way. 'He was selling guns. To anyone who wanted one. He was selling to gangsters, storekeepers, frightened people who felt the law wasn't protecting them. And he said he didn't want to do it any more, and gave me the business. He was getting the guns from some Mafia guy, and as long as this guy got his cut, I was a free agent. I sold them out of the back of a van.

'I thought I was making easy money – guns and Lindy. And no taxes to pay. I mean, man, you can see why people do this for life; they got it made. And you think it's so easy. But it never ends well.'

It started to look like it wouldn't end well for Steve when a local pimp – a friend of Lindy's incarcerated pimp – had promised his friend that *he'd* take care of Lindy for now. When he discovered that Steve had muscled in on his business, he cornered him in a men's room of a bar.

'This mother-fucker was a huge grease-ball,' said Steve. 'Just so *fat*. He could have squashed me like a fly. He told me to beat it and stay out of his neighbourhood – like he *owned* it, so I told him he didn't own it, and he said, "I can find you a piece of ground *forever*, and that's me owning this part of town, and you'll own only your grave, which nobody'll ever find."

'I didn't wait for him to hit me. I hit him as hard as I could in his huge stomach. He was fat but hard, and I don't think he felt a thing. But coz he was fat he wasn't fast, and I was small and *very* fast. I flew outta there, got in my car and drove back to my apartment, where I hoped he'd never find me.'

Steve could have just laid low and stayed out of the fat pimp's way, but he kept thinking of Lindy, and he felt he was letting her down. 'I had to go and find her, and tell her she needed either to come with me or I'd have to leave her to her new fat pimp. She was really kind of calm. She asked if she went with me, what would she do, and I told her, "Work in a shop, anything but this," and she said, "But this is what I do best." I couldn't make her look at things any other way. It was whoring or nothing, and she just sort of resigned herself to her new boss.

'But I wasn't happy, so I went to see my [gangster] friend and told him what was going down. He said to leave it to him.'

Steve said his friend paid the fat pimp a visit. 'Just him on his own. No back-up. I didn't know just how tough he really was, and he pulled a gun on the fat guy and told him that *he* was going to be Lindy's pimp and he'd kill anyone who said otherwise.' Steve only learned a year later, when he bumped into Lindy by chance at a party, that his friend was still her pimp and taking very good care of her. 'She said I did her a great favour finding her a good man to take care of her. It just shows, nothing's black and white. We're all shades of grey.'

Steve's friend did him another favour. 'He told me to stop selling guns and get out of the racket for good. He said, "You're not cut out for any of this. You want to be a movie-star. So go be one. Pretend you're like us but in the movies. You'll be great at it." And I knew he was right.'

That might be the key to Steve's sudden decision – for it had not been a lifelong ambition – to have a go at acting. Rather than ever really thinking seriously about acting, Steve had identified with his screen heroes, particularly Humphrey Bogart, followed closely by James Cagney – or rather, he identified with the kind of characters they often played. 'I didn't fantasise about being a movie-star,' he told me. 'But when my life was shit, or when I was out of my depth, I thought, how would Bogie deal with this?' By doing that, he had managed to overlook, or just failed to foresee, the hazards of getting involved with gangsters and prostitutes. 'I thought there was glamour there. Then I saw the blood and I got scared. But for a while, it was like being in the movies.'

Steve also conceded that he figured being an actor would be a better way to make a living than just about anything else 'that busted my ass', and he also figured it would be a great way to meet 'the best-looking chicks'.

CHAPTER 5

—

Cocky Young Actor

After retiring from crime, Steve's life began to centre more on what went on in Greenwich Village rather than outside of it. 'People there were kind of wild, but not like the wild I had been. And the chicks were wild too. Not whores. Just girls who were looking for fun.'

Steve took advantage of the girls looking for fun. 'I hardly ever went back to my flat,' he said. 'I was spending nights in girls' flats.'

For a while, Steve was a lot calmer, a lot less angry. 'I was learning to be cool,' he said. 'I had to learn to hold back. Stay cool. I'd been through so much. I was an old man by the time I was 19 . . . 20. I had to learn to be young. Not to want to bust people wide open.'

But even though he was learning to be cool, it didn't take a lot to ignite his anger – and he stayed that way most of his life. He felt he had a chance at overcoming his rage when he met a girl from a good family. 'I really dug her. I mean, I think I loved her. But her parents didn't like me. They were a "good" family, and I was from the wrong side of the tracks. I figured this time I wouldn't run out when things were getting good like I did before [with Sue Ann]. But her parents hated me, and stopped her seeing me. I just saw red.'

His attempts to overcome his anger were defeated by the girl's father's attitude towards him, and he got his revenge. 'I stole his car and wrecked it. I made sure it was unfixable. That decided [it] for me – no more nice girls. No more love.'

Having decided he wasn't going to fall in love again, Steve began to explore his avenues into the acting profession seriously. He discovered that being an ex-marine, he could take advantage of the GI Bill, which allowed him to study for a trade. He applied to Sanford Meisner's Neighborhood Playhouse in June 1951; Sanford Meisner was an actor who had adopted an acting methodology known as the Meisner Technique (which, to put it simply and briefly, required actors to react truthfully rather than mechanically to any line of dialogue or action).

Steve got his interview with Meisner. 'I didn't think I had a chance. I thought he'd take one look at me and kick me out.'

But Meisner didn't kick him out, and is on record as saying, 'He was an original – both tough and childlike, like Marilyn Monroe, as if he'd been through everything but had preserved a certain basic innocence. I accepted him at once.'

Steve didn't prove to be the most disciplined or even enthusiastic of actors. 'I was just giving it a try,' he said. 'When I got up in front of everyone, I felt like a fool. It was embarrassing. It was like playing silly games.

'I didn't get on with the other students. They took it so *seriously*. I didn't give a rat's ass about art. I thought about giving it up, and even cut classes sometimes. It was too much like being back at school. I thought I'd be kicked out, and didn't care, but the funny thing was that when I had to do a scene, I gave it my best shot, and my teachers were impressed. I think they saw all that truth or whatever gig it was they wanted from me, but all I was doing was putting myself into it. I didn't find it that hard.

'The only problem I had was when I heard my voice played back on a tape recorder, and I thought it was lousy and I *knew* I could do better than that, so I worked on my voice. But mostly I found the best technique was to not give a damn.'

Steve often said in later years when he was a success that he wasn't an actor but a reactor. That was certainly true in those early days at the Playhouse. He was improvising a scene with a girl and she suddenly slapped his face. He reacted by punching her out cold.

He had to work part-time to earn enough to live on. He drove a delivery truck from seven in the evening, well into the night, and turned up tired for class each day.

To pass the exams, students appeared in scenes from plays, and in one of them, from *Truckline Café*, Steve played the role Marlon Brando had played on Broadway. There is no filmed record – that I know of – of Steve's early stage work to be able to judge how good he was at that time, and his early film work doesn't always reveal the star quality waiting to leap off the screen to grab an audience. Ultimately it took a good film director to be able to lead Steve in the right direction, and that director was John Sturges, who would direct him in *Never So Few*, *The Magnificent Seven* and *The Great Escape* (and almost *Le Mans*, but they had a permanent falling-out). Sturges told me:

Steve was too inhibited to be a really good actor on stage. Acting teachers are okay for some, but not for others, and Steve really didn't come out too well. He could *act*, but it wasn't exciting. He wanted to be Marlon Brando and do all that Method Acting stuff. But what Steve really needed, for film if not the stage, was someone to get him to play honestly, and, let's face it, Steve had lived a lot of life in not a lot of years, and he had a lot of life experience, and *that's* what made him a star, because what you saw was honesty, not clever bits of technique. It took time to find that in him. It wasn't really until *The Great Escape* that it came through, and that's why he's still the most memorable of all those stars in that movie – not just because of the motorbike jump. *That's* the movie when he really became a great screen actor and a star. It also brought out all the things that are worst about Steve, because he had come to realise he only wanted to do what made him look *good*. And that put demands on everyone. He wasn't a team player. Everyone had to play *around* him.

Steve told me that he credited John Sturges with teaching him more about acting than anyone ever did at the Neighborhood

Playhouse. But to become a professional actor, he needed some formal training, just to get him started, and he got that at the Playhouse. After six months' training, he landed a small role in a Jewish repertory company during the summer break, speaking three words – in Yiddish. He was fired after the fourth night. 'I guessed it was my lousy Yiddish,' he said. But the truth was, he conceded, he really wasn't very good.

He had some good luck though. An agent, Peter Witt, would watch the annual productions put on by the Neighborhood Playhouse, had seen Steve in the scene from *Truckline Café*, and was impressed enough to tell him to call him when he completed his studies.

Steve continued at the Playhouse, which provided him with a chance not only to study drama but to meet lots of girls. 'I think Steve went into acting because there were plenty of girls available,' laughed Jim Coburn. 'He was known as a fuck 'em and leave 'em kind of guy.'

Contrary to legend, Steve didn't jump on the bones of *every* pretty girl. One girl he ran into at an actors' party was a 14-year-old brunette, Suzanne Pleshette, who became one of his closest lifelong friends. She said, 'I was like his baby sister and he had to look after me.'

Even on their first meeting, at that party, he became over-protective of Susanne, which mystified her. 'I was with an older guy,' she recalled, 'and Steve knew this guy but he didn't know me. He just thought I needed protecting and he pulled me aside and said he'd give me a ride home. He took me outside and there was his motorcycle, and he said, "Get on," but I told him it wasn't necessary and I was all right. He said, "Okay, but any time any of the guys give you trouble you come to me," and from that day he always treated me like his baby sister. Did that until he died. I have no idea why he decided he needed to be my protector. Maybe I reminded him of someone.'

I think she reminded him of the young teenage girl he saved from being raped when he was in the marines. Like Susanne, that girl was dark-haired, dark-eyed, pretty, young and, at the time, in need of protecting.

When I pressed Susanne about their relationship in later years, she insisted, 'It was always platonic. He had this reputation with the girls, but he wasn't like that with me. At first I thought, "What's wrong with me? Why doesn't he want me?" But I guess I was too young for him. He looked out for me, and whenever boys annoyed me he'd deal with them. It's funny, because one boy he chased off I kind of liked, so I got annoyed with Steve and said, "Are you my brother?" And he thought about that a moment and said, "Yeah, I am. And no one's gonna mess with my kid sister." And that's how it was. He was so sweet. People have this image of him being such a rebel and some kind of punk, but I found him just totally sweet.'

At the end of Steve's first year of studies he went with a friend to Miami to scuba-dive. With no experience but a never-ending drive to seek thrills, he found a new thrill – swimming with sharks. He kept a speargun handy just in case, and with each dive he went lower until he went too far and punctured his left eardrum, causing it permanent damage so that he was almost deaf in that ear.

He was accepted for a second year at the Playhouse and awarded a half-scholarship of $350. To earn enough to survive, he competed in motorcycle races each weekend at Long Island City raceway.

'That was more fun than acting,' he said. 'That was the gig that drove me. I could have done it professionally coz I won a lot of races and won a couple hundred bucks each weekend. I even bought a Harley-Davidson.' He no longer had to drive trucks at night.

I wondered why Steve didn't just quit acting there and then and actually become a pro racer. He said, 'I'd started something and for once I was going to finish it.'

Steve just refused to quit acting, no matter what, and accepted the offer made by agent Peter Witt. That led to small acting roles in *Time Out for Ginger* and *Peg o' My Heart* in Fayetteville, New York. 'I was nervous and forgot my lines. One of the actors told me, "You were just plain embarrassing." I figured I could either quit or learn from it and get better, so that's what I did.'

Despite being able to earn money as a motorcycle racer at weekends, Steve still somehow managed never to have enough money to buy food, so he made a deal with the chef at an Italian restaurant called Louis's that he would pay for all food with what he earned from the first acting job he got. The chef, called Sal, set Steve a limit of $20. From his earnings in *Time Out for Ginger* he paid off his bill in full, then ran up another tab and paid it off with his earnings from *Peg o' My Heart*.

Witt then landed Steve a role in *The Member of the Wedding* in Rochester, New York. It starred the great actress and jazz singer Ethel Waters, who won the New York Drama Critics Award for her performance in that play. Steve could see why. 'She was wonderful. She really made the audience care about her [character]. I learned more from watching her than I ever did at drama school.'

Going on the road with the play, Steve was getting regular pay cheques, much of which he blew on good food, another motorbike and a used British MG sports car. He had to pay for the car in instalments, but it wasn't delivered until payment had been made in full. Steve and the play were in Chicago when the MG arrived. 'I loved that car. It was *beautiful*. But it cost me every penny I had, so I asked the producer for a raise, and I was fired.'

That was Steve's version – brief and to the point. But the truth was, Steve had become cocky and was upsetting a lot of the company. When Peter Witt heard this, he warned Steve to calm down, but it did no good. Finally, Melvyn Douglas, the veteran actor who was in the cast, decided enough was enough, and demanded the producer fire McQueen. The producer contacted Witt first, and Witt begged him not to fire his client, knowing it could damage Steve's career beyond repair, and said that he would persuade Steve to resign. Which he did. But the damage was done, and word spread that Steve McQueen was trouble. No theatre or producer would hire him, and he didn't get another part for three years.

Out of work and broke, Steve moved to a cheaper apartment, sold his beloved MG and worked as a mechanic. 'I figured my acting career was over,' he said, 'but then one day in comes James

Dean, and I serviced his car. I felt humiliated because I knew I should have been making money acting, and now I was servicing Jimmy Dean's fucking car. So that made me mad enough to hang in there.'

He had to hang in there a long time. Meanwhile, Julian came back into his life.

When he first arrived in Greenwich Village, he had called her and told her he was going to learn to be an actor. She had told him, 'Let me know when you flunk.' He never heard from her after that, until she called him from Bellevue Hospital, where she was being treated for alcoholism, asking him to come and discharge her. He went, discharged her and walked her home. She insisted on stopping at one of her favourite taverns for a beer.

The same happened again, and then a third time. Each time, Steve went to collect her, driven by an impulse that had nothing to do with love but was simply duty. She needed him, he answered the call. It did nothing, however, to repair the broken bond of mother and son.

But he never turned his back on her when she needed him and he resolved to stay in touch with her. 'He always kept her at arm's length,' said Don Gordon. 'But he didn't feel he could just abandon her.'

Neither did he abandon his almost nonchalant notion not to give up trying to become an actor, which is surprising since he didn't work as an actor for around three years. 'I had to show 'em,' he said; he always had to show them – whoever they were at the time. Before it had been the marines. Now it was anyone who thought he couldn't make it as an actor. Above all else, Steve was determined to prove to *himself* that he could stick at something and become a success. It was either that or, as he said to me, 'I was going to end up in jail as a professional criminal.'

Although he didn't work as an actor again until 1955, Steve did appear as an extra in a 1953 film, *Girl on the Run*. He suggested to me he did some other work as an extra but said he couldn't even remember what those films were. 'You just turned up early in the morning, waited for hours, did your bit, got paid and went home.'

In 1955 he applied to join the Actors Studio, where James Dean and Marlon Brando had learned Stanislavski's Method, taught by Lee Strasberg. 'The Actors Studio was where you really had to go to make it as an actor in New York in those days,' said Steve. 'I thought I could learn to act like Brando.'

Joining the Actors Studio at the same time was Martin Landau. He recalled, 'Steve and I were the only two accepted by the Actors Studio that year. Two thousand auditioned and Steve and I were the only ones accepted. So he had to be good enough even then or he wouldn't have got in.'

The same year Steve joined the Actors Studio, his agent Peter Witt managed to get him good role in a TV drama, *Chivington Road*, and an episode in a series called *Goodyear Television Playhouse*, which featured original plays.

The work trickled in. Steve landed the second lead role of a longshoreman in a stage play, *Two Fingers of Pride*, set in the New York docks, after convincing the writer, Jim Loghi, and director, Jack Garfein, that he was, like the character he played, half Italian. The play was performed in summer stock, in 1955, in Ogunquit, Maine. The *New York Post* gave his portrayal of the longshoreman a warm appraisal, and Garfein, impressed with McQueen, managed to get him an appointment to meet with the MCA agency. Steve claimed he arrived at the interview on Madison Avenue by riding his Harley into the lobby, into the lift and up to the 11th floor. MCA signed him.

'I wanted to show them I was no ordinary guy you could put in a suit,' said Steve. 'I was a guy of the streets, and I could play that part.'

MCA put him up for a small role in the movie *Somebody up There Likes Me*, which starred Paul Newman in a role originally intended for James Dean, who had recently died in a car crash. Newman was playing a small-time criminal who fights his way out of crime as a boxer.

'That was *me*,' said Steve. 'That was almost *my* life. I should have had the part.' He was envious of Newman, and although McQueen and Newman became friends in later years, they were never great buddies.

'I didn't like Steve too much when I first met him,' Paul Newman said. 'He wanted my part, and he made it clear. He was a cocky kid, but that's what his part needed, and it was a good start for him in pictures.'

Of Newman, Steve told me in 1970, 'I couldn't afford to be his friend. He was ahead of me, and I had to catch up. I did. Now we're the two biggest stars around, and I want to be *bigger* than him.'

The film's director, Robert Wise, remembered Steve as a 'cocky young actor, fresh and wanting to do well. When I auditioned him, he arrived in a sport jacket and wearing a little cap kind of on the side. Maybe he was trying to impress me that he *was* the character, a punk with a knife.'

I told Wise that Steve said he didn't try to play the part but *was* the part. Steve never dressed to impress. He just showed up for interviews, whether it was with MCA or with Robert Wise, in his own persona as a guy on a motorbike.

And yet I can't help thinking that Steve, who could be arrogant and charming at the same time – he just had this faint air of innocence that was appealing even when he was cocky – knew he only had to enhance his own persona and almost challenge agents and directors, as if he was saying, 'Come on, I dare you *not* to give me the part.' Wise said, 'He made you feel like he could slug you just as fast as he could smile. He was tense, ready to spring, but he was also very likeable.'

Once he had the part of the punk, called Fidel, Steve put everything into it, according to Wise.

'He was going to prove he was not just right for the part, but a *good* actor. He liked the new breed of actors like Brando and Montgomery Clift, and he wanted to *be* them. He played the part the way he thought Brando would play it. He really wasn't very good. But he *wanted* to be good. He said, "You can be a great actor, but to be a great *movie* actor you have to study men like Humphrey Bogart." I think what was special about Steve was that he managed to combine the qualities of Brando and Bogart. Not in *Somebody up There Likes Me*, because he was really terrible in that small role, but later. Maybe it was intentional, maybe that's just the way he was. Every actor takes a little of what rubs off on them from watching other actors they admire. I'm sure a lot of actors have since let some of Steve McQueen rub off onto them. But there's no doubt, he was an original, and even though he was bad in *Somebody up There Likes Me*, I knew he was going to do well.'

The word was now spreading that a new actor on the block called Steve McQueen was on the rise, and he quickly landed another TV role, in an episode from *The United States Steel Hour* called *Bring Me a Dream*. Television plays, usually taped live in those days, were a good training ground for potential movie actors, although it was considered dangerous ground for established movie-stars to tread. Movie stars didn't do television.

But Steve wanted to get back on stage, especially when he heard about a new play on Broadway, *A Hatful of Rain*. He lobbied for the lead role of Johnny Pope, a Korean veteran addicted to morphine, but was beaten to it by Ben Gazzara, who proved a hit in the part. Then, as luck would have it, Gazzara had to leave the play to fulfil a film commitment, so Steve hassled MCA and the play's producers to give him the part.

But he still had to compete with others for the role, namely George Peppard and John Cassavetes. Steve beat them to it through sheer hard work, which included spending time among junkies, and sending flowers to the wives of the producers. 'I scammed my way into the part.'

Steve worked hard at rehearsals, wanting to be not just good, but better than anybody else could be. Even better than Ben Gazzara had been.

After working hard, he liked to relax. He drank beer and smoked marijuana. Many actors took drugs. And so did directors and writers. They had been taking drugs from the days of silent movies, and to my knowledge they've never stopped. That's just a privately accepted, though publicly unaccepted, part of show business. Recent research has shown that long use of marijuana can cause excessive moods swings and paranoia. Steve had certainly suffered from all that before he used marijuana, but it does seem that it got worse over the years. Certainly by 1970, when he had reached a crisis point in his marriage to Neile, and was experiencing almost uncontrollable violent outbursts against her and John Sturges, he was, by his own admission, 'so angry and so wild that even I hardly know myself'.

But when he first met Neile, he was less angry, less paranoid, and even able to fall in love.

CHAPTER 6

—

The Bandido and the Girl

In June 1956, Steve was walking down a street when he saw a beautiful woman in a red dress walking in the opposite direction. 'I knew I liked her immediately,' he told me, 'so I stood in her way. I said, "You're pretty," and she said, "You're pretty too." Then I saw someone I needed to see and said, "Okay, well, see ya," and I left her standing there. I think she was kind of puzzled by my approach.'

The girl he had puzzled was Neile Adams, a professional dancer who was about to open on Broadway in *The Pajama Game*. She had just come from a dance lesson for that show when Steve saw her for the first time. Neile had already noticed him. She often caught sight of him, usually riding his motorcycle, often without a shirt on. He had become a regular sight in the village, on his motorbike and shirtless when the weather was good, in a leather jacket when it wasn't. He was a rebel without a cause, a wild one. He was also 'the Bandido'. That's the nickname people around Greenwich Village gave him, according to Suzanne Pleshette. 'He was called the Bandido because he was a real master at managing to get beer and food for free from bars and diners. He always had a scam.'

Steve told me, 'One of my greatest talents is how to scam. It might not be respectable but it saved me from going hungry a lot.'

Just a few evenings after Steve saw Neile in the street, he saw her again, at Downey's Restaurant. 'She walked in and I just looked her up and down, and the shape of her fabulous dancer's legs in tight pants – just beautiful. And she had such a beautiful smile. But she was with some guy, and she looked like she was having a good time. I tell you, as she walked past me, I was so taken by her that I dropped a forkful of spaghetti in my lap, and she said, "Wow, good one, kid." Anyone else said that, I would have gotten mad, but she just kinda took my breath away, and I had to laugh.'

Friends who sat with Neile noticed her interest in Steve, and warned her that he had a reputation for sleeping around. Her friends knew he was rehearsing for A *Hatful of Rain* and, according to her own account in her book *My Husband, My Friend*, they told her, 'He's not so hot.' Whether they thought that because word was out that he wasn't doing so well, or his reputation for being trouble had gone ahead of him, it was an indication that in the world of theatre Steve McQueen was still an outsider. And he didn't care. 'I wasn't in it for the art,' he said. 'I was in it because I wanted to be somebody.'

If Neile's friends thought they could dissuade her from showing any further interest in him, they were mistaken. Destiny, Steve's determination and his smile were to take care of things. That smile had melted the hearts of many women. A lot of them he only ever saw once, but they all found the Steve McQueen smile irresistible. 'He had the cutest smile,' said Suzanne Pleshette. 'His face really kind of changed when he smiled. He could look so moody and angry, even if he wasn't, and he had a lot of lines in his face even when he was young – just so much living was done in so few years – but when he smiled, he was like a boy. He had so much charm. His eyes smiled too, and his face lit up, and girls just fell in love with him. He was so darn cute. And he knew it. He learned that he only had to smile and girls fell at his feet.'

Neile didn't exactly fall at his feet, but she had been charmed enough so that when she turned up again at Downey's with an actor, Mark Rydell (later to become a really fine movie director), and saw Steve sitting with Ben Gazzara, she gave him a smile – one which was just as endearing as his, according to Don Gordon. He told me, 'Neile has this dazzling smile with perfect teeth, and she's like a beacon when she smiles. She just floored Steve with it.'

As well as the attraction he had for her, Steve couldn't resist his competitive nature; he figured that he would challenge this young actor Mark Rydell for her affections. So when she left her table to go to the washroom, Steve went over to Rydell and told him that he was going after Neile, declaring, 'All's fair in love and war.' He patted Rydell on the back and returned to his table. Neile returned, and when Steve saw Rydell excuse himself temporarily, he quickly moved in on Neile. However, he wasn't ready to ask her out on a date. 'I wanted to be somebody before I asked her out,' he told me. 'She was already on Broadway, and I wanted my name in lights before asking her on a date.' He was competing even with Neile, determined not to ask her out until *Hatful of Rain* was running with him as the star. Steve had to be a bigger star than her.

When he opened in *A Hatful of Rain* he was a big success. Robert Culp recalled seeing him in the part. 'That's where he really came alive – on stage. He was transcendent on stage. It was visceral. It was instinctive. Almost primeval. This was the real thing. You could feel it.'

Once his name was on the marquee, he turned up at the theatre where Neile was in *The Pajama Game* and asked her out. She accepted, and he told her he'd pick her up after her show that night.

Neile made sure she was in her prettiest dress. Steve arrived on his motorcycle wearing jeans, T-shirt and a leather jacket. He told me, 'She must have thought I was a wild man. She said, "Are we going for a walk in the park?" I said, "No, we're going for a ride on my motorcycle. Just climb on behind, hold onto me with one arm and with your other hold onto your dress and your high heels." I thought she'd tell me to drop dead, but she just did what I said, and I rode as fast as I could, wondering if she could take it. I didn't want a girl who would cry. But she loved it.'

Don Gordon observed, 'I don't think Neile ever had another man tell her what to do before. He just gave the orders.'

That first date was spent speeding through Greenwich Village and in a coffee shop. It didn't occur to Steve to take her to dinner. 'Those coffee shops were cool places,' Steve told me. 'Just places to sit and talk. It was perfect for us, coz we could talk about our lives. I told her about my childhood, she told me about hers.'

Neile had been born in the Philippines in 1933 shortly after her parents married. Her mother was of Spanish and German descent, and her father was part Chinese and part Filipino. Then it was discovered that her father was already married, and so he left and neither Neile nor her mother ever saw him again.

When the Japanese occupied the Philippines during World War Two, nine-year-old Neile and her mother were placed in a prison camp, where Neile learned to speak Japanese and became a messenger for the Allied underground. Steve told me that Neile and her mother were tortured and, as he put it, 'made to do unspeakable things'. But not all of this was revealed by Neile to Steve on that first date. But she told him just enough to convince him that she was someone he had more in common with than was immediately obvious.

'They hardly seemed like a perfect match,' said Don Gordon. 'I didn't know them when they first met, but when I did get to know them, I thought that she was such a lively chick, always ready to laugh, and Steve was such a moody guy.'

Even in 1970, during a crisis in the McQueen marriage, Steve still thought he and Neile were the perfect pair. 'We have so much in common coz both our dads left us when we were young. And we both had our problems when we were teens. From that first date I thought we were perfect together.'

Other than that, Steve wasn't able to articulate what it was that made him believe that he and Neile were a perfect match. He said, 'I dug her – really dug her, and she dug me. That's all there was to it.'

'They were soulmates,' said James Coburn. 'That's why they stayed friends after they divorced.'

Suzanne Pleshette said, 'They were such a beautiful couple. They were both so exotic in their own way. She was dark and he was blond, this dark and light – they were just gorgeous. There was an incredible vitality that came from the both of them. You could feel the love and the sexual chemistry between them.

'I told him once, "So, the Bandido got the girl." He said, "I can't believe how lucky I am." He really knew he was lucky.'

There was something else about Neile that fascinated Steve, thought Jim Coburn. 'She had a worse time than he did when they were kids, and he couldn't believe anyone could have had it worse than him.'

In fact, while Steve felt there might have been a certain amount of soul-sharing, there was also competition. He *had* to compete with her when it came to sharing bad experiences. And he lost. If anything, that made him love her all the more, because he couldn't believe such a sweet soul as hers had been through so much hell and come through it all intact. And, he admitted to me, she was a better person than him. 'I was ready to hate the world, or at least take it on. Neile just loved the world.'

Neile did have the advantage of a loving mother who was able to give her a good education and encourage her to become a dancer. Steve never had anything like that, and that was where he trumped Neile. I think he had to trump her in something, otherwise I don't believe it would have ever worked in the first place.

In 1977 Steve acknowledged that they weren't so perfect after all. '*She* made it work for as long as it did. She's the outgoing one. Not me. She can laugh at herself. I just get mad at myself, and at everyone else. I guess we fell in love and then became friends. But it wasn't enough.'

Although that first date had Steve enthralled by Neile, it wasn't actually love at first sight for him. In fact, Steve had nothing more noble on his mind than getting her into bed.

'Steve had a lot of girls before he met Neile,' said Don Gordon. 'Girls almost threw themselves at him. He told me that before Neile he just wanted girls for screwing. And that's all he wanted when he took Neile out. What really got to him was she said, "No." No girl ever said that to him before. So he took her out again and she still said, "No." I guess she finally said, "Yes," because then he moved in with her.'

According to Steve it was only a week after their first date when he said, 'Let's move in. Your place or mine?'

She asked him, 'Where do you live?'

'In a cold-water flat.'

Neile had a nice apartment on 55th Street, so she said, 'Mine,' and in he moved, along with a bus stop he used as a barbell.

In the apartment above them was actor Rod Steiger, who was often away because his career was burgeoning. Rod recalled to me, 'I couldn't see Steve making it as an actor. He didn't seem to care about acting. All he cared about was having a good time.'

When Steiger was away he let a journalist friend, Lionel Olay, stay in his flat. Steve liked Olay, and he and Neile would visit with him. There Steve rolled a joint of marijuana, as if he were demonstrating it as a special craft to Neile, who had never encountered the narcotic before. Steve's moods were, even at the best of times, unpredictable, but they were not helped by his daily use of marijuana.

'Steve smoked the stuff. We all did,' said Jim Coburn. 'My experience was it just makes you feel good, but when Steve came down off a high he could be a real son of a bitch.'

Don Gordon observed, 'Steve could get in a real temper and then you better watch out, but when he was in a good mood, he was your best friend. But I think he related better with guys than with girls. Neile was a bit of a mystery to him. And I guess he was to her too.'

When Neile asked Steve if he liked trees, and warm air, and the spring, and just feeling like life has promise and hope, he told her, 'That jazz is for women and children.' Then, after a moment or two, he asked her, 'What do you mean, love and hope?' That, apparently, was enough to make Neile understand him – he was innocent about love and didn't know what it meant. And that might be what made Steve fall in love with Neile, because she actually loved him, and he felt it very strongly. 'Scared the hell out of me,' he admitted to me. 'I'd had a couple of girls say they loved me before but I never hung around long enough to see what that meant. But Neile hung with me. From the first day we met. She never gave up on me. We talked about love and life, and I was kinda "Yeah, so what?" and she cried. That moment I knew I loved her. But I wasn't one for all that sunset and roses jazz.'

He might not have been a romantic, but he still felt the necessity to introduce Neile to his mother. 'I thought a lot about taking her to see Julian,' he told me. 'I think for once in my adult life I wanted some kind of approval from my mother, and I wanted her to like Neile, and for Neile to like her. But I'd told Neile so much shit about Julian I was sure she'd say she didn't want to meet her. But she was okay with it, so I took her to meet Julian, and for the first time I can remember, Julian actually seemed pleased about something I'd done. I'd brought her my girl. Neile said she liked my mother. Julian was a lot more sober, and she didn't have a man to knock her about, so I guess she was . . . settled. Maybe even as happy as she'd ever been.

'She said to me once, "Can we try and be like a real mother and son?" and I said, "You had all the chances. Now we have what we have, and let's settle for that." I just couldn't love her. But I couldn't forget she was my mom. Some things can't be healed.'

Neile was still in *The Pajama Game* and Steve was still in *A Hatful of Rain*, and even though he had come to some kind of resolution about love, he was still competing with her. 'I didn't want to be better than her,' he said. 'I just didn't want to be worse.'

But then things suddenly went downhill for Steve. Neile was offered a screen test by director Robert Wise for a role in *This Could Be the Night* in Hollywood when her run in *The Pajama Game* ended in September 1956. That was the weekend Steve's run in *A Hatful of Rain* ended suddenly and unexpectedly. He had begun strongly in the lead role, but over time he found he was unable to maintain the strength and freshness the role demanded. Perhaps it was because, as Robert Culp observed, Steve was visceral and lacked enough technique to be able to sustain it. And so he was being replaced. He had lasted just six weeks.

He made out to Neile that it didn't matter to him – but it hurt him. 'I just didn't want to be a baby,' he said. She begged him to go with her to California, but he said he'd stay in New York the 10 days she'd be in Hollywood.

He actually saw her absence as a chance to take off himself. 'I needed to take stock,' Steve said. 'I wasn't sure I liked being in love. It hurt when Neile went away and I didn't like how I felt. So I took off with some buddies on our motorcycles to Cuba. I take a road trip now and then to sort out my head.'

His buddies, he said, were 'kinda crazy– all kinda wild'. He told me about this road trip:

Lionel Olay was in Cuba writing articles about Fidel Castro, who was shooting it out with Batista, so me and an actor friend, and a poet and a guy who was more crazy than the rest of us all got on our motorcycles and we went to Havana to try and find Lionel. I thought, how hard could it be to find an American journalist in the war zone? Crazy! So down in Havana we get juiced up and I got into a fight and thrown in jail. But it wasn't too bad coz the guard was a real friendly guy and let me out the cell so I could have lunch with him. Cheese and wine!

Trouble was, I was due to be back when Neile got home, and I was in jail, and she didn't even know I'd gone down there. My buddies have all split, and I was about to get out of jail, but my motorcycle was gone and I had no way to get home. So I sent Neile a telegram in Hollywood asking if she'd send me money.

She didn't send it. I had to get back without her help. I thought she had spunk for doing that. It wasn't that she didn't care. She knew I would only spend the money hanging around Havana and then cable for more. I admired her for standing up to me. So I had to make my way home. I sold my motorcycle helmet and anything I had for hash, hitched rides, walked a hell of a lot.

I got back and she had been home for four days. She was out when I got in, and when she came in and saw me, she looked worried and said she was sorry for not sending me any money. I said, 'It's okay, baby. I love you and I'm just glad to be home.'

Everything was fine again, but then Neile heard that she had passed the screen test and was needed back in Hollywood. She was to play a minor role of a stripper. She urged Steve to go with her, but he said he just wanted to stay at home. He recalled:

I really did need time to think coz I really was feeling like I loved this girl and I needed to decide what to do about it. So she left for California and she was scared that was it between us – and I wondered if it might be too, coz I didn't know what I needed to do. I smoked dope and drank beer and thought hard and long for three days, and I realised all I wanted was her. Nobody had ever loved me so much.

Feeling like that surprised me. And I was surprised when I asked Julian to come over for supper and that's kind of when I made up my mind I wanted to marry Neile. So I phoned her and said, 'I'm gonna come out and be with you and make an honest woman of you.' That was the best I could come up with as a proposal. But I wanted to marry her just straight away if we could.

I needed a ring and I had no money – Neile paid for food, the rent, everything – and paid a jeweller I knew to design one for me with a $25 deposit, promising him Neile would pay the balance.

I pawned the gold watch Claude had given me and bought a plane ticket to Los Angeles. I loved that watch but I loved Neile a whole lot more. [Later he was able to buy the watch back.] I went to MGM and found her on a sound stage, where I picked her up in my arms and kissed her – like a scene from a movie.

But despite this uncharacteristic and romantic behaviour from Steve, Neile was suddenly unsure about rushing into marriage. She was the breadwinner, not only paying off the balance of the wedding ring but also other debts Steve was constantly running up. Her agent, Hilly Elkins, warned her that Steve was only marrying her for her money. Steve insisted he was not. 'I just wanted to be with her,' he told me.

She finally gave in and agreed to get married, so three days after he arrived in Los Angeles, they hired a Ford Thunderbird and headed for San Juan Capistrano. A nun at the mission there told them they had to wait for six weeks for the wedding banns to be published, so Steve told her, 'Then we'll live in sin.' Neile actually felt relieved that there would be more time to make sure they were doing the right thing, but Steve was in a hurry, and he got Neile back into the car and drove off to find the nearest justice of the peace.

'I was in a hurry and broke the speed limit,' he said – not that Steve ever worried about speed limits – 'and we got pulled over by two cops in a patrol car. These were big guys, hands on the handles of the guns, just in case. I said, "Look, fellas, we just want to get married straight away," and one of them said, "Follow us," so I followed them. I was kinda worried when we pulled up outside the police station. They said, "It's okay, we got a captain here knows a minister," so we found the captain, who said he would call him. It was late, gone 11, and the minister was still up and said he'd marry us. He opened up the church, and these two big cops were our witnesses, standing there with their pistols in their belts, and we were married.'

It was 2 November 1956. Neile was on the threshold of a career in movies, Steve seemed to have no prospects, and the marriage had begun the way it was to go on, at high speed with Neile giving in to everything Steve wanted, and Steve scamming his way to an inevitable conclusion.

Their honeymoon was just a weekend in Ensenada, Mexico, then it was back to Hollywood because Neile had a film to make. She began bringing Steve to the studio each day, which irritated the film's director, Robert Wise. He recalled, 'He [Steve] was just hanging around, lost, nothing to do, getting bored. I said to him, "Get out of here and find something to do," and he said, "No, I'll just hang out here." I said, "No, you won't. Get your ass off my set and don't come back." He should have been going from stage to stage, hassling directors, casting directors, anyone to give him a job. He just didn't seem like a hungry actor to me.'

If he wasn't hungry, it was because Neile was paying for everything, and he didn't need to earn money.

'I just hadn't dug what I needed to do,' Steve said. 'I thought she'd be earning money like this forever, and I couldn't be doing with getting off my ass and finding work. It didn't occur to me then that I was just using her, like she was my banker. And she never complained.' If Steve thought he was being smart at the time, he didn't think so by 1970. He said, 'I think she deserved better and I deserved none of it.'

He wasn't entirely idle though. 'I got it into my head that I might be able to find my dad [Bill McQueen]. I had all this hatred inside me for him, and it was eating me up, so I figured I ought to try and find him and see if I can sort my head out. I didn't know what I expected but I figured I should try.'

It was the beginning of a search that Steve would only periodically get enthused about. He really had nothing much to go on except that Julian had told him the last she heard of Bill McQueen he was in California. His efforts, such as they were, proved fruitless.

Unable to remain permanently in Los Angeles, Steve returned to New York and flew back to Los Angeles every weekend, all at Neile's expense. She continued paying for everything he needed, or wanted, including a new Corvette, and his gambling. She wasn't earning great money, but it was more than Steve had ever had, since he considered what was hers was his own, and he was spending it almost faster than she could earn it.

One weekend in Hollywood, Neile, tired from work, presented Steve with a TV dinner, making the mistake of trying to disguise it as home-cooked. He flung the dinner at the wall. It was one of many times when his temper overtook him.

In desperation, Neile begged her agent, Hilly Elkins, to find him work. Elkins took Steve to lunch, where Steve failed to endear himself to the agent with his coarse manner and selfish attitude. Elkins called Neile and told her he thought Steve was crude and obnoxious. Nevertheless, as a favour to her, he got Steve a small acting job, as a man on trial for murdering his psychiatrist's wife, in a Studio One TV drama, *The Defender*.

'Neile really helped me,' Steve told me. 'I think she saved me, coz I thought I was going to be like Brando and James Dean, and I tried to be like them, but she saw it and said, "You know, you can smile a little, like in the scene when you talk to your mother. Show us something about you. Don't just get mean and moody."

She coached me, and she made me good enough that when the show aired I got fan mail.'

Even Hilly Elkins was impressed, and promptly signed him up. He landed Steve a role in the movie *Never Love a Stranger*, in which he played an unlikely Jewish district attorney. Based on a Harold Robbins novel, it took a serious look at anti-Semitism. Robbins's books had sold around 14 million copies and the company producing the film, Allied Artists, thought the picture would be welcomed by Robbins' readership.

It was, however, very much a B-movie, costing just $700,000 to produce. Harold Robbins adapted the screenplay and co-produced, determined that this one would not end up like his last filmed book, *A Stone for Danny Fisher*, which became *King Creole*, starring Elvis Presley.

Although the film was set in New York, most of it was shot around Los Angeles. Neile had left Hollywood and gone to Las Vegas to appear in a revue. Their temporary separation by work so soon after their wedding caused insecurities on both sides, and their numerous telephone conversations occasionally ended with a phone being slammed down. Among Steve's numerous insecurities was the fact that, while he was hopeful about embarking on a real career as an actor, Neile was still earning 10 times what he got.

Steve was soon playing around with the film's leading lady, Lita Milan. He even admitted the affair to Neile after filming was over. It was the first of many affairs he would have which Neile tolerated. Some took her toleration as approval, but she never approved, according to James Coburn. 'I don't think you could say Neile was okay with it, but she couldn't stop it. I don't know what she said to him about it because she was lady enough to not talk about it to anyone else that I know of. But I will say that he needed her more than she needed him.'

Steve was laconic about his reasons for cheating on Neile. 'When you have girls really putting it on to you, you can only say no so many times.' I asked him how Neile had reacted when he told her about his first on-set fling. 'She was hurt. But she kind of accepted it.'

Neile wrote in her memoir, *My Husband, My Friend*, that she might never have known about what Steve called 'meaningless fuck-flings' had it not been for his need to confess to relieve his guilt. By doing that, she felt he transferred all the responsibility of making it all right onto her. She said that she was always able to rationalise his behaviour as something that disrupted an otherwise 'spectacularly successful marriage', and blamed his mother for treating him so badly.

It's curious that even having admitted to me that he cheated now and then on Neile, Steve felt the need to express how bad he felt about it all. 'I always felt guilty,' he said. But that had never stopped him. 'It wasn't all the time,' Steve told me. 'Just now and then.'

A lot of movie-stars I've known were unfaithful, and some almost made a career out of it. The best I can say for Steve is he didn't make a career out of it.

He appeared in more television dramas, and finally even his film career seemed to be taking shape, although it wasn't anything he felt proud of. 'When they gave me *The Blob* they were just looking for any guy who didn't look any worse than the special effects,' he said.

Steve couldn't have known how much of an impact the B horror flick would have on moviegoers *and* his career. He was lucky that he had Hilly Elkins to wheel and deal him through low-budget movies. Most actors of Steve's generation usually began with a studio contract that at least ensured them work for a while before they either made it or went into obscurity. So getting work in independent B movies wasn't an obvious building block as an actor, and most actors in those kinds of pictures usually didn't last long (rare exceptions include Jack Nicholson).

The Blob in question was a giant jelly monster from outer space, and Steve was the hero who saves mankind. While he was the leading man in the picture, it was the Blob that was the real star. As *Variety* noted, 'Neither the acting or direction is particularly credible. McQueen, who's handed star billing, makes with the old college try while Aneta Corsaut also struggles valiantly as his girlfriend. Star performers, however, are the camerawork of Thomas Spalding and Barton Sloane's special effects.'

Steve may have got star billing but his salary was hardly star-studded at just $3,000. He was offered 10 per cent of the profits and a smaller up-front fee but, convinced the film would never make a profit, he decided to take a flat fee instead. 'How was I to know the film would gross millions?' he said, grinning at his own lack of foresight.

When he'd first read the script, Steve didn't want to do it. 'It was shit! But Neile said, "Why not do it?" I said, "It'll kill my career." She said, "No, it won't. No one'll see it. No one'll know you were in it." I figured she was right.' He laughed and added, 'Man, *everyone* saw it.'

The film's budget had been a mere $240,000, much of which went into producing the special effects which, for its day, were just good enough to scare teenagers. In fact, when producer Jack H. Harris showed the film to Paramount, they were impressed enough to buy if for $300,000, and then spent another $300,000 promoting it. The film took $5 million in its first month. With re-releases and overseas markets, the film earned around $12 million, very lucrative for Harris and Paramount. If Steve had accepted the percentage offer, he would have become a millionaire from that film alone.

What Steve lacked in foresight, he made up for in tempera-ment, according to the film's director, Irvin S. Yeaworth Jr, a minister who directed a number of sci-fi horror films in the late 1950s before turning to making religious films. He said, 'I can't count the number of times I had to call Jack Harris and say, "Your star is giving us trouble again." I'd leave it to him to deal with Steve.'

When I asked Yeaworth to be specific, he said, 'He just wanted someone to tell him they liked him. He seemed to need approval, and all I could do was say, "Steve, you did just fine in that scene," but that wasn't good enough. He'd walk off the set and refuse to come back, so I'd leave it to the producer to make him happy. Jack Harris was very good at dealing with him. Steve would come back to the set and we'd carry on. I'd say to Jack,

"What happened?" "Oh, he was going to call his agent and everyone else, but when I told him how wonderful he was, he was fine."

'I didn't get to know Steve well, but what I can say is that you knew he was going to be a big star because he not only looked like a star on the screen but he behaved like one,' and with that Yeaworth laughed.

Steve admitted he was difficult, not just in his early films, but throughout his career. 'I only ever wanted to be good, and I didn't always know if I was any good, especially in those first movies. When you want to do your best, you're not always a nice guy.'

Don Gordon, who knew Steve as well as most, said, 'Steve can be difficult but he can also be the most generous guy. I knew him when he first started and saw how he could drive directors and producers crazy, but only because he wanted to do his best, and if he didn't think he was being allowed to do his best, he'd give them hell.'

That's true of a lot of major stars – Kirk Douglas, Burt Lancaster and William Holden were all known for their often difficult behaviour, and like McQueen none ever behaved in a way that was detrimental to their work. But when Steve made *The Blob* he wasn't even a *minor* star. He was the low-paid leading man in a picture in which the monster jelly was the star. And that was why he was difficult on the set – he wondered how a movie like that was ever going to be any good. Steve said, 'I guess a lot of actors in those movies just get paid and do their job, but I can't work that way. I want the picture to be good, and that means *I* have to be good.' He didn't know that as far as *The Blob* was concerned, it wasn't Steve McQueen who had to be good. Irvin S. Yeaworth Jr was convinced he saw a spark of the star quality McQueen had. 'It isn't easy to stand out when you're competing against a special effect, but you can see that Steve McQueen had *something* about him.' Perhaps spotting star quality is always easy with hindsight.

There was, I think, something else that drove Steve to behave the way he did. He'd never had a father to show him approval, and suddenly here were directors and producers – men (and sometimes women) who were often seen as surrogate parents by insecure actors.

On top of that, Steve was undoubtedly worried that he just might not be good enough to become a successful actor. 'I didn't know what the hell I was doing,' he told me. 'How did I know if the lighting they gave me was any good? Actors are supposed to know that. I didn't know if I was overacting or standing on the wrong mark. I guess I blew off steam because I was scared.'

But McQueen wasn't always throwing tantrums. Yeaworth told me, 'Sometimes Steve would walk over to me and I'd think, "Here we go," and he'd say, "Thanks for what you did," and he was actually showing gratitude to me, for what I never usually knew. I just did my job, and something I did or said affected him and helped him in a shot.'

Neither Harris, Yeaworth nor Steve could have known when they made the movie that part of its success would be due to the popularity of Steve McQueen who was about to become a major television star.

CHAPTER 7

—

Faster, Better, Going to the Edge

Just a few months after finishing *The Blob*, Steve landed the lead role in *The Great St. Louis Bank Robbery*, which was based on an actual robbery. Steve was ideally cast, as the driver of the getaway car. 'I knew what that was like,' he said, having been a real-life wheelman. 'I knew the thrill and the terror of the getaway.'

United Artists agreed to finance the film, but it was on a very tight budget, so Steve's salary was still minimal, and the movie was another B picture. It was shot in a semi-documentary style on location in St Louis. Unfortunately, being so far away from Neile led Steve to stray again. As with the previous separation, Steve and Neile kept in touch by phone calls every day, a lot of them ending in arguments. But Steve always followed up with incredibly heartfelt telegrams to Neile, expressing his love in almost poetic terms.

'I loved her so much,' he told me in 1970. 'I couldn't imagine my life without her.' He added, 'I still can't.'

Steve hoped for much from *The Great St. Louis Bank Robbery* but it didn't quite deliver. As Howard Thompson of the *New York Times* noted, 'The entire cast, excluding Steve McQueen, is unfamiliar, hence a freshness of faces. Likewise, the good photography and semi-documentary flavor of its actual St. Louis backgrounds. The pacing is far too slow and the neurotic clashes of the four thieves make the actual robbery anticlimactic and slightly absurd.'

Important Hollywood producers were not knocking on Steve's door, but Hilly Elkins had to keep finding him work because, said Steve, 'Elkins let me borrow his motorcycle and I jumped a hill on it and smashed it up, so the only way I could pay him back was if I got better-paid work.'

Elkins knew that a feature-length pilot for a TV show about a bounty hunter in the old West was to be presented as a special episode in a Western series called *Trackdown*, made by the Four Star Company and starring Robert Culp, who was another of Elkins's clients. Culp recalled, 'Hilly talked to me, asked me if I'd mind Steve being in an episode, and I said, no problem. I mean, I *hated* this guy and here he was guesting on my show.'

When I asked Culp why he hated McQueen, he said, 'Because whenever I arrived at a girl's place, he was going out the back door as I was coming in. I didn't know who he was then, and I asked, "Who is this guy?" But, you know, when we worked together, I *liked* him. I hated him for stealing all the girls, but he was so likeable. So I didn't hate him forever.'

Elkins approached the series' producer, Vincent Fennelly, about casting McQueen as the bounty hunter, whose name was Josh Randall. Fennelly gave Elkins a script to give to Steve, who had misgivings about it straight away. Fennelly made Steve understand that this character was very different from other leading characters in Western shows. A bounty hunter was looked down upon by lawmen and hated by criminals. He was the underdog. And that appealed to Steve, because he felt he had always been the underdog. The challenge Fennelly gave Steve was to win the audience over.

'That scared me,' said Steve. 'But my agent told me that if it came off, there'd be a series in it with me as the star. I wasn't sure I wanted to do television, but, as my agent made plain, I wasn't getting good money in movies, and the money in a series would be pretty good. So I did it.'

For a man who preferred motorbikes to horses, Steve felt out of place at first in a Wild West setting. 'He couldn't draw a gun fast enough,' recalled Culp, 'and I could, so I said I'd show him how to do it, which I did, and I told him, "It really takes a long time to learn how to do it, man," and the next day he came to the studio and he outdrew me. I said, "Ooooh, man, that's not right!"'

Steve wasn't prepared to be second best to Robert Culp. 'I had to be the best at drawing a pistol,' Steve told me. 'Be the fastest gun. So I practised until I was the fastest gun in Hollywood.'

That might not have been an idle boast. Jim Coburn said, 'I don't know anyone faster on the gun than Steve. He'd outgun John Wayne any time.'

But other actors I've met claimed to be the fastest gun in Hollywood. Lee Van Cleef was one. And Eli Wallach told me that he never saw anyone draw as fast as Clint Eastwood. 'Although Steve was pretty good too,' Wallach said.

After the feature-length episode aired on 7 March 1958, CBS picked it up as a series of half-hour shows. And Steve McQueen was its star. The series was called *Wanted: Dead or Alive*. 'You couldn't deny that this guy jumped right off the screen,' said Culp. 'He was an actor waiting for the right part in front of the camera. Man, he was a *star*. And I even got to like him.'

Steve said he felt he 'just about got away with it with the gun and the horse in the pilot, but for the series I needed to be better ... proficient. I was a bounty hunter. I had to be the best gunman there was. I wanted a special kind of gun. I thought a sawn-off carbine would be good. That kind of gun didn't exist, so I took a carbine to a friend of mine who worked with guns, and he did the job. It was a one-off. And powerful. First time I used it, it knocked me down and blew off the cameraman's hat. They had to put a plastic shield over the camera to protect it. And I had to make sure I stayed on my feet.'

Steve also had to learn to ride a horse proficiently. 'Not too many of them in New York,' he said. 'I prefer a motorcycle. But I got so I could stay on a horse and look good. I picked my own horse coz the one they gave me was so old they almost wheeled it out on roller skates. I picked a horse from a cowboy I knew who had a black horse which threw me as soon as I got on him. I knew that was the one. We called him Ringo in the series. He was a crazy horse. He bit all the other horses, kicked over the lights, he broke my toe stamping on it the first day . . . on purpose. He bit my back four times, so I punched him in the nose. We had three years fighting, and he'd kick and bite me and I'd punch him, but he always stood his ground. That horse was a lot smarter and had more courage than me.'

McQueen learned to ride as well as many of the Hollywood cowboy stuntmen. 'When Steve had to do anything technical, he practised until he was the best,' said Jim Coburn, who guest-starred in the show, becoming one of McQueen's friends.

Few actors became Steve's life-long friends. One of them was Don Gordon. That's probably because Don also rode a motorcycle. Gordon told me:

I lived near Steve and Neile, and he'd pass my door on his way to work. He saw me and kind of stared at me, then the next time he waved, and then one day he stopped and said, 'I've seen you on TV,' and I said, 'I've seen you too.' Next thing is, he got me a guest spot on *Wanted: Dead or Alive*. When he became a really big star he got me a lot of roles in his pictures. I never asked him to do that. He did it because we were friends . . . and probably because I never asked. He doesn't like people who ask things of him. He likes those who don't ask.

We really became good friends because I rode a motorcycle. Not as good as he did. We'd go off into the Palm Springs desert, where he taught me to ride in the dirt. One time we went down a hill and just took off and I decided I'd catch him up and pass him. And I did, and when he saw me pass him he just went crazy because he was Super-rider and I had managed to catch him up and overtake him, but then he passed me. We had to stop and we laughed about it. You had to compete with Steve.

He loves talking about bikes, and we'd often just get on our bikes and into our leathers and take off. He'd turn up in the middle of the night, and we'd ride off.

McQueen knew that getting stuck in a TV show could be the death of any aspiring movie actor. But he recognised that as well as earning him good money, *Wanted: Dead or Alive* was a chance to hone his skills in front of the camera. He also determined not to let it get in his way of becoming a movie-star.

'I only saw the show as being temporary,' he said. 'What I wanted to do was be in the movies. My agent made a deal with Dick Powell [one of the heads of Four Star] that if I got offered a movie they'd arrange my schedule so I could do it.'

On the first day of filming the series, Steve had three stuntmen fired. He was discovering the power of stardom and exercising it. He insisted that he wasn't playing a power game, saying, 'They just didn't look right. They didn't look like they could double for me,' meaning the audience would know it was a stuntman and not Steve McQueen.

After he fired the first three stuntmen, the fourth, Loren Janes, a legend among Hollywood stuntmen, was given the job, and he and Steve hit it off, and they often worked together from then on, until Steve's last movie, *The Hunter*.

'I have a lot of respect for stuntmen,' Steve said. 'They lay their lives on the line a lot, just to make the rest of us look good. I like to hang out with them.'

He was now earning $100,000 a year, and he and Neile decided that she would give up her career so they could start a family. 'I had it with that shit about me marrying her for her money,' said Steve. 'Soon as I could, I told her I wanted her to stop working and we can have kids. And she liked that.'

Was Neile really happy just being what McQueen referred to as 'his old woman'? Said James Coburn, 'I never heard her complain.'

John Sturges had an opinion. 'She had a career all her own. She was McQueen's counsellor and adviser. She guided him in his career choices. She had her work cut out for her.'

Coburn agreed. 'She helped him make the right choices. He relied on her. I don't think he would have made it without her.'

The success of the series coincided with the release of *The Blob*. Steve suddenly had a fan base from the TV show which loyally went to see *The Blob*, making it not only a hit but something of a classic among B horror movies.

Unhappily for the makers of *Never Love a Stranger*, they released their film in July 1958, weeks before *Wanted: Dead or Alive* turned Steve into a star attraction. The picture played well in the northeastern urban areas but its pro-Semitic theme made many exhibitors cautious about showing it, and in New Orleans it wasn't shown at all.

The Great St. Louis Bank Robbery, released in 1959, also benefited from Steve's TV stardom and did especially well at the drive-ins.

With *The Blob* being a surprise hit, and *Wanted: Dead or Alive* also a success, Steve began making demands upon the writers and directors of the series. 'It wasn't that he wanted to cause trouble and prove he was a star,' said Don Gordon. 'He wanted to make sure it was not just different to all the other Western shows but *better*. It drove directors crazy and they complained, "Who does this guy think he is? He's just a television actor." But he was more than that and he knew it. He worked hard at it, and when he worked hard he wanted you to work just as hard. Nothing wrong in that.'

Martin Landau, another guest star in the series, said, 'He worried a lot about the script. He corrected things. He'd say, "I would never say this."'

Jim Coburn recalled, 'Whatever Steve did, he always wanted it to be done *his* way. That was Steve. He kinda knew what was best for him and what he could best bring to any movie or the series *Wanted: Dead or Alive*, and so he argued a lot with his directors. If they wouldn't do it his way he'd just go back to his trailer or his dressing room. He didn't care too much about being popular. He just wanted to be good. No, *better*.'

McQueen regularly watched the 'dailies', which was the film shot that day. 'I had to do that coz I had to know what I did that worked and what didn't,' he said. 'That's how I learned on that show.'

Steve even became something of a coach for some of the actors still new to the TV medium, like Don Gordon, who recalled, 'We'd do a scene and he'd say quietly, "You're doing too much, man. Let the camera do the work." He was right. He taught me a lot.'

I think what Steve always tried to bring to his roles was his own life experiences. He knew he could reflect what he felt was true, and that can be clearly seen in moments from films like *The Great Escape* when he is locked up in the cooler for the second or third time, or in *Love with a Proper Stranger*, in which he played a man who meets a girl, has a one-night stand, but doesn't love her. 'I've always felt I've done my best work when I find something I *know*. If I can ride a motorcycle or drive a fast car I'm doing what I know. If I can wheel and deal or run a scam, then I know that groove. If I need to knock the shit out of somebody, then I know what that feels like. And getting it knocked outta me.

'When I did that Western show on TV, I told the producers that if I have a scene where I'm going to get the shit kicked out of me by eight men, then I'm not going to fight fair. I'll do whatever it takes to survive. I think I helped give that show an edge. My whole life has had a kind of edge to it. I'll do whatever it takes.'

Steve was a new kind of screen hero. He wasn't tall, and he never stood up ramrod straight, was always slightly round-shouldered. He was somehow ordinary in an extraordinary way. Martin Landau recalled, 'He'd come onto the set and he looked like he'd wandered in off the street and put on the hat and started saying his words, and it looked easy, but it took hard work to do that and make it seem that way.

'His character was always in some kind of jeopardy but Steve made Randall someone who approached all that with a kind of casualness. I think that's appealing.'

These were happy times for Steve and Neile. She was now pregnant with their first child, while he was finding. TV stardom. She had sacrificed her career, seemingly willingly, to raise a family with him. She was for him the perfect wife, keeping the home tidy, cooking dinner by day and sleeping with him at night. She also overlooked his occasional indiscretions.

She gave birth to a daughter, Terry Leslie, on 5 June 1959. Steve had hoped for a boy. Nevertheless, he doted on Terry and decided he'd like another girl. The next child was a son, Chadwick Steven, born 28 December 1960. He was over the moon to have a girl and a boy.

Steve didn't say too much about his children to me, one late night in an upstairs room in an English country inn, but I could see in his face and hear in his voice how proud he was of his children. 'I never wanted them to go through what I went through. They were always going to have the best of me.' I think he succeeded in being a good father, and was determined they wouldn't be typical Hollywood brats. 'Neile and me just wanted them to have their own identities and not be "the son and daughter of . . ." I think we did that.'

It was hard at first for Steve to connect with his children. 'I didn't have any idea what to do with babies. They don't *do* anything. I needed them to grow a little with personalities, and then I figured out what a father should do . . . should be . . .' When he told me that, I could hear the bitterness in his voice as he trailed off at the thought of what a father should do and be.

He hadn't given up hope of finding his own father. He said that he got a tip some time in 1959 which led him and Neile to a house in a small town just outside of Los Angeles where an old lady answered the door. 'I told her who I was and that I was looking for Bill McQueen. She let us in and it turned out she'd been my father's lady friend. He'd died just three months earlier. She said that every time my show was on TV, he sat and watched it and said, "I think that might be my son." Then she gave me a photo of my dad and a lighter with "Red" engraved on it.

'I didn't know what to think or feel. I had so much anger and resentment. But then I never knew what happened between him and my mother. Maybe she drove him crazy . . . drove him away. But he never came to see me. I can't know why. If I had met him I might have asked. I don't know it's any of my business coz whatever happened with him and Julian was between them.'

When he told me that, I said, with absolutely no experience of what it was to be a parent, 'Of course it's your business.'

'Yeah, I guess so. And after I met that lady and heard about him and that he died, I felt pretty upset. It was a loss.'

Steve had a lot of mixed emotions about his dad. In 1977, when we were discussing fatherhood (I was about to become a father), he told me he was frustrated that his dad died before he had a chance to say to him, 'Look what I did without you. I'm doing great and you're just a drunken bum.'

I don't think Steve really knew for sure exactly what he would have said to his father, had he had the chance. There were many things in his life he found hard to articulate, sometimes because his feelings were too mixed up, and sometimes because he simply had trouble with words. He wasn't an intellectual, but he was a deep thinker. Sometimes he simply thought too much. 'I try to understand things and get frustrated when I can't,' Steve told me. 'I figure there has to be a reason for everything.' Perhaps he tried too hard, and perhaps there doesn't always have to be a reason for everything. But he was sure there was, and when he got to the point where he couldn't think any more and became frustrated, he had a simple solution. He got on his motorbike or into his car and drove as fast as he could.

I asked Steve why he felt it necessary to ride and drive so fast. He said, 'It gives me freedom. I love the rush. It's like a drug. The faster the better.' Well, I certainly noticed that, as we sped through Cornwall, Somerset and Devon, breaking speed limits and weaving in and out of the traffic that moved a lot slower. It was one of the most dangerous experiences of my life. He was exhilarated. I was scared to death. But I never let on. Jim Coburn later told me, 'He was testing you. He didn't care if you were scared. Just so long as you did it. Hang in there, man, that's what it's about.'

Hanging in was what McQueen did. Not for anyone else, but for himself. 'I don't want to prove how brave I am to anyone. I don't care what anyone thinks. I only want to prove something to myself. I want to prove I'm not scared.'

I've no idea what the bike was that we were on. He talked about a Bonneville he once had, and I pretended to know what kind of a bike that was. He told me how he would ride his Bonneville to a motorcycle shop on Ventura Boulevard. The store owner was Bud Ekins. 'I hung around his store quite a bit,' said Steve. 'He knew who I was but all he ever said was, "Oh yeah, seen you on TV." He wasn't impressed. He just talked motorcycles. I liked that. We became good friends.'

They went to cross-country motorcycle races together, and soon McQueen was taking part in the races. There he could go as fast as he liked without breaking any laws. Going fast was what it was all about. But he also liked the skill factor involved. 'Anyone can go fast,' he said. 'It's going to the limit and surviving that counts. I like to go fast, and I like to have control. I like to polish that skill. Racing does it for me.'

Steve began hanging out with other racers and bikers and, apart from them, he seemed to make few friends, especially among actors. Don Gordon was one of his few actor friends; probably the best friend he had among actors, but that was because he rode motorbikes too.

James Coburn was never as close to McQueen as Gordon was. 'We only really got to like each other down the line,' said Coburn. 'I did a couple of guest spots on *Wanted: Dead or Alive* and then we seemed to work in the same films quite a lot. But he was very private, very paranoid about people, which is why I guess he was so demanding. He was like a kid who had all these toys, driving fast cars and motorcycles. That was his trip.

'We weren't great buddies to start with. You have to have something that he either likes, wants or has to compete with. When I got into martial arts and my teacher was Bruce Lee, then Steve and I got closer. That was the bag we had in common.'

Coburn may not have known it, but McQueen had a sneaking admiration for him. He told me in 1970, 'Jim speaks his mind. Says what he thinks. He's no "yes" man. I like him for that. If I asked Jim what he thought about something, he'd tell me straight. No bullshit. At first, I was kind of wary of him. But he was always open, always honest. It took a long time for us to become friends, but he is still one of the best friends I have.'

I think he also liked Coburn because Jim never became such a big a star as Steve. He preferred his actor friends to be lesser stars. One actor friend was Tom Gilson. Gilson was no competition for Steve because he never became a star. He had something Steve liked; a drug habit. Unfortunately, McQueen had his own, and it got worse over the years. He and Gilson would go off into the desert to buy peyote from the Native Americans.

Peyote is made from a small, spineless cactus and has been used for centuries by Native Americans in religious rituals and as a medicine. When they brought it back to the McQueen house, Neile would prepare it for them, boiling it first, letting it simmer for half an hour, and adding salt and pepper, like it was some recipe for one of Steve's favourite meals. This was a recipe to get him and Gilson high for up to 12 hours. Neile never took it but would watch Steve and Gilson getting totally stoned.

Gilson remained one of Steve's closest friends until Gilson's wife, model Sandra Edwards, shot him dead in October 1962. A coroner's jury ruled it justifiable homicide.

Steve explained his preference for racers over actors or anybody else. 'At the studio everyone waits on me. They always tell you what they think you want to hear and you end up thinking you're some kind of superman. But when you're racing, the guys on the bikes don't care who you are. He wants to beat you, and if he does, he's the better man and he's not afraid to tell you that you're a lousy biker. So racing really keeps my feet on the ground and I know I'm not a superman.'

He got Bud Ekins to build him a bike for dirt racing, and they went racing together at every opportunity. Ekins believed that Steve would have been placed in the expert class but remained in the amateur rating because he would miss races when he had a picture to make.

'He loved to race as much as he could,' said Don Gordon. 'I think he did it because he wanted to find out what kind of person he was. It was just him in a car against somebody else in a car, or on a motorcycle. He was on the edge, man. Always on the edge, seeing how far he could go. And it was the mechanics who could make that bike or car go and hum and purr. Just a purist kind of thing. It was like nothing else for Steve. He never got that hum from acting.'

Steve entered his first automobile race at Santa Barbara in 1959, winning in a Porsche sports car .

'I'm happiest when I'm racing,' he said. 'Alone on a bike just humming along at high speed, I just know that's where I want to be. I want to do that more than act in movies.'

That might have been the case but, since he was an actor, and making a good living at it, what Steve wanted now was to be in movies – and not B movies. His chance finally came when director John Sturges cast him opposite Frank Sinatra in *Never So Few*. He was actually a replacement for Sinatra's Rat Pack pal Sammy Davis Jr, who had committed the cardinal sin of saying on radio that he was a bigger star than Sinatra.

As soon as Hilly Elkins heard that Davis was out of the Sinatra picture, he went to John Sturges and asked him to meet with Steve. Sturges told me, 'As soon as I saw Steve I knew he looked right. I like to meet people in person and when I do I can usually gauge if they are right or not without a screen test. In fact, I wasn't impressed with him in *Wanted: Dead or Alive*. But in person he looked good to me. As soon as he walked into my office, he had the same thing that you saw in *The Magnificent Seven* and *The Great Escape*. He was brash but insecure. He was just a big bundle of contradictions. But he had an immediate scene sense – he could get the scene you were telling him about, and knew what to do with it.'

Sturges was so impressed with McQueen that he signed him to a three-picture deal; few directors signed actors to a contract. The second and third Sturges movies would be *The Magnificent Seven* and *The Great Escape*. McQueen described working with Sturges as 'the best education I could get in movies. He showed me how to be my best.'

Sturges hated to admit it, but he had to get Frank Sinatra's approval before casting Steve. 'He almost ran the picture,' Sturges said of Sinatra. 'He had his best friends in the film, like Peter Lawford, and Sammy was supposed to have been in it. I've no idea where Dean Martin was at the time. So I set up a meeting between Frank and Steve. Frank liked him. That was it. He got the part.'

Sinatra immediately took to Steve. He once told me, 'Steve has a fuck-you attitude, and so do I.'

Of Sinatra, Steve said:

Not many people impress me but he did because I knew he was

like the King of Hollywood. And he'd have your head cut off if he wanted. Or your knees broken. So when we started on the picture I had trouble figuring out how I should be towards him. I guess at first I was like, 'Yeah, well, okay, so you're Frank Sinatra,' like I didn't care.

He was the one who kind of broke the ice. We were filming on location in California and he snuck up and put a firecracker in my gun belt while I was trying to study my script. It went off and I jumped three feet in the air, and Frank thought it was hilarious. When I realised he'd played a joke I decided to play one back right then, and I grabbed one of the Tommy guns and I yelled at him, 'Hey, Frank! Eat lead!' and I squeezed the trigger, and those bullets hit the dirt all around his feet.

Everyone just stood in silence. We looked like we were in some kind of a showdown. No one knew what he'd do, and I didn't have a clue. But then he started laughing. He had a childish sense of fun, and so did I. We were like two big kids who didn't grow up, and all through the picture we tossed firecrackers at one another.

Sinatra once told me, 'Never back down, even if you don't want me to kill you. Don't back down and I'll respect you.' That's why Sinatra liked Steve, who instinctively knew that if he hadn't played Sinatra's game, it would have been hell for him from then on. 'Frank tests people,' observed Steve, and added, 'So do I.' Well, I knew that, spending hours on the back of his motorcycle, wondering if I would live or die.

For the duration of the filming, Sinatra had a sort of mini Rat Pack with Steve McQueen and Charles Bronson, who played a supporting role in the film, and was another of Sturges's regular actors. 'I think Frank was lost without Dean and Sammy,' Charles Bronson said. 'He had [Peter] Lawford on the picture, but I felt that Lawford wasn't Frank's favourite buddy, and so me and Steve became his newest best buddies.

'The three of us had a lot of fun with cherry bombs. We'd throw them in each other's trailers. It's a wonder nobody got hurt. We nearly killed Loren Janes, who was a stuntman. We let off so many firecrackers and cherry bombs in one go his trailer caught fire, and then we realised he had to be in there. We couldn't find him and then he turned up outside. If he'd been inside he would've been killed for sure. So me, Steve and even Frank apologised to him.'

Bronson and McQueen got along well. 'When you discover the fun side of McQueen, he's great to work with,' said Bronson. 'But when he's in a lousy mood he's a bigger pain in the ass than even me.'

There was no being a pain in the ass in a Sinatra picture. Even Sinatra behaved, according to Sturges. 'He wanted to make a good picture as quickly as possible,' Sturges told me. 'He liked me because I get on with things. I can work however my actors want to do it. And Frank was really a generous guy when it came to sharing a scene. He said to me, "Steve's really got something I think the kids will go for, so I don't care if you want to cover him more than me," and so I got as much of McQueen in the coverage as I could.

'Sinatra always said, "Take all the time you need to light a scene and block it, but when I get in front of the camera I only want to do one take. So everyone better be on the ball." And McQueen liked working that way too. He got better at it over the years, so he could prepare and then do just one or two takes, and he was never going to get it better.'

Sturges thought that Steve had it in mind to become a bigger star than Sinatra. 'Steve was a different guy then to the one he became by the time we did *The Great Escape*, when he made a lot of demands. He was a major supporting co-star with Sinatra and he knew his place. And anyway, he knew he couldn't be bigger than Sinatra. Nobody is.'

That didn't stop McQueen from trying. He told me, 'On a Sinatra picture nobody is bigger. So I watched and learned, and figured that I'd be the biggest.'

What really impressed Steve about Sinatra was the fact that 'nobody pushes him around. But he's fair if you're honest with him. One guy in the picture told a pretty dirty story about Sinatra to some of the crew and this guy thought it a blast to make fun of

Sinatra in this way. Then one of the guys who heard it snitched on him to Frank, who found this guy and knocked him on his ass. That guy got fired. Then Frank had the snitch fired too. I said, "Frank, why'd you do that?" and he said, "Nobody likes a rat." So you had to be careful with Frank. But he was generous too. He heard about one of the extras whose wife was in a car crash and badly busted up, and Frank paid all her medical bills.'

Sinatra became a role model for Steve, while at the same time John Sturges became Steve's mentor. 'He took a real interest in me,' Steve said in 1970, just a few weeks after having a violent bust-up with Sturges on the set of *Le Mans*. Sturges had begun directing the film but Steve had become, as Sturges told me, 'a way over the top control freak', and they argued, then fought and then Sturges quit. For Steve, it was almost like losing his father all over again.

'No film director ever gave me the confidence that he gave me,' said McQueen. 'And he always showed his approval. He didn't actually say it, but it came out, and I picked it up. Right from the Sinatra film, John helped me find my angle in front of the camera, and helped me with just little bits of direction. "Just a little bit more," or "a little bit less." Like, "Turn your head just an inch." He cared.'

By the time the film was in the can, Steve had accepted a part in Sinatra's next movie, *Ocean's Eleven*, which was essentially a Rat Pack movie, with Dean Martin, Joey Bishop, Peter Lawford and Sammy Davis Jr (now forgiven by Sinatra) all cast. 'I thought it a lousy idea if Steve did that picture,' said Sturges. 'He would have just become one of Sinatra's cronies, so I said to him, "You don't want that. You can be a big star on your own," and Steve said, "Bigger than Sinatra?" I said, "Yeah, why not?" although I had no idea if that was really true. But Steve believed it, and so he didn't do the Sinatra film.'

Steve told me that Hedda Hopper, the Hollywood gossip columnist, gave him the same advice. She also enthused about him in her column, writing, 'He excites. I took one look at that hardened face and knew he had a past.'

Never So Few, released in 1959, was moderately successful, thanks largely to a public interest in action films and Frank

Sinatra. Film critic Bosley Crowther, observed in the *New York Times*, 'John Sturges has directed it for kicks.' He likened it to an Errol Flynn swashbuckler, with Frank Sinatra trying 'to succeed Errol Flynn as the most fantastically romantic representation of the warrior breed on screen'. He commented that the 'swashbuckling antics' of the co-stars, including Steve McQueen, were 'played almost beyond comprehension'.

Overall, McQueen came out better in the reviews than anyone else. Paul V. Beckley of the *New York Times* wrote, 'Steve McQueen looks good as the brash, casual GI sergeant. He possesses that combination of smooth-rough charm that suggests star possibilities.' *Variety* also enthused about McQueen in its review of *Never So Few*: 'Steve McQueen has a good part, and he delivers with impressive style.'

Steve always credited Sturges with helping him find that impressive style. He carried it with him back to the set of *Wanted: Dead or Alive*, but now he felt that doing the TV series was a comedown from having co-starred in a Frank Sinatra film, and he began to lose interest. He said that he worked longer and harder on the TV show than he did on the Sinatra film. 'Every day you were up at five in the morning to get to the studio by six thirty, and sometimes you didn't get home until around nine in the evening. Too many pressures . . . and the quality wasn't great.'

It was during the second season that James Coburn played a guest role and met McQueen for the first time. 'Steve had become bored with it,' said Coburn. 'He'd say, "Let's go to my trailer and get high." So we did. He'd have marijuana in his trailer. You could get high just breathing in there.

'He'd get so bored he'd take off on his motorcycle and, when they called him, he wouldn't be there. He'd come back 15 minutes late, but that was expensive time not to be filming on a TV series. Naturally the producers weren't happy.'

His behaviour did him no favours when John Sturges and producer Walter Mirisch offered Steve a role in a Western they were going to shoot down in Mexico, because Four Star refused to give him time off. For a while it looked like Steve would never be one of *The Magnificent Seven*.

CHAPTER 8

—

Magnificent Among Seven

Since his Oscar-winning film debut in *The King and I* in 1956 Yul Brynner, with a semi-mythical Mongolian background and his distinct shaved head, had become one of the biggest stars on the planet. He always played vaguely exotic roles, such as the biblical king in *Solomon and Sheba*, the Pharaoh in *The Ten Commandments* and a Russian army officer in *The Brothers Karamazov*.

But what he really wanted to do was play a cowboy. But nobody thought he could. 'Producers then didn't think a gunslinger would have a shaved head and an accent nobody could quite figure out the origin of,' Brynner told me. 'So I decided to find myself a Western, and when I saw *Seven Samurai* I realised it could be remade as a fantastic Western.'

Actually, the origins of how *The Seven Samurai* came to be remade as *The Magnificent Seven* are somewhat vague. Anthony Quinn insisted it was his idea, which he revealed to Brynner when he directed him in *The Buccaneer*. But it was Brynner who paid $112,000 for the rights to remake *Seven Samurai*. He planned to direct the film, with Quinn playing the lead. Plans changed when Tyrone Power died midway through filming *Solomon and Sheba* and United Artists, producing the film, sought Yul Brynner to replace him. Brynner agreed if United

Artists made *The Magnificent Seven*. Anthony Quinn felt like he was being pushed out and tried to sue Brynner and United Artists. When he failed, he just pulled out, and the way was left for Brynner to negotiate with Walter Mirisch, who, as one of the Mirisch Brothers, had a deal with United Artists. By the time he had finished playing King Solomon, Brynner decided he didn't want to direct the movie but just play Chris, an enigmatic man in black coming from nowhere in particular and heading nowhere when he is asked by poor Mexican peons to hire men to protect them from the bandit Calvera and his men. So Chris hires six other gunfighters.

Brynner told me he passed on the rights of the film to Walter Mirisch for the $112,000 he had paid for them. Mirisch, who had admired John Sturges's *Gunfight at the O.K. Corral* and *Bad Day at Black Rock*, immediately asked Sturges to direct. Sturges remained convinced that the film had always been Brynner's idea. 'Nobody would have ever dreamed it up but Brynner,' he said. 'It seemed like a mad idea, but I liked that mad idea when Walter Mirisch came to me and said he wanted me to direct it.'

Mirisch seemed very sure, when I interviewed him in 1978, that he had been the one to acquire the rights to remake *The Seven Samurai*. 'I had seen [Akira] Kurosawa's great movie *The Seven Samurai*, and it immediately resonated with me as a Western. I made the deal with the Japanese film company for the rights. So I called John Sturges and asked him to direct and he said he'd love to do it.'

Sturges was intrigued by the idea of taking a samurai film and turning it into a Western. (The director of *The Seven Samurai*, Akira Kurosawa, had said that his film was inspired in part by the Westerns of John Ford.) 'It was kind of fantastical,' said Sturges who, with movies like *Bad Day at Black Rock* and *Gunfight at the O.K. Corral*, had been creating a new style of movie, taking realistic backdrops and turning them into something almost fantastical that proved very successful. In the case of *The Magnificent Seven* it was taking a samurai story and setting it in Mexico, where the poor peons had to send for American gunmen to protect them from the evil Mexican bandits. 'It could never have happened,' said Sturges. 'Those peons would never have paid gringos to solve their problems. So we began with a premise that was pure fantasy. As for there being seven gunmen, that's just a magic number Kurosawa thought up. It's not real. It's a fantasy, and I liked that idea. So I thought, let's put Yul Brynner in a cowboy hat and see what great characters we can surround him with.'

One of Sturges's first decisions was to cast Steve McQueen as Vin, who would essentially be Brynner's second-in-command. He needed to convinced two people about casting McQueen, one being Walter Mirisch and the other being Yul Brynner, who had casting approval. Mirisch recalled, 'John Sturges said, "I want you to meet Steve McQueen." So I met with him for a couple of hours as soon as I could, and I told John, "He's got to be in our picture."'

Yul Brynner said that it was his son, Rock, who recommended Steve McQueen to play Vin. 'Rock told me he had seen the Western series McQueen did on television. I knew Rock had an instinct for picking actors, so I watched an episode of the show, and I liked what McQueen did in it. So I chose Steve McQueen.'

It was impossible for me to tell by 1980, when I interviewed Yul Brynner – two years after I interviewed Walter Mirisch and four years since I worked with John Sturges – who exactly cast Steve McQueen, but I'm inclined to believe Sturges when he said that he had made up his own mind. There's no evidence that Yul Brynner ever held any kind of audition to cast the other actors, or met with any of them to discuss their roles.

But one thing is for sure, and that is, despite the stories that have been told and retold by some surviving members of the cast of *The Magnificent Seven* about how much Steve McQueen supposedly hated Yul Brynner – and I've no doubt that McQueen did despise him at times – Steve was always grateful to Brynner. He said, 'Brynner could have had me fired, but he never did. I did everything I could think of to needle him, but he never went to Walter Mirisch or John [Sturges] to complain.' But when it came to casting him as Vin, McQueen had no doubt that it had been Sturges's decision. 'I was under contract to John for three pictures, and as soon as he got the job directing [*The Magnificent Seven*] he had my agent send me the script.'

When he read the screenplay, which was an unfinished draft, Steve counted no more than a dozen lines and thought the part would be too small, but Sturges convinced him that it would grow, and that it would be a springboard for him into stardom. Trusting Sturges, Steve accepted.

But there was a major problem. The schedule for *The Magnificent Seven* would delay the start of the next season of *Wanted: Dead or Alive* and, despite the verbal agreement Dick Powell had given Hilly Elkins that they would work around Steve's movie schedule, Tom McDermott, now in charge of production at Four Star, refused to give McQueen the time off he needed, effectively robbing him of his part in *The Magnificent Seven*. James Coburn, also cast in *The Magnificent* Seven, as the knife thrower, thought this was McQueen's punishment 'for giving Four Star hell', like not turning up on time, and making too many demands on the writers and directors.

Hilly Elkins got in touch with Steve, who was in Boston with Neile at the time, and said, 'Have an accident.' So Steve drove into the side of a bank, only just missing a policeman, with Neile in the car. She was all right but Steve suffered what may have been an authentic neck injury – or there again it might have been fake – but in either case, he returned to Los Angeles with a neck brace on.

News of his car accident reached Dick Powell, who sent Steve flowers and best wishes. Finally, Tom McDermott, possibly unconvinced by the injury but taking no chances, called Elkins and told him that Steve could do the movie. 'Double his salary,' Elkins demanded. McDermott swore at him but conceded.

The Magnificent Seven was shot entirely on location in Cuernavaca, Mexico, where the cast and crew arrived to begin filming in late February 1960 for three months. Along with Brynner, McQueen and James Coburn, the magnificent seven were completed by Robert Vaughn, Charles Bronson, Brad Dexter and Hungarian actor Horst Buchholz as young hot-headed Mexican Chico, a part that McQueen coveted because it was much larger.

Brynner and Buchholz stayed in adjoining villas. The rest of the cast and crew were put up in the Hotel Jacarandes. 'It wasn't a dump,' recalled Coburn, 'but it wasn't four star either. But most of us didn't care, except Steve, who saw Brynner and Buchholz living in luxury and he didn't like that.'

Things were fairly cordial between Brynner and McQueen to start with. Steve even helped Brynner learn how to handle a gun, but typically he was also playing a game designed to put one over on Brynner. James Coburn recalled, 'Yul Brynner didn't know how to draw a gun, so Steve gave him lessons. He taught him to draw a pistol in what is an ordinary way, while Steve was doing all this fancy stuff with his pistol.

'Yul realised that Steve's fancy gunplay would get all the attention, so he asked him to use a rifle, but Steve refused because he knew Yul didn't want to be upstaged. I think Steve felt his greatest con was tricking Yul to do just a simple ordinary fast draw which anyone can learn.'

The first scene shot was Chris and Vin's ride to Boot Hill in the funeral coach, with Chris at the reins, chomping on a cigar, and Vin riding shotgun. Brynner turned up with a huge entourage, including a secretary, two gofers, and a barber to keep his bald head smooth and shiny. He also had his own luxury and very large mobile home to rest in, while the others had to make do with canvas chairs and a communal make-up trailer.

'Yul Brynner was the king with this entourage – all these people to dress him and put a chair down for him and light his cigarettes,' said Coburn. 'He'd snap his finger and they'd come running. I never saw a movie-star so *royal*. I think Steve just hated the way Brynner was and yet I think he was also jealous and would have liked to be a bigger king than Yul.'

When Sturges called for action and the cameras rolled, McQueen, sitting on the coach next to Brynner, began shaking the gunshot shells. Then McQueen took off his hat, held it to the sun, and put it back on again.

Eli Wallach, who had been cast as Calvera, recalled, 'They did this scene on the hearse, and Steve would take out the shells for his shotgun and go like this . . . [Wallach mimed holding the shotgun shells to his ear and shaking them] and then he took off his hat and held it up to the sun and then put it back on his head, making a big thing of it. And Yul looked at him as if to say, "If you do anything like that again, I'll kill you." Steve was clever. He would do anything to steal a scene from Yul Brynner.'

John Sturges recalled that scene, and said, 'Steve was just catching flies . . . just doing bits of business, like pushing his hat on the back of his head, but he did it as a response to something. Steve always worked out bits of business. Actors are supposed to dream up these things, but Yul was convinced it was scene-stealing, always fussing with something like his hat or his gun behind Yul's close-up. So Yul had a guy watch McQueen's hat, and finally I said to Yul, "For crissakes, *you* watch his hat. It will look good for the scene." You can't explain everything to an actor. You just have to be the boss. If something didn't work, I'd cut it out later or change the dialogue.'

And so began an uneasy relationship between Brynner and McQueen, which grew into what might be the biggest rivalry between any actors in film history. Sturges said, 'They were bitching about each other day and night. Yul didn't understand Steve, who felt he had to assert himself. He was trying build up his part so that it meant something.

'Brynner and McQueen are such dissimilar characters. Yul's a rock. Steve's volatile. Steve mainly behaved on *The Magnificent Seven* with me, but he tried to gang up on Brynner by getting everyone to hate Brynner.'

The problem with Steve's methods was, according to James Coburn, that he didn't really care how it affected other actors. 'You could never call Steve a giving kind of guy. He loved to play games with people, and I guess that's because an abandoned child always tests everything. And he sure tested Yul.'

For years, people who worked on the film loved to talk about the feud between McQueen and Brynner. Robert Vaughn said, 'Steve and Yul had a much publicised feud. There was a sense of Yul being the old champ, and there was this newcomer come to take a crack at the old champ. Every morning at about six o'clock Steve would knock on the door. "What is it?" He'd say, "Did you see how big Brynner's gun is?" I said, "No, actually I didn't notice." "He's got a big gun, man. Big damn gun." Next morning, knock, knock, knock! "Did you see Brynner's horse? He's changed horses. Now he's got a bigger horse than anyone. Big as an elephant." He never asked me for any kind of help. He just wanted to sound off about it.'

'There was only rivalry between Brynner and McQueen because Steve wanted to be Yul's rival,' said Coburn. 'Steve's main aim was always to promote Steve McQueen. He wasn't interested in being part of an ensemble. He wanted to be the star, but of course Yul was the star and we were the co-stars. So Steve did everything he could think of to upstage Yul.'

Before long, every member of the cast was trying to upstage everyone else. Walter Mirisch talked about a scene where the seven cross a stream. 'Brynner is at the head, then comes McQueen, who suddenly takes off his hat, leans right down from his horse, scoops up some water and drinks it, and behind him is Charles Bronson with his shirt undone and showing his muscular chest, and then James Coburn doing three versus of *Hamlet*, and they were all doing something, and it was just hilarious.'

The stream-crossing story has been much repeated by other members of the cast and crew, and Mirisch was convinced that shot was in the film, but it isn't there. Presumably it ended up on the cutting-room floor.

Eli Wallach watched from the sidelines, having only a few scenes with Brynner, McQueen and the rest of the seven. 'I really enjoyed watching the magnificent seven – those seven actors – compete. I wasn't involved because I was with my bandidos for most of the time.' And they were real bandits too, from the mountains, whom Sturges had hired to play Calvera's men. 'They took care of me,' said Wallach. None of the other actors dared to mess with Eli Wallach.

When Brynner married his fiancée, Doris Kleiner, on the plaza set, everyone in the cast and crew were invited. Sturges and all the actors went except for McQueen, who boycotted the event. He made every attempt to get the rest of the cast to hate Brynner, but at first it was McQueen who wasn't popular with everyone. 'I thought Yul was okay and actually when we started making the film a lot of us didn't like Steve too much,' said Coburn. 'We didn't like the way he'd seem to be kissing Sturges's ass all the time, but while he was doing that he was getting a line changed here and there and making his part better, and the rest of us were so busy hating him that he stole the movie from the rest of us. So he may have been a kissass but he was smarter than everyone else.'

Coburn preferred to spend time with Robert Vaughn, who liked to discuss Russian theatre with Brynner, who, in turn, enjoyed entertaining everyone singing Russian songs and playing guitar. Only McQueen and Charles Bronson stayed away from Brynner, finding some almost perverse pleasure in comparing notes on how deprived their childhoods were.

Said Bronson, 'McQueen wanted to be the biggest star, and he wanted to be the biggest loser. We had a lot of discussions, he and I. We both had it tough as kids. He *had* to have it tougher. But then, so did I.'

Robert Vaughn recalled how McQueen and Bronson would spend hours telling each other how bad their childhoods were. 'It was like, "I had it worse than you." "No, I had it worse." Steve talked quite a bit about his childhood. He certainly thought he'd gone to the school of hard knocks.'

John Sturges was, of course, aware of the problems quickly developing among his cast, and he encouraged it. 'The more they competed with each other, the more they became like their characters, and the more each character became more defined, the better it was for the movie, so I encouraged it.'

Sturges recognised that McQueen was the more demanding of his cast, but he was willing to put up with it because, he said, 'Steve delivered on screen.' Sturges also recognised that McQueen was often like a child, demanding and spoilt, and, knowing about Steve's background, he made allowances. 'A director sometimes has to be a father to some actors,' said Sturges. 'Steve needed someone to tell him he is a good boy, that he did well. I liked Steve very much because he was such a likeable guy, very charming when he wants to be, and very funny. He's like the child who wants to be the centre of attention the whole time, but he's got the talent to back it up.'

I thought what Sturges said was very true, because Steve had said to me, 'When a kid doesn't have enough love, he begins to wonder if he isn't good enough. I thought that if my mother didn't love me and I didn't have a father, why then, I must be not very good.'

I think Steve spent much of his life, if not all of it, trying to be 'good enough'. It became his nature to try to get his own way on every film he made, to do what was good for him. He agreed he demanded much, saying, 'If my name sells a movie, then I want to make sure that I don't disappoint my fans, because if I do, they'll stop coming.'

However, sometimes his approach tended to lead to childish behaviour and tantrums, and he would reach the point where he threw all his toys out of the pram, as happened when he made *Le Mans* – and not only threw out his toys but threw a punch or two at his mentor John Sturges.

Sturges saw no sign of what was to come when he directed *The Magnificent Seven*, and he and McQueen talked about making a movie about car racing that would eventually become *Le Mans*. The project had a different title then, *Day of the Champion*. Sturges recalled, 'We decided we'd make that picture when we were in Mexico, when I was the mentor and he was the student.'

When *The Magnificent Seven* wound up filming, Steve went straight back into *Wanted: Dead or Alive*. But he went back into it lacking enthusiasm, because now he wanted to leave TV to make movies, despite getting a cool $100,000 for the season.

He returned in a belligerent mood and everyone suffered, especially the executives. Steve made demands, walked off the set, came late to the set, and did everything to make himself as unpopular as anyone could be. 'I think he just made it impossible for everyone to work with him,' said James Coburn.

When *The Magnificent Seven* was released late in 1960, it wasn't an immediate hit, and influential New York critics, never keen on Westerns, were unimpressed by it. Howard Thompson of the *New York Times* said it was 'a pallid, pretentious and overlong reflection of the Japanese original'. Outside New York, there were some good reviews. The *Los Angeles Times* called it 'genuinely magnificent – a Western to rank along with *Shane*, *High Noon* and *Stagecoach*.'

It didn't get a rave from *Variety*, which, although describing it as a 'rip-roaring rootin' tootin' western with lots of bit and tang and old-fashioned abandon', found that 'the last third is downhill, a long and cluttered anti-climax in which "The Magnificent Seven" grow slightly too magnificent for comfort'.

It did not bode well for the picture, especially as United Artists, according to John Sturges, didn't think it was very good and so released it without proper first-run engagements at major theatres. It went into the suburbs virtually unnoticed. But in Europe, especially in France, and then in Japan, it was an immediate and phenomenal success. In the UK it became a 'must-see' picture, with rave reviews. Dilys Powell of the *Sunday Times* wrote, 'The big screen is filled in a deeply satisfying manner. The battle is made up of the extravagant acrobatics, the leaps and dying falls which are the stuff of Western gun battles. They are the ritual movements of the Western, as stylised as the Samurai, and should be accepted with as much respect.'

Back in America, theatres where the movie did good business rebooked it, and people who saw it kept going back to see it again, and the word spread. It was what is called in the business 'a sleeper' in that its success began to grow very slowly. United Artists had to produce more prints of the film and, by 1961, it had become a huge success.

By then, the makers of *Wanted: Dead or Alive* had become so sick of McQueen's difficult behaviour that they cancelled the show in March 1961. Steve was deliriously happy to be free. The trouble was, no one up to that time had successfully moved out of television into movies. James Garner came close, when he shot to fame on TV as *Maverick* and then starred in some fine films in the 1960s, but he moved back into TV in the 1970s with *The Rockford Files*. When I saw Steve in 1977, he said, 'Jim Garner never made it in movies the way I did. It's hard to break into movies from television. I think the people who watched my television show and liked it are really the ones who put me where I am because they came to see my movies.'

That was a rather simplistic view but often Steve took the simplest view. If he hadn't had a real movie-star presence, he wouldn't have been a success in movies and might have returned to television – or more likely, just quit acting and stuck to racing cars and bikes. James Garner, a really fine and also very personable actor, was at his best in movies when he had a good co-star, or a whole host of them like in *The Great Escape*, or when he was with Clint Eastwood and Donald Sutherland in the 2000 picture *Space Cowboys*. But Steve didn't need a major co-star. He could hold a movie on his own. (Clint Eastwood would become the greatest example of an exception to the rule about TV stars not becoming major movie-stars, but that would happen after McQueen did it.)

The ironic thing was, by 1977, Steve had gone into semi-retirement and wasn't making movies of any kind, and James Garner was on television as Jim Rockford and earning a fortune, as well as ensuring his career had longevity. That didn't bother McQueen. 'I don't want to be miserable making lots of money,' he said.

—

CHAPTER 9

War Is Hell

Becoming a movie-star when you didn't have a studio to back you wasn't easy in the early 1960s. Steve did, however, have a non-exclusive contract with MGM, which he had had to sign as part of his agreement to be in *Never So Few*, and MGM called on him to play a part that had been turned down by Cary Grant. The script was called *The Golden Fleecing* but would change to *The Honeymoon Machine*. His part was that of a navy lieutenant who uses the ship's computer to break the roulette table at a Venice casino.

The film's leading lady was MGM's brightest young star, Brigid Bazlen, who had played Salome in *King of Kings* and a river pirate's daughter in *How the West Was Won*. She was young, just 16, and as volatile as Steve. There was a mutual attraction leading to a tempestuous affair.

This was Steve's first starring role in a studio film, and his first comedy role. 'The thing with Steve was, he was funny when the humour came out of a situation,' said John Sturges. 'But he was no comedy actor.' Some critics agree. The *New York Herald* observed, 'There is little to laugh at. Steve McQueen confuses posturing with entertaining.' The *Saturday Review* suggested McQueen should 'go back to TV westerns'.

Joseph Morgenstern of the *New York Herald Tribune*

complained, 'In addition to indulging or encouraging Mr McQueen, the director wasted the talents of several other actors in his concern for the obvious.'

One critic who liked both the film and McQueen was Arthur Winstein, who said in the *New York Post*, 'It moves fast and easy and everyone in the cast seems to be enjoying it, and so does the audience. One can also say a good word for Jim Hutton and Steve McQueen, both of whom. represent something new in Hollywood casting.'

The film did poor box-office, proving that Steve was not yet a star. Steve specifically asked Hilly Elkins to find him an action story, wanting to avoid another comedy, and Elkins suggested a World War Two script he'd been sent, *Hell Is for Heroes*. It was written by Robert Pirosh, who based it on a true story of seven men who were ordered to hold their position until replaced. To survive, they used various tactics to persuade the Germans they were a much larger force. McQueen's role was perfectly suited, as Elkins knew, because the openly rebellious character he was to play was very like Steve.

Pirosh, who had written the Oscar-winning screenplay for *Battleground*, was slated to direct *Hell Is for Heroes*, which he had been trying to write for seven years but had to wait for the US Army to declassify material he needed to include in his screenplay. McQueen initially liked Pirosh, who described the character Steve was to play as 'off centre, a misfit', which Steve responded to positively.

While Pirosh was polishing his script, Steve made suggestions for changes to the dialogue to suit him better. Pirosh felt Steve's suggestions improved the script, but as Steve delved further into the script he began to realise that it was very much an ensemble piece and that his character didn't stand out as much as he felt it should. As James Coburn, who was in the cast, said, 'Steve felt that he was the star of the picture but was crowded by the rest of us and he wanted to shine. He said to me, "Why the hell can't they just do the picture about one guy – me!" I said, "I don't know, Steve. Maybe because the picture is about seven guys?" But he wanted it to be about one guy.'

Steve thought he was justified. 'The studio (Paramount) paid me to star in their picture. They wanted my name to sell it.' Steve was yet to discover, after the failure of *The Honeymoon Machine*, that his name alone didn't sell a picture. He demanded more changes to the script to enhance his part, and when Pirosh refused, Steve insisted that Paramount replace him. The studio, obviously feeling their director was not as indispensable as their young star, fired Pirosh as director *and* screenwriter.

Writer Richard Carr was put to work with Steve to make his part bigger. To direct, Paramount chose Don Siegel, although he had to be approved by Steve, who was flexing his less than developed star muscle power.

'Steve wasn't the hardest actor I ever worked with,' Siegel told me. 'He wasn't the easiest either, but I was just a studio director doing what I was told. I think, though, we made an honest picture and Steve was right to get a little more screen time than the others.'

Jim Coburn believed that Siegel was making life easier for everyone by agreeing to what Steve wanted. 'When Steve asked for something, Siegel said, "Yeah, okay, Steve, let's do that," and when Steve wasn't around Siegel would shoot something else, so he didn't get any opposition from Steve.'

But Siegel told me that he stood up to Steve at the beginning, laying down the law as to who was in charge. 'He pissed me off with his attitude of him being the only one who bore the weight of the picture's integrity, while the rest of us were just company men who were selling out to the studio. So I told him that I was as interested as he was in making a good picture and the sooner that idea sunk through his thick skull the sooner we'd all get along. He was pretty pissed off about that. Moped around, gritting his teeth, but then he calmed down. I think what really pissed him off was not that I'd stood up to him but that I'd knocked him down before he could knock me down – verbally, not physically – and he just didn't know how to come back at me. From then on he was a pussycat.'

Filming began with interiors being shot on the Paramount sound stages, and then the unit moved to the woods of Redding in California for exteriors. 'That's when the picture really began for me,' said Siegel. 'The studio stuff looked like a studio set. Up in Redding we were able to get some good footage. But there was a time limit and we were still getting the script right. I could only do the best I could.'

Siegel conceded that Steve made some good changes to the script. In one scene he had a speech to make when asked by one of the characters, played by Fess Parker, 'Were you right?' Steve hated the long speech he had to give as an answer, and finally decided on the briefest response – 'How do I know?' McQueen's strength on screen was often in what he didn't say and, as he often pointed out, he let the camera do the work. But there was more to it than just standing in front of a camera. 'Steve knew how to give just enough for the camera to relay his thoughts. And that's the mark of a good screen actor,' said Don Siegel.

Filming on location in the summer of 1961 was uncomfortable due to the heat of the day, so a lot was done at night. 'This meant Steve had nothing to do in the day,' recalled James Coburn, 'and he was just buzzing all the time. So he had a rented car which Paramount had agreed he could have, and he wrecked it, and then two more. The last one was a Mercedes convertible which he was driving up these winding roads too fast as usual, and he turned off the road to drive down a dirt track that led to our location, through all this thick brush and bushes and, as he came to the location, right ahead of him were two tractors, and he didn't have time to stop so he swerved off into a huge tree, which wrecked the car. Steve walked away with scratches. He got a memo from the studio telling him if he wrecked another car he wouldn't get another. He didn't wreck another.'

Coburn said it was taking him time to get to like Steve, but what really impressed him was the way McQueen stood up to studio executives who were anxious about how well Don Siegel was doing up there in Redding. 'When he heard that studio executives were coming down to see how things were, he said, "Those guys will shut us down and we'll have a film that's just shit," so I said, "Well, what are you gonna do, Steve? These guys have the power, man," and he said, "Oh yeah?" They turned up and Steve drew a line in the dirt with a branch and said, "Anyone steps over that line gets the shit knocked out of him." They backed off quick.'

Siegel credits Steve with possibly saving the production. 'The studio could have said, "Enough, you got all you need," and the picture would've been terrible. But he stood up to them. They didn't stand up to him. You have to stand up to him first, but I'm glad he beat them to it.'

Siegel was able to finish the film on a limited budget of $2.5 million and come up with a typically good, rugged Don Siegel movie, full of tension, strong characterisations and violent action. The critics generally liked it when it opened in 1962. The *New York Daily News* called it 'an unstintingly honest depiction of the hell of war. Among the more memorable men in the squad is Steve McQueen whose word-at-a-time speech indicates an undercurrent of hostility.'

The *New York Times* proclaimed, 'An arresting performance by Steve McQueen, a young actor with presence and a keen sense of timing, is the outstanding feature. *The Times* said, 'Steve McQueen is extraordinarily good.'

But for some inexplicable reason Paramount failed to showcase it and instead put it out in neighbourhood theatres as a double feature with another action movie, *Escape from Zahrain* (starring Steve's nemesis Yul Brynner), and so it failed to make the impact it deserved.

Upon finishing *Hell Is for Heroes*, Steve narrated and appeared in a 30-minute documentary for the pubic relations wing of the Marine Corps. He also set up a company of his own, Solar Productions. But he didn't really intend to make movies, it was simply a tax shelter, and in time it would become an active production company. Then Steve went to Britain to make another World War Two picture, *The War Lover*. Steve later claimed, 'I'd made eight films up to then, and only one, *The Magnificent Seven*, was any good. I just wasn't making the right connections, so I tried doing a film in Europe.'

American studios had to make a certain number of films in Britain – called quota quickies – or the British government simply wouldn't allow American movies to get shown. Hollywood usually sent its less valuable stars to make British films. Columbia had the idea of making a film about American pilots based in Britain, and they signed Steve McQueen as the star and Robert Wagner as the second lead. Wagner had been a leading man in Hollywood since the early 1950s, but was no longer doing well, so he decided to find work in Europe. McQueen was struggling to establish himself, so neither he nor Wagner was a major Hollywood star at that time. If the film was a failure, it wouldn't harm Hollywood, but it could potentially harm the careers of its leading men.

I don't know if Steve was really aware of this when he signed to make *The War Lover* – he certainly never gave the impression he did. He said to me, 'I only did the movie so I could be next to Brands Hatch.'

Paid a reasonable $75,000 and provided with a three-storey house in London's plush Knightsbridge, Steve brought Neile and his children over to England. When he wasn't working he spent his time at Brands Hatch. It was, I think, more of a perk rather than the actual incentive to do the movie. Columbia had realised that their star would want to have a go at racing, and so they tried to protect themselves against his injury or even death by inserting a clause in his contract saying he wasn't to race before filming was over. In the case of a non-fatal injury sustained while racing cars, they would sue McQueen for $2.5 million. Steve said, 'They tried to stop me, but they couldn't. I don't threaten easily.'

Steve's part was ideally suited to him, playing a hell-raising, competitive and cocky American fighter pilot. 'He was a complex guy, selfish and also selfless,' said Steve. English actress Shirley Anne Field played the girl McQueen and Wagner compete for. Steve decided he needed to stay in character even when the cameras weren't rolling and was often brash and arrogant towards Shirley Anne. All he did was make her actually, dislike him intensely, according to the film's publicist, Mike Frankovich Jr (Mike's father was president of Columbia Pictures at the time of *The War Lover*.)

Robert Wagner felt he got along well with Steve, but that's probably because Wagner is the kind of guy who is easy to get on with. He even tolerated it when Steve made sure that he arrived on set after Wagner. 'That's an old trick of Steve's,' said Jim Coburn. 'He makes sure you wait for him.'

Towards the end of filming, and to Columbia's dismay, Steve crashed a car at Brands Hatch. The Cooper he was in was a write-off but Steve miraculously walked away. He had bruises, cuts and a fat lip, and still had one last scene to shoot, in the cockpit of an aeroplane. The film's director, Philip Leacock, hid the bruises, cuts and fat lip by having Steve wear an oxygen mask.

Leacock was one of the directors who stood up to Steve from the beginning of the shoot, telling him, 'You may want to do it this way, but this is not what I want, and the overall importance is the picture.' According to Frankovich, Steve behaved from then on.

Unfortunately, Leacock failed to get a good performance from Steve, as Richard L. Coer of the *Washington Post* observed. 'One would have thought Steve McQueen ideal for the title role, and he might have been, had he been imaginatively used.' Coer thought *The War Lover* went to 'remarkable trouble to avoid what it is talking about'.

Variety felt the film's major failing was a 'lack of proper penetration into the character referred to by the title. That the central character emerges more of an unappealing symbol than a sympathetic flesh-and-blood portrait is no fault of McQueen, who plays with vigour and authenticity, although occasionally with too much eyeball emotion.'

The film didn't do well in the States but was a big hit in the UK when released in 1962. That wasn't good enough to make him a Hollywood star, and when Steve returned to California he actually considered quitting acting to become a professional racer for the British Motor Corporation. 'I'd driven at John Cooper's racing school in Britain and he said he wanted me to work for him,' Steve told me. 'He gave me a weekend to make up my mind. I couldn't get into my head if I was an actor who raced or a racer who acted. I was close to ditching it all in coz I just wasn't making it as a movie actor and really didn't think I'd ever get *the* picture.'

He joked, 'They say war is hell. It was for me.'

To make matters worse, Hilly Elkins announced he was quitting Hollywood to have a go at producing plays on Broadway. However, he did put McQueen in the care of a very good agent called Stan Kamen at the William Morris Agency.

Steve told me, 'I stuck with acting because I had my wife and kids to look after and I could make good money still acting.'

It wasn't as straightforward as that. John Sturges told me, 'Steve's career looked like it was over before it had begun. I think he would have quit as no studio wanted him. But I did.'

The best thing that ever happened to Steve as an actor was when John Sturges wanted him in *The Great Escape*. It was the film that changed everything for Steve McQueen.

When Sturges offered him the part of Captain Virgil Hilts, Steve said, 'I dunno, Johnny. I just did two World War Two flicks and they both died.'

Steve told me, 'The problem with the role . . . when I saw what there was of the script, which they hadn't finished . . . was it had no juice.'

Sturges laughed when I told him what McQueen had said about the problem with the script. 'It was McQueen – his career – that had no juice. He wasn't in a position to quibble.'

But quibble Steve did.

Hilts, nicknamed 'The Cooler King', was based on a British soldier, George Harsh (although Harsh, unlike Hilts, never tried to escape on a motorcycle. In fact, in those early drafts, there were no motorcycle sequences.)

When Sturges asked Steve to play Hilts, he had already cast James Garner as 'The Scrounger'. Sturges told me, 'When McQueen read Garner's part, he said, "He's got the best part." And I told him that Hilts was a great part for him because he was a loner. I said, "That's the part for you."'

Sturges promised him his part would be improved. What McQueen didn't understand was that the film was an ensemble piece, much like *The Magnificent Seven* had been, only that movie had a star, Yul Brynner. There was no central character in *The Great Escape*. Steve accepted the role of Hilts with reservations, but trusting Sturges and, perhaps, misunderstanding Sturges's promise to improve his part – taking it to mean he would expand the role. It helped that McQueen got paid a cool $100,000.

Sturges had wanted to film *The Great Escape*, based on Paul Brickhill's book about a mass escape from a Stalag Luft III during World War Two, for more than a decade but no studio had shown interest. Now, because of the phenomenal success of *The Magnificent Seven*, the Mirisch Brothers and United Artists were happy to finance *The Great Escape*, which Sturges personally produced as well as directed. He gathered cast largely from Britain to play the more major roles – Richard Attenborough, Donald Pleasence, David McCallum and John Leyton – as well as many of the more minor roles – Gordon Jackson, Nigel Stock, Angus Lennie, James Donald and Tom Adams. There were just a few American actors (since the POW camp was largely populated with British and Polish airmen), namely Steve McQueen, James Garner, Charles Bronson (who played a Pole) and James Coburn (who played an Australian).

In early June 1962, the cast and unit arrived in Germany, where the film was shot just outside of Munich where Stalag Luft III had been faithfully recreated in full. Interiors were to be shot at the Bavaria Film studios in Geiselgasteig.

The script had gone through various drafts by various writers and because of that, as well as weather problems, filming began to fall behind schedule. Morale in the cast sank, so Sturges decided to screen what he said was 45 minutes of roughly assembled footage. James Coburn was convinced it was only 20 minutes of footage. In either case, what little film there was mainly featured James Garner and hardly any of McQueen, which upset Steve so much that he disappeared on his motorbike for several days. Mirisch said that McQueen thought 'he was being upstaged', and of course, he was.

James Garner recalled what happened after that screening. 'Steve didn't like my turtleneck sweater. He wanted it. I just picked it out of wardrobe. I thought it looked right. When he saw it he got a little upset. If he'd asked for it I would have given it to him. He was very competitive, same when we were racing. He was always competitive with me, and I was always hoping he'd do well.'

Sturges recalled, 'When Steve saw Jim in that sweater after he watched the footage, he said, "Nobody's going to be looking at anybody but Garner in that damn sweater."

'It was a big picture with a bigger cast than we had in *The Magnificent Seven*, in which Steve was just one of the seven, but in this he wanted to be the *whole* picture, and when he realised this wasn't going to happen, he took off. So I gathered the whole cast and crew and I said that I was going to combine the McQueen and Garner characters into one, and word got back to Steve and he called his agent and manager and they came over to Germany and we thrashed it out.'

There were a number of days when filming was stopped while John Sturges spent time with Steve, trying to work out scenes for him. David McCallum recalled, 'John and Steve had a history with two other films and, when the film didn't work, rather than plough on, John would stop and we'd have three or four days off while John went away with Steve and they'd work very hard to get the scenes right before they shot them.

Sturges even assigned writer Ivan Moffat to come out to Germany and work on additional scenes for McQueen. Among these was McQueen's first scene in which he tosses a baseball bat at the fence, leading to his first spell in the cooler. Another scene was when Squadron Leader Roger Bartlett, played by Richard Attenborough, and Flight Lieutenant Sandy MacDonald, played by Gordon Jackson, try to persuade Hilts into becoming their advance scout by escaping and allowing himself to be caught.

'Oh, how he loved that idea,' said Gordon Jackson. 'Suddenly he had a scene which would lead to him becoming the hero of the film.'

Also written in was the climactic moment when Hilts, escaping from Germans on a motorcycle, makes the daring leap over the fence before being captured. That scene, more than any other, appeased McQueen enough to keep him in line.

James Coburn, who remained friends with Steve for many years but never had an easy relationship with him, said:

> Steve demanded things and if he didn't get them he didn't go to work. He was hard to figure. A complex guy. He saw all these British actors who were all very good, and I think he felt a little intimidated by them. But he couldn't show them that. They were able to play their characters based on the script, but Steve based his character on what Steve McQueen would do. He was complex and simple at the same time. He was selfish but he didn't think he was being selfish. He thought he was protecting himself. That's from being an abandoned child. He was testing everyone.
>
> One day me and Richard Attenborough were waiting on the set for Steve, who always made sure everyone arrived before he did. Richard asked me why Steve did that, and I couldn't tell him why. It seemed he didn't like anyone else being in control. He imagined that other people would dominate him and that he would then be put into a bad position. He worried a lot about bad things coming after him. That's paranoia, man. And it made everyone uptight, but he didn't care – he probably didn't even realise it.
>
> He fought to make the role what it was. The film wasn't th character, so he made sure that he was separated from all the other men except one, which was the little Scottish guy (played by Angus Lennie) who becomes his partner. Just this little guy who Steve's character looks after. But he had to be in a cell on his own.

Being in that cell was a part of the real Steve McQueen, harking back to the time he was in jail and felt lonely and abandoned. 'That was easy for me to play,' he said. 'And that baseball. That was all me. I just had to go back to that place in my life. I think it had an impact.'

I think it certainly did. Of all the great scenes in the film, including the motorcycle race, the image that lingers longest in the memory is Steve McQueen in solitary confinement, endlessly throwing that baseball against the wall. And in fact, that's how the film ended, with Hilts back in the cooler after his failed motorbike escape and, while we don't see him in the cell, all we hear is the lonely and monotonous sound of that baseball. That baseball was a metaphor for Steve's life.

Like Coburn, James Garner had an uneasy friendship with Steve. 'It kind of began on that movie,' Garner told me. 'We both came from successful television shows and were making it into movies. He hated me in that white turtleneck sweater because he thought it made me look better than him, so I said, "Take the sweater, Steve. *You* have it." Of course he wouldn't take it and put his own wardrobe together, and he looked great in that kind of torn T-shirt – just like someone who'd ride a motorbike.

'A few years later, when we were both making good money, we were both living in Brentwood on the hill – almost neighbours. He lived just above me, and he'd throw beer cans down into my drive. I didn't know where the damn cans kept coming from. Every day there would be more of them. Finally figured out it was McQueen.'

Steve recalled his childlike practical joke. 'Jim kept his lawn so tidy all the time, and he had to have everything so spic 'n' span. So I began tossing empty beer cans down onto his drive, and it drove him crazy trying to figure out where they kept coming from.'

Garner finally discovered it was McQueen when, after a beer can bounced on the ground next to him, he looked up and saw McQueen above him, laughing. 'Okay, it *was* funny,' Garner told me. 'I wasn't mad at him. And he stopped throwing the damn cans.'

Richard Attenborough had to go through an initiation ceremony when he met Steve – much like I did. He told me, 'Steve was on his bike, and he said, "Hey, Dick, like a ride?" I felt absolutely terrified but I knew that if I didn't accept, that would be the end of any possible prestige and self-respect the British contingent would have with Steve for the rest of that movie. So I said, "Of course, Steve, I'd love to," absolutely shaking with terror on the inside as I got on this bike and off we went.

'When we came back, I was never more delighted to get off

any vehicle of any kind. But it resulted in a relationship with Steve that I've treasured all my life.'

Many of the actors from that movie had generally fond memories of Steve; I don't think any of them considered him a rival in the way Yul Brynner had on *The Magnificent Seven*, and they all had stories to tell about his driving.

'When we made *The Great Escape* he crashed a 300SL, a convertible,' recalled James Coburn (who assumed I knew what a 300SL was). 'He was driving at 90 mph, and suddenly there were two trucks in his way, and it was either crash into these guys at 90 mph or head off the road and into the forest, so he headed in the forest and hit a tree that just smashed this SL. He had just a few scratches on him.'

Donald Pleasence recalled that story. 'Steve said he did a "controlled crash,"' laughed Pleasence.

James Garner recalled, 'He crashed more than one car. They had to put up roadblocks for him because they knew he was coming and he'd just fly down the road. Finally they said, "No more driving for McQueen," and they took away his driver's licence.

'One time he went to lunch and took one of the German motorbikes with the sidecar we had for the movie, and it had swastikas all over it, and the German people yelled at him in the street. He didn't get it, I guess.'

David McCallum remembered McQueen getting arrested by the police. 'The local chief of police was tired of all the actors speeding through his village, so he set up speed traps. I always drove slow, and I remember that Donald Pleasence wasn't feeling well so he drove slow, but a lot of people got caught, and so of course did Steve, who was in a racing car he described as being like a "bullet". He was late, as he usually was, and came flying through and was stopped. The chief of police opened Steve's car door and saluted and said, "Good morning, Herr McQueen. We have stopped a lot of your friends this morning but I am pleased to tell you, you have won the prize," and they put him in jail. So we had to stop filming until they let him out.'

More than any other aspect of the filming, McQueen enjoyed

the motorbike chase sequence. 'That was a gas,' he said. 'I could ride as fast as I liked, and I knew there were people thinking, "Jesus Christ, he'll kill himself. How will we finish the movie?"

'John [Sturges] must have been scared, so when we got to the jump, he said, "You can't do this." I said, "I can." He said, "No way." So I asked my buddy Bud Ekins to make the jump for me. I coulda done it. I coulda made it.'

Apart from the actual jump, Steve did all his own riding, right up to the point where he was about to take off over the fence. Brilliant editing made everyone believe McQueen did the jump himself, but Steve never took credit for it. He always made it clear that it was Bud Ekins, with his hair dyed yellow, doing the jump and crash-landing on the other side of the fence.

Steve did keep one secret for many years about that scene. He doubled for one of the German motorcycle riders. 'I told John this guy wasn't driving fast enough. He didn't look like he wanted to catch me. I said if I put on a German uniform nobody would recognise me on screen, and John said, "Go ahead," so I did and, when the movie was finished, I was chasing me and nobody knew it.'

The Great Escape was not envisaged by Sturges as a realistic portrayal of a World War Two POW camp. It was, like his 'fantastical' Westerns, a piece of sheer entertainment. *Variety* caught the spirit of the film, saying, 'John Sturges has fashioned a motion picture that entertains, captivates, thrills and stirs. There are some exceptional performances. The most provocative single impression is made by Steve McQueen,' and acknowledged that 'British thespians weigh in with some of the finest performances in the picture,' singling out Richard Attenborough and Donald Pleasence.

Judith Crist of the *New York Herald* called it 'a first-rate adventure film, fascinating in its detail, suspenseful in its plot, stirring in its climax and excellent in performance. Steve McQueen plays a familiar American war-movie type – brash, self-interested, super-brave emoter. For sheer bravura, whether he's pounding a baseball into his catcher's mitt in solitary or stumping cross-country on a motorcycle with scores of Germans in pursuit, Steve McQueen takes the honours.'

But Bosley Crowther of the *New York Times* didn't like the film or McQueen. 'There's Steve McQueen, surly and sophomoric, tediously whacking a baseball into a glove, one of the most moronic running gags in years. The film grinds out its tormenting story without a peek beneath the surface of any man, without a real sense of human involvement. It's strictly a mechanical adventure with make-believe men.'

The public didn't agree with Crowther, and the film grossed $16 million. And it finally proved to be *the* film Steve was looking for. His dedication to creating that part, even his selfishness in making sure he stood out, resulted in Steve McQueen becoming one of the biggest stars of 1963. Hilts was a character that defined Steve – or maybe it was the other way around – and it established that 'cool' manner which was to earn him the tag 'The King of Cool'. I mentioned to him once that there was some irony in him being called 'The King of Cool' because he had played, 'The Cooler King'. He laughed and said, 'I just played that character as me. That's where I'm at. There is more Steve McQueen in that picture than in any other.'

That again was a simplistic view of himself, but I think there *is* a lot of the real McQueen in Hilts. Maybe that's why Hilts remains my favourite McQueen character.

CHAPTER 10

—

In Search of the Ultimate Trip

The Great Escape changed Steve's life. And Neile's. They bought a $33,000 stone house in the rather exclusive Brentwood neighbourhood which Steve called 'the Castle' because it was in the Spanish style. It had a fabulous view of the Pacific, with three and a half acres featuring trees and a large swimming pool, all protected by 15-feet-high and 30-feet-wide gates.

His agent, Stan Kamen, set Steve's fee at $300,000 a film and, as there was no shortage of scripts coming his way, he spent money almost before he had it. 'I had to buy what I wanted before they took it all away,' he said. He bought classic cars, ending up with a collection that included a Triumph, a Lincoln, a Porsche, a Ferrari, a dune buggy, and a D-type Jaguar in mint condition.

It was Neile's job to furnish the house. She purchased paintings, rugs, chandeliers and antiques. And she bought him a US Army Land Rover for his birthday present.

As if to confirm Steve's new superstar status, *Life* magazine arranged to do a spread of him, with photos of him camping with friends. It didn't matter that he never went camping with friends. James Coburn said:

He called me up and said, 'You gotta come camping with me for these photos,' and I said, 'Steve, none of us know dick about camping,' and he said, 'You gotta make me look good, Coburn, so come and do it.'

So we went – Bud Ekins and Don Gordon – and we had this photographer called John [Dominis], who was an actual outdoors guy, and we went up to the Ojai mountains, which were about an hour from Los Angeles, and Steve brought along a fancy tent and all these utensils, and he was cooking up beans, which exploded, and this guy John said to me, 'Does he know what he's doing?' I said, 'I guess he does. Who knows?' It was so funny. None of us knew how to camp and so we ended up sending for hamburgers. We stayed up there a few days, and we'd go out in Steve's Land Rover, which was like a tank, and we smoked some joints because we were getting bored with this *Life* shoot, then head back to camp for some more photos.

McQueen appeared on the cover of *Life* the same week other important magazines, such as *Time* and *Look*, were covering President Kennedy's meeting with the Pope. *Life* sold more copies than the others.

The story *Life* wrote on Steve came to the attention of the FBI and an agent from the New York office wrote out a file on him, dated 1 August 1963. It detailed his life as a 'bad boy' and quoted him from the article, in which he had said, 'I could have wound up a hood instead of an actor.' The report concentrated on Steve's 'rough world' and detailed how 'his mother sent him away for rehabilitation' and talked about his days working in a brothel.

It was as though the FBI expected him to be mixing with criminals or, worse, Communists, and they continued to watch him. I don't think he ever knew it. The FBI drew up files on many celebrities. For many years, J. Edgar Hoover, director of the FBI, was paranoid about celebrities and made sure the dirt was dug up on as many of them as possible.

Another FBI file mentioned Steve's name as one of a large group of movie-stars who intended to attend the famous march in Washington in 1963 to hear Dr Martin Luther King speak. It's as though the FBI considered this some kind of threat. Among the stars named were such obvious subversives as Charlton Heston, Debbie Reynolds and Gene Kelly.

Ultimately, Steve didn't march with the other film stars, although he did make his views on politics and civil rights known. He told *Variety*, 'Though actors who mix into politics want to do good, they must be sure that the stand they are taking is valid. We have a lot of kitchen cleaning to do in Hollywood, and I think we're doing it. As for the problems of employing Negroes, I think you should use a Negro actor because he is good at his craft and not simply because he is a Negro.'

The FBI would continue to keep an eye on McQueen and add further reports to the secret files of J. Edgar Hoover.

After *The Great Escape*, Steve wanted another stab at comedy, and unwisely chose to do *Soldier in the Rain*, a well-written (by Blake Edwards from a book by William Goldman) farce about the relationship between a fatherly master sergeant, played by Jackie Gleason, and a cornball Southern supply sergeant, played by McQueen. Steve broke his rule about making the part like him because this character was nothing like Steve, so he tried to be like the character. He went way over the top with his acting, producing a terrible Southern accent.

He was actively involved in the production of this movie, having dusted off the cobwebs from his Solar company and put it to use, making him an uncredited co-producer. That made it especially difficult for the director, Ralph Nelson, who had only made one previous film, to control Steve, either in front of or behind the camera.

Again Steve did his Frank Sinatra trick of making sure his co-stars were on set waiting for him to arrive. This didn't endear him to Jackie Gleason, who told the director that *he* would not arrive on set until *after* Steve McQueen. So for a day or two neither showed up. Finally, they agreed to arrive together.

Ralph Nelson's problems increased when Steve said to him, 'Are you going to be shooting master shots?'

Nelson replied, 'Yes, of course.'

'Well, I don't do master shots.'

Steve's first foray into producing, as well as an attempt to play a non-McQueen-type role, was a complete failure. Judith Crist, who usually liked McQueen, didn't like *Soldier in the Rain*. 'McQueen, one of the more exciting actors around, is totally suppressed as a mush-mouthed stupid [sic] devoted to dawg and buddy to the point of tears,' she wrote in the *New York Herald Tribune*.

Bosley Crowther agreed with Crist, writing in the *New York Times*, 'McQueen is simply callow with his striking of foolish attitudes, his butchering of the English language, and his sporting of hick costumes.'

Wanda Hale, who liked Steve's comedy turn in *The Honeymoon Machine*, was disappointed, writing in the *New York Daily News*, 'McQueen, with phoney accent, jumps around as if he had ants in his pants, overdoing it so much that I could hardly recognise the fine comedian of *The Great Escape* and *The Honeymoon Machine*.'

Variety blamed the film's director Ralph Nelson for 'failing to detect or delete the artificiality of McQueen's approach'.

Bad reviews and the fact that it was released on 27 November 1963, just five days after President Kennedy was assassinated, didn't encourage the public to want to see what is arguably the worst film McQueen ever made. And it was only bad because he was miscast. 'That picture was a mistake,' he told me. 'I made a bad mistake thinking I could do it. It wasn't my bag and I was careful never to make that mistake again.'

As for his behaviour, not just on that film – which demonstrated his behaviour at its worse – but on all, he told me, 'I always feel like someone will come and just take it all away. I don't know why I feel that way. But I have to protect myself, take control. I guess to some that made me aggressive or hostile, but I don't mean to be. I'm just watching my back the whole time.'

Even when Steve behaved badly, he often won people over because, said James Coburn, 'he had so much charm, and also because he was a child, and you could get mad at him but you couldn't hate him for it'.

He was, as Coburn had said, both complex and simple.

Trust was always a major issue for Steve. He even put his best friends to the test.

Don Gordon recalled after Steve's death, 'Steve changed his phone number every week or so and you could never get hold of him. He'd come by my house on his bike and he'd tell some crazy wild story about – something like he's got into a fight and he thinks he's killed this guy, and he'd be absolutely straight about it. But he'd tell only me that story, and then he'd read the newspapers to see if there were any stories about this fight, and of course there weren't because I'm not telling anyone, and then he'd call me and say, "Here's my new telephone number." He was always checking to see if people were trustworthy. And I understood because he needed to protect himself. He was a big star and people were going to use him. He wasn't interested in anyone who wanted something from him just because he was a star.'

Don told me before McQueen's death, 'If he doesn't like you, he doesn't hide it.'

I think McQueen particularly enjoyed being in the company of just one other person, so he could study them and discover what he could from them, as he did with me. From what I gathered from speaking to those who knew him, you would be left in no doubt what he thought of you. If he didn't like you, you knew it, and you never had his attention again.

Soon after *Soldier in the Rain* wrapped, Steve began filming *Love with the Proper Stranger*, with Natalie Wood as an Italian girl who gets pregnant after a one-night stand with a young Italian musician (played by McQueen). Together they try to raise money for an abortion but in the end he decides to marry her.

It was a controversial subject for its time, but in the hands of its director, Robert Mulligan, it was a bittersweet romance with touches of both drama and comedy. For McQueen, it was a role that allowed him to show his very macho side, yet also his vulnerability. His performance was perfectly balanced by Natalie Wood, who was always at her best when playing a vulnerable young woman caught up in circumstances which she battles to control.

Filming began in New York in March 1963. Natalie, then divorced from her first husband, Robert Wagner, was just coming to the end of an affair with Warren Beatty, and she was instantly attracted to Steve. Natalie once told me informally, 'I was on the rebound and there was Steve McQueen, who I thought might be the perfect antidote for getting over Warren.' More formally, in an interview, she said, 'There was nothing between me and Steve McQueen then. That came later. But when we made *Love with the Proper Stranger* he had his wife Neile with him in New York, and I was only interested in making a good picture with him.'

She would later have a brief affair with Steve after his divorce from Neile but, despite her attraction for him, she never made a serious play for him on that movie. She admitted she wanted to, and made a few vain efforts, but she said that for her, going to bed with a man was a commitment, and she knew Steve wasn't going to be making any commitments to her or anybody else in the near future. She did, however, enjoy teasing him, and made a game of flirting with him. 'I'd hear him coming by my dressing room and I'd stick my leg out the door which made him laugh.'

Steve told me he liked Natalie. 'A very cute girl, very funny, kinda crazy. I heard she was with Warren and I was at a good place with Neile.' Considering that he usually made a play for his leading ladies, I'm surprised that he didn't do the same with Natalie, but while he managed to keep on the straight and narrow, he did enjoy what he called a 'warm friendship' with her. 'It was better that way,' he said. 'We worked well and had some laughs.'

Natalie recalled her time on that movie as 'one of the most rewarding experiences of my career. I had nothing in my life but the picture because my personal life wasn't happening then, and the picture was it for me. I loved Steve and Robert Mulligan and Tom Bosely [who played her boyfriend]. We were like a family.'

Midway through April, the unit moved from New York to Hollywood to film interiors, where Natalie continued her flirting games. She and Steve remained good friends but not great friends, since Steve rarely had really good female friends, Suzanne Pleshette being one of the rare exceptions. All of Steve's best buddies were men, and few of them were actors. One of his closest was hairdresser Jay Sebring, who began his friendship with Steve when he styled his hair and lightened it to make it even more blond for *Love with the Proper Stranger*.

Jay Sebring was known for his free lifestyle, with plenty of women and drugs. Steve was already a regular user of marijuana, and Sebring had no problem providing Steve with the best grass on the market. They also shared a young, beautiful actress, Sharon Tate.

Love with the Proper Stranger split the critics. Bosley Crowther of the *New York Times* never liked much of anything McQueen did, and wrote, 'He's a face-squinching simpleton, for my money.'

Andrew Sarris in the *Village Voice* wasn't endeared either: 'McQueen is more mannered under [Robert] Mulligan than he has ever been before.'

Variety thought differently. 'McQueen displays an especially keen sense of timing,' they conceded, but 'he's probably the most unlikely Italian around. The characters could and should obviously have been altered to Irish Catholic. He is an appealing figure nevertheless.'

The *New York Herald* thought, 'Steve McQueen is first rate as the musician.'

In Britain Philip Oakes, writing in the *Sunday Telegraph*, found the film 'fresh, funny and endearing. The performance that catches the eye is Steve McQueen's, mainly because it's so busy. In relaxed moments, however, he does act with real charm.'

It was a box-office success and earned Natalie Wood a Best Actress Oscar nomination. Steve was not nominated, and he wondered what it would take to get a nomination. 'I wasn't a part of the Hollywood establishment,' he told me. 'All that Hollywood shit wasn't my groove.' Perhaps the Hollywood establishment recognised how Steve felt and so chose not to honour him, in which case Hollywood and therefore the Oscars were, at least then, very elitist.

Steve liked working with Robert Mulligan and did so again, in *Baby, the Rain Must Fall*. He played an ex-con who returns to his wife, played by Lee Remick, and their daughter, and tries to start his life over again as a singer. Like many of Mulligan's films, such as *To Kill a Mockingbird* and *Love with the Proper Stranger*, it was in black and white, sensitive and somewhat downbeat.

Steve put a lot of energy into learning to play the guitar. He always had boundless energy which he had trouble using up. When I asked him once how he relaxed, he replied, 'I relax at speed.' Lee Remick perceived that for his role he had little chance to expel his energy. 'My feeling was he likes action films better,' she told me. 'I think he wants to be a good actor, and he *is* a very good actor, but my feeling is he felt that this part wasn't right for him.'

I don't know if Steve felt that way about this film, but I was aware, during my four days with him in 1970, that he rarely sat still, unless he was watching the sunset, or lost in some distant memory, or was high on pot. He always had to be on the move, even if it was just moving from the sofa to the floor and then to a chair. He was hyperactive and, although the term Attention Deficit Hyperactivity Disorder hadn't been coined back then, I think it's possible that's exactly what he had. In a television documentary about Steve McQueen made in 2005, Suzanne Pleshette used that very term to describe him.

'He was hyperactive,' Susanne said. 'I mean, really hyperactive. I said to him once, "Steve, you should see a doctor," and that got him mad. He said, "I'm not sick. Just active." But he was more than active. He could get very anxious and that made him worse. So then he'd smoke some dope and he'd calm down. Then it would wear off and he'd be hyper again.'

Having AD-D would certainly fit his background as a child who never had the attention of his mother, or almost anybody else, and so got himself into trouble, leading to his time in the Boys Republic. I think all he ever craved was attention, and by the time he was an adult it had ingrained into his psyche and never left him. Most children with AD-D grow out of it to some degree, but if he did truly have that disorder, then he never grew out of it but, rather, it grew with him.

When I saw him in 1977 he was a man in search of something else in his life which he found hard to define. 'Like something spiritual,' he said. 'Something to make me stop.'

He was convinced that his craving for speed and even danger – or rather the threat of danger – was driven by a peculiar notion he had that he would not live into old age. Both his parents died at the age of 50, and he had a conviction that he wouldn't live beyond that age either. In 1970 he told me, 'I got to live all I can before I die 20 years from now.'

In 1977, he said, 'I only got a few years left and I've been chasing my tail all my life, but now I got to slow down before it's all gone.' But he found it hard to slow down.

I don't know if Steve really believed he would die at 50 when he made *Baby, the Rain Must Fall* in the early spring of 1963. He was only 33 and, for anyone at that age, being 50 is a long way off.

After the film wrapped in May, Steve decided he would take a break and didn't work for more than a year, retreating into his Castle with his family.

'I felt kinda burnt out,' he said. 'I didn't know what to do as an actor any more. But most of all I wanted to give my kids my time. That was important to me.'

It may be that, even before *Baby, the Rain Must Fall* was released, Steve knew that the film didn't work as well as he'd hoped, and that he wasn't as good as he'd hoped. Wanda Hale of the *New York Daily News* wrote, 'McQueen, a fine comedian with a disarming smile, wasn't chicken when he took the part of poor Henry, sad sack, ill-fated, emotionally immature. This vital actor just isn't the type to portray such a long-suffering fellow.'

Variety, however, thought, 'Chief assets are outstanding performances by its stars and an emotional punch that lingers. Steve McQueen is exactly right as the irresponsible rockabilly singer, Lee Remick portrays his wife sensitively, and newcomer Kimberly Block is charming and unaffected as their six-year-old daughter.'

His year off 'was kinda odd', he said, and that being a major star 'was just weird'. Steve said, 'People come at me and go kinda crazy because they see I'm a movie-star and they just got to make their move, because if they don't this movie-star is going to go past and the chance of a lifetime for them is gone, so they move in on you, wanting a piece of you. And soon these crazy geeks are all the same person. They flip out just because of who you are.'

His paranoia about fans increased when, in May 1964, his doorbell rang at three in the morning. He grabbed his 9mm Mauser – he always kept a gun handy – and went to the door to find a stranger called Alfred Thomas Pucci who had managed to get into his grounds and up to the house. Steve marched him to a tree at gunpoint and told Neile to call the police. Pucci was charged for prowling but defended himself by telling the police, 'All I wanted was refuge and peace of mind. I am a good judge of character and thought this guy would understand me, as I have seen many of his movies.'

Apart from having an intruder in his grounds, Steve was shaken by the realisation that there were a lot of people out there who couldn't distinguish between the man on screen and the man in real life. In fact, they couldn't even *know* the man in real life. Most movie-stars accept that as part of the job. As Charlton Heston once said to me, 'It was ever so. They think I opened the Red Sea and when they asked how I did it, I said, "I had a big stick." That made them happy.'

But Steve didn't want to make people happy – not in that way. He felt he had more he could give to society as a celebrity, and that year he supported a lot of concerned Americans by openly opposing a plan by New York corporations to buy up mountain land and build homes on it. He told councilman Karl Runberg, 'I'm representing juvenile delinquents here, and I want to see that children have an opportunity to play in the mountains. This plan will kill that opportunity.'

As a result, the plans were cancelled. Realising the power he had and also believing his description of himself as someone 'representing juvenile delinquents' was sincere, Steve began visiting the Boys Republic to meet and talk to the boys. 'I don't preach. I just talk and listen. I let them know I was one of them and how that place helped me.'

He made frequent visits to the place he sometimes referred to as 'my reform school' and made financial contributions. I think he also made personal financial contributions when he discovered a boy in particular need. 'I don't want people knowing everything I do for them,' he told me. 'I'm glad there are some young fellas out there who I was able to do something for – sometimes just talk, sometimes pay for what they need.'

As I've said, Steve was always trying to escape his childhood, but I don't think he ever tried to escape his time at the Boys Republic. It stayed with him, and he remained a boy from Chino. It meant he could do something positive. 'You have to put back what you took,' he said. 'I took a lot from that place.'

Steve's hiatus from acting continued through the summer of 1964. In August, he and Natalie Wood were asked by President Lyndon Johnson to co-host a cocktail party in Los Angeles for Johnson's re-election campaign. McQueen was merging into the establishment.

A greater honour for him was when, in September, he was accepted as a member of the American motorcycle team to take part in the six-day trials in East Germany. Also in the team were Bud Ekins and Bud's brother Dave. The American team arrived in London, where they were provided with a team van. Catching the ferry to France, they drove all night to Germany, where, the next morning, they were held up at the East German, border. They finally arrived at Erfurt and took part in the parade of nations in the stadium. Steve recalled, 'It was one of the greatest moments of my life. I held the American flag, stood right between the Russians on one side, the East Germans the other. I was proud. Very proud.'

Steve survived the gruelling first day, riding for 200 miles. Then the second. On the third day, Bud Ekins broke his leg, and Steve crashed into a spectator's motorbike which was in the way, sending the bike into a tree, while Steve flew through the air and headfirst into a rock. He gashed his face and the skin from his knees was shredded, but he was lucky to be alive. Bud and Steve were out of the race, but Dave Ekins and fellow teammate Cliff Coleman took gold medals, while another from the team, John Steen, won silver.

The American team drove to Frankfurt, where they were joined by Neile, then went on to Paris for the French premiere of

Love with the Proper Stranger, where Steve was voted France's favourite foreign movie-star. The gala premiere was followed by a party at Maxim's Restaurant, where Bud (his leg in a cast) and Dave Ekins, Cliff Coleman and John Steen were among Steve's bodyguards – he had six in all, and all were motorcyclists.

After the party, Steve, with Neile and his cycling buddies, made their way back to their hotel and were recognised by members of the public, who began to scream his name and follow their favourite star. Steve started running, so did the crowd, so did the bodyguards, Bud Ekins hobbling behind them. They made it to the safety of the hotel and were unable to leave for the remainder of their stay as mobs gathered outsides. 'It was crazy,' Steve told me. 'It was like Beatlemania but it was McQueen mania.'

When he got back to America, Steve discovered *The Blob* had been re-released to cash in on his stardom. It was taking more money than ever, and Steve regretted having turned down a slice of the profits.

In November 1964 Steve's name again appeared in an FBI report, this one specifically reporting on the activities of a Sunset Strip club, the Whiskey a Go-Go, run by an ex-cop, Elmer Valentine, who, shortly after Tom Gilson's death, became Steve's regular peyote buddy. Valentine's club was being investigated for racketeering, and Steve's name was mentioned on a list of people who frequented the place.

Since the days when he and Gilson bought peyote from the Native Americans, Steve had taken a more philanthropic interest in the Navajos. David McCallum, one of *The Great Escape* stars, told me, 'I didn't really know Steve well but when I was down in Arizona filming *The Greatest Story Ever Told* I ran into Steve, who was visiting the local Navajos and bringing them clothes and other things.'

Steve had become fond of the Navajos, who lived in the reservation near the place called Four Corners, which was where Colorado, Arizona, New Mexico and Utah all met. From 1963 until 1970 Steve and Elmer Valentine visited the Navajos, taking them clothing and medicine. Steve told me a little about his experience among them.

'They weren't in a hurry like the rest of us. The land is everything. They have a saying: "Where there is room enough and time enough." Made me want to get back to the land. Some place to be free and at peace. Sometimes I just kind of scream out for some peace. I got it all because I'm supposed to be a movie-star, but sometimes I think it's wrong to be able to earn so much money from acting. There's got to be more noble things to do. Getting out in the desert and sleeping under stars, forgetting all that Hollywood shit – that's what makes my life real. The rest of it isn't real, if you know what I mean.' I told Steve I did, but frankly I hadn't a clue back then. But I think I understand it more now. Steve always thought his life as a movie-star was a fantasy come true, and that some day it would suddenly end. It would all be taken from him, which scared him because he enjoyed not so much being rich, but not being poor. His intention was to make as much money as he could as quickly as he could, so that if the time came when it all stopped, he and his family would be financially secure. Only then would he have escaped the deprived childhood he was forever running from.

Ironically, it did all come to a stop. Only he stopped it himself in the early 1970s. His time as a really major star lasted a relatively short time. If you count *The Great Escape* as being the film that really shot him to stardom, and *The Towering Inferno* as the movie which he made for the money so he could retire, which ended his time as a major star, that was a mere 11 years.

He was sure it would come to an end, and he was sure he would die when he was 50.

It seemed to me that Steve McQueen was not someone who was ever optimistic. In fact, his paranoia was increasing, partly because of his background, and probably because of his growing use of narcotics throughout the 1960s. Jay Sebring gave him LSD, and in turn Steve persuaded actress Mamie Van Doren to try it when they had a brief affair.

They had met at the Whiskey a Go-Go and then gone back to her place. They met up again at the Whiskey a couple of days later, and then partied at Jay Sebring's house, where Sebring provided Steve with two LSD tablets. Steve persuaded her to take one and then they made love while tripping – Steve told me that making love while on acid was like 'the greatest climax in the universe'. I took his word for it.

After that, Van Doren refused to take any more LSD with him, and when she realised that he had no intention of ever leaving Neile, she broke off the affair.

Neile tolerated his womanising and his drug taking. She put on a brave face and made the best of what she had. But Steve's indulgences were becoming ever more extreme, namely sex and drugs. Curiously, a lot of his close friends, especially those who shared his interest in racing motorcycles and cars, didn't know that Steve was adding LSD and even cocaine to his choice of narcotics. Most of them knew that he smoked grass, but it came as a shock to a lot of his friends after he died to learn he was into more extreme drugs.

'He was like an expert in keeping from you what he didn't want you to know,' said James Coburn. 'We smoked grass together but I never knew he was into acid and other hard stuff. I have sometimes thought there was more than one Steve McQueen – kind of different personalities for different friends which he could turn on and off. He talked about drugs in interviews, saying he opposed them. He was outspoken about it. I just thought, "Yeah, Steve just uses grass and really hates stuff like cocaine," and you *believed* him. But he was using acid at Jay Sebring's house, where they had some *wild* parties, man. That wasn't the McQueen I knew. They were sharing girls. Passing the girls back and forth. I didn't know that Steve McQueen.'

Steve was full of contradictions. He was bemused at first by the growing hippie movement springing up from around 1967. He told John Sturges, 'They want to be free but they're just bumming around and tripping out. That's no life.'

But he began to envy their life. 'I figured hippies were where it's at because they want only love and peace, and don't we *all* want that?'

From the beginning of the 1960s getting stoned and tripping out were among Steve's ways to escape reality, although he insisted, along with a lot of drug users, that the drugs gave him reality. He told me in 1970, 'Sometimes I feel like I got to find the ultimate trip. Acid may be it. And a thing called peyote which the Indians drink. I find those things expand my mind – give me a new kind of reality – kind of more real than reality.'

Steve said that the first time he took peyote, it was such a strong high that he fought to beat it by getting on his bike and riding as fast as he could through the desert. 'I jumped every bump in the ground, leaped over every gulch, came off my bike a few times, got caught in the cactus, got ripped up pretty bad, and kept going till the gas ran out, and then I just lay on the ground tasting blood, sand up my nose, waiting for it to pass.' Despite that experience, he got to like the sensation. He sought all kinds of highs, and tried all kinds of illegal narcotics.

He thought it was funny that, at the age of 17, I'd never tried any kind of drug, but he didn't, as others have, try to pressure me into trying it. He just said, 'What blows your mind?'

I said, 'Movies.'

He said, 'That's cool. If that's all you need . . .'

He always had marijuana in his house, hidden in secret places he built, just in case the law ever came searching.

Neile tolerated his drug use, but didn't like it. 'Neile knew she couldn't stop him,' said James Coburn. 'No one can stop Steve doing anything. But she made life as sweet as she could for him. I think she was the most stabilising force in his life.'

When I was getting to know Steve on that four-day road trip, his life with Neile, his stabilising force, was falling apart, and he took solace with dope . . . and me. I don't think there was a link. He obviously forgot that he smoked weed often on that road trip because, in 1974, he said to me, 'That was a groove we had. You're a groovy guy. I didn't need any shit to chill on. You did that for me.'

Well, that might be how he remembered it, and maybe I contributed in some way, and if so, I'm glad I did.

But the drugs, the pseudo-hippie lifestyle, the wild parties with Jay Sebring would very nearly be Steve's undoing.

CHAPTER 11

The First Comeback

After a year-long break from acting, Steve went back to work at MGM. He was paid $350,000 to play *The Cincinnati Kid*, a raw young stud poker player in New Orleans. He liked the project so much that he agreed to do it even before a script was written. He'd hustled during his early days, playing poker among other things, and he felt the part was perfect for him. And because the screenplay had not been written, Steve felt he could make sure it was written to suit him, telling the film's producer, Martin Ransohoff, to inform screenwriter Paddy Chayefksy, 'I'm much better walking than talking.'

Ransohoff wanted the film to have its action centred around the card table, a showdown with a deck of cards rather than guns, but when Chayefsky's screenplay proved to be more of a character piece, Ring Lardner Jr was brought in to rewrite it, and then Terry Southern to write the final draft.

Steve hoped Spencer Tracy would play the role of card master Lancey Howard, against whom the Cincinnati Kid plays, and wrote personally to encourage him to do it. Tracy replied that he wasn't enthusiastic about the part. Meanwhile, Ransohoff brought in Sam Peckinpah to direct. Peckinpah, to Ransohoff's dismay, insisted the film be made in black and white – this at a time when audiences were demanding films be shot in colour.

Then Peckinpah rejected Ransohoff's choice of female lead, Sharon Tate, whom Steve was enthusiastic to have in the film; he met her on a casual basis for sex. Tuesday Weld was cast in the role, which McQueen didn't object to; they had worked well together on *Soldier in the Rain*.

Filming began – without Lancey Howard being cast – during the first week of November 1964 and was stopped four days later when Ransohoff discovered Peckinpah filming scenes not in the script, such as a nude scene with a black prostitute and a riot scene with 300 extras. Apart from the extra cost involved – the film was already budgeted at $2.6 million – Ransohoff and MGM didn't want the film to have an X rating, which it would most certainly get with the sex scene.

Peckinpah was a maverick who did what he liked, but only because he thought it was best for the film. He just didn't believe he should be made to work according to studio rules, or what the producer wanted. So he was fired. McQueen never came to the defence of Peckinpah, which is why Peckinpah was baffled when McQueen turned up in Cornwall in 1970 hoping for some solace with the director. In 1976, Peckinpah told me, 'He could have told them, "If Sam don't do it, I don't do it." They would have changed their minds.'

Steve told me in 1977 he didn't defend Peckinpah because he agreed with Ransohoff, but insisted that he and Peckinpah had got along fine and had shared a few hard-drinking sessions just prior to filming *The Cincinnati Kid*. Steve said he had no reason to believe Peckinpah disliked him so much in 1970, especially since they were soon to work together on two films, *Junior Bonner* and *The Getaway*.

The delay in filming increased the budget to $3.5 million. A new director had to be found quickly. Steve was on edge, his nerves demanding action while the film was held up, so MGM agreed to give him $25,000 cash to spend in Las Vegas. Steve's agent, Stan Kamen, suggested to Ransohoff that one of his clients, Norman Jewison, direct the picture. Jewison had directed a good deal on television but only made four feature films, two of them, *Send Me No Flowers* and *The Thrill of It All*, Doris Day comedies.

Ransohoff decided to set up a meeting between Jewison and McQueen for when Steve returned from Las Vegas.

'When I first met Steve he was very cool, and kind of testing me,' said Jewison. 'I said, "Tell me a little bit about yourself," so he started talking about his childhood, and I felt that he was a loner and troubled and always looking for a father. I told him, "I can be your older brother and I'll always look out for you," and I think he bought that idea.'

Edward G. Robinson was cast as Lancey Howard, which made Steve so nervous that when he heard the news he was unable to sleep that night. He told me, 'When Robinson came on the set I just felt like I'd never acted in my life. It was like, this man is one of the greatest actors and I'm gonna screw up.'

Jewison said, 'Steve had this vulnerability, and he wasn't afraid to show it. He'd often look down at his feet, as though he couldn't look Robinson in the face, and Robinson didn't like that. He said, "He never looks me in the eye." That relationship was interesting, because you got Eddie Robinson, who was a *star*, a very cultured man who spoke four languages and knew all about art with this fabulous collection of masters, and here was Steve McQueen, a young rebel, the motorcycle rider. The edge in their off-camera relationship made the dramatic confrontation between the two of them on screen really wonderful.'

I'm sure that Steve was looking at his feet not to show he was vulnerable but because it was his way of taking the attention away from Robinson; he didn't want Robinson to steal the picture from him.

Steve told me he liked working with Tuesday Weld again, but I don't think she became one of his conquests. He told me, 'She was the best actress I've worked with up to that time.'

Jewison felt they worked well together. 'There was a wonderful chemistry between him and Tuesday Weld. I felt they were both loners, both kind of lost. Both were vulnerable. I loved his vulnerability on camera. I felt he'd been hurt as a child and he had difficulty with relationships. When I looked through the camera, or watched him in the dailies, I *believed* him. He had such believability.'

There was another good actress in the film, and a major sex symbol in her time, Ann-Margret, whom Steve once described as 'everybody's wet dream'. Norman Jewison thought that McQueen and Ann-Margret didn't get on well.

Considering that Jewison was relatively new to movies, he managed to keep a tight rein on McQueen. Said Jewison, 'Steve wanted to view the dailies, and I knew he was worried that Robinson was stealing the whole picture, and we also had these other wonderful actors like Karl Malden and Rip Torn, and so I said, "Steve, I don't think that's a good idea," and then tried to explain why he shouldn't watch them, and he just blew up. "You're twistin' my melon, man, you're twistin' my melon. You're getting me all mixed up. Fucking with my head, man."' Jewison laughed when he told me this. 'I didn't know what he was saying half the time. He talked so *hip*. I did my best to soothe his insecurities, but I still refused to allow him to see the dailies.'

Shortly after the film wrapped, Jewison showed Steve a rough assembly of the film, and Steve liked what he saw. 'Norman Jewison is one of the best directors for me,' Steve told me. 'John Sturges is number one, Norman Jewison number two.'

The Cincinnati Kid became one of the biggest hits of 1965, bringing in around $10 million worldwide. The critics didn't fail to see the connection with *The Hustler*, which had starred Paul Newman as a sort of poolroom Cincinnati Kid. 'The film pales beside *The Hustler* to which it bears a striking resemblance of theme and characterisation,' thought Howard Thompson of the *New York Times*. Judith Crist compared the two films as well, writing in the *New York Herald Tribune* that *The Cincinnati Kid* 'is quite literally *The Hustler* in spades. McQueen is at his *Great Escape* best, embodying the surface cool and high intensity of the man who'll go for broke but hasn't had to.'

Variety found the film to be 'a tenseful [sic] examination of the gambling fraternity. In Steve McQueen, [producer Martin Ransohoff] has the near-perfect delineator of the title role.'

While McQueen finished *The Cincinnati Kid*, he and John Sturges made a start on *Day of the Champion*, their cherished dream of a film about racing. Sturges had been spending his own money – $25,000 so far – on pre-production and, in the summer of 1965, he, Steve and racing legend Stirling Moss, hired as technical consultant, flew to France to tour the Formula One circuit. They engaged Porsche and were even able to mount Panavision cameras on some cars. A second unit crew filmed races at Reims, Monaco and Nürburgring, while in America Edward Anhalt worked on a screenplay which was about a driver who must win at any cost. Warner Brothers announced a May 1966 start date.

In the autumn of 1965, Steve started his next picture, *Nevada Smith*, back in the saddle for the first time since *The Magnificent Seven*, unless you counted the final episodes of *Wanted: Dead or Alive*. Nevada Smith was a character from Harold Robbins's novel *The Carpetbaggers* who hunts down the three men who murdered his parents, becomes a cowboy and, in his autumn years, becomes a movie-star. But the bulk of the book, and all of the film version of *The Carpetbaggers* (in which Nevada Smith was played by Alan Ladd), had focused on silent-movie days, and since the movie had been such success for Paramount and producer Joseph E. Levine, they wanted some kind of sequel to it. So a decision was taken to make a film just about the early days of Nevada Smith.

Harold Robbins was to be a co-producer, but when the screenplay was expanded to the point where the film's plot bore little resemblance to Robbins's concept, he backed away from the project completely.

Veteran director Henry Hathaway was brought in to make the picture. His credits included many successful action films, such as *The Lives of a Bengal Lancer*, *The Desert Fox*, *North to Alaska*, *How the West Was Won*, *The Sons of Katie Elder* and, a couple of years after *Nevada Smith*, *True Grit*. He was a man whose movies were full of action if little subtlety. 'I make movies, not art,' he told me. 'I'll entertain you, I hope I won't bore you, but I won't try and amaze you.'

Hathaway was a craftsman, and a tough director who had a reputation for yelling at supporting players, extras and crew but not the stars. 'I don't have time to be a nice guy,' he said. 'I have a few million dollars to make a picture that the studio wants to earn 20 million or so from, and I have to get the job done any way I can.'

Henry Hathaway was not the kind of director Steve McQueen was going to be able to intimidate. John Wayne once told me, 'The only son of a bitch who ever intimidated Hathaway was *me*! And that was maybe just once.'

Hathaway and McQueen had a meeting before filming began. 'I want you to know something, Mr McQueen,' Hathaway began. 'I'm the boss. Nobody argues with me. I'm not putting up with any shit from you, and if I do get any shit from you I'm going to deck you. I'm the meanest son of a bitch there ever was.'

When Hathaway finished, McQueen sat in silence, then smiled and shook hands with Hathaway and said, 'All right, Dad, you've got a deal.'

Hathaway told me, 'I never had any trouble with Steve McQueen. I just made sure he knew who was boss.'

Of Hathaway, Steve said, 'He's of the old school. You have to respect someone who was making movies before I was born. He was like my Uncle Claude. They were both tough, lovable, cranky.'

I asked Steve if he saw Hathaway as a surrogate father. He thought about that, looked kind of embarrassed – because Steve never liked to show too much emotion – and then said, 'Yeah, he was.' He also thought the same of John Sturges. McQueen had as many surrogate fathers as he could find, but Hathaway filled that role more substantially because he saw himself as the patriarch of his whole cast and crew.

'When I work it's like a family,' Hathaway said. 'I'm the head of the family. I can love my family or I can chew their nuts off. I heard all about McQueen and thought I'd be chewing his nuts off all the time. But he was great to work with. He called me Dad. I think that said something.'

The family atmosphere of filming *Nevada Smith* was heightened by the casting of the leading lady, Suzanne Pleshette. She was the one who broke the news to Steve that they would be acting together. She told me, 'There was a party before filming and there was still some casting to do, and I said to Steve, "By the way, guess who your leading lady in *Nevada Smith* is." He said, "Who?" I said, "Me." He said, "*Who?*" I said, "Me." Well, I was still his baby sister, and it had never occurred to him that I was an actress and we might one day work together.

'When we had to do the love scenes we looked at each other and were just horrified. It was like incest. "Oh, my God, I can't kiss you." "Well, I can't kiss you," and Hathaway was saying, "For Christ's sake, will you two kiss already?" I'd kiss him and then kind of cough and spit, like I would vomit. What the hell was I thinking? He was *gorgeous*.' She laughed. 'Turned out I was his only leading lady he didn't sleep with. I don't know if I should be flattered or pissed off.'

She saw a very different side to McQueen from the one other women saw. He usually showed little or no respect for women, and he certainly didn't want to hear their opinions – except for Neile's. Women were there for his pleasure, and there were plenty who were happy to give him pleasure, which, I suspect, only added to his negative attitude towards women. He knew he could pour on the charm if he wanted something from a woman. But in the case of Suzanne Pleshette – whom he always called Suzy – he was, as she put it, 'generous and loving and always respectful'.

She recalled a scene in which he had to pull her from a canoe and lay her on the ground. 'Where he laid me was a bed of dry leaves with pointed stems which stung me like bees and made me sit up and start screaming. He grabbed a blanket and put it around me to comfort me but they also had these leaves so I got stung even more, and I just got up and ran away, and Steve was left standing there horrified that I was in such pain. And he felt even worse when I told him the blanket he put round me was full of those leaves, and he thought it was his fault. He was so upset, and he showed such love and kindness to me. He always did.'

Paramount wasn't skimping on this picture. They put $4.5 million into the budget and paid McQueen a handsome $500,000. He was also provided with a comfortable mobile home for the location at Hathaway's insistence.

Suzanne Pleshette said, 'Henry handled Steve so wonderfully.

He gave him a boat with a motor on it – like a putt-putt motor – so he could use all this energy riding up and down the river when we weren't shooting, otherwise he was going crazy out where we were filming with nothing to do.'

Hathaway bought him the boat when they were filming in Louisiana by the Amite River. Steve recalled, 'The river had leeches, there were mosquitoes and it was too hot. I couldn't hang around.'

Hathaway told me, 'When we finished a scene, Steve got on his motorbike, revved that goddamn engine so it scared the horses, and then rode off, doing wheelies through the woods. No shirt on. No helmet. I yelled, "Get that goddamn idiot off that goddamn bike." If he got hurt that would be the end of the movie. So when we shot in the swamps I figured I had to do something to keep him happy, so I bought him a putter motorboat to play around in, and Steve just loved that.'

Susanne was of the opinion that his deprived childhood contributed to his hyperactive nature, and that it also made him insecure all his life when it came to anything that cost money. She said, 'He wasn't comfortable in fine places where the food was rich and you had to be rich to pay for it. I remember in New Orleans we went to a dining club, and he ordered two steaks, and I said, "Just order one, and if you're still hungry you can order another," and he said, "What if there isn't another one?" And I think that was very telling, because there had been so many lean years. It also made him incredibly cheap. He always said, "I don't have any money on me," so I always had to pay the bills.'

Susanne remembered how she and the rest of the cast and crew had to make do with meagre bagged lunches – a sandwich and an apple – while Steve was being served chicken and vegetables in his motor home. 'Steve had it first class compared to the rest of us, and after he'd had lunch every day he'd leave his trailer and come over to me and ask for a cookie, and I'd just give it to him. I didn't think about it, but Hathaway caught on and said to me, "Just hang on and let me negotiate this for you, Suzy." He said to Steve, "What are you going to give up for this cookie?" And Steve didn't want to give anything up. That was the psychology of this very poor boy who had almost nothing to begin with. He was always very giving in other ways, but he never picked up the check.'

That was true to some degree. I think Steve never picked up a bill when he was around people who could pick it up for him. But during my road trip with him he paid for everything. He *had* to. I didn't have more than enough to pay for my train fare home, and Sam Peckinpah was paying for my bed and breakfast (although he obviously saved money by getting Steve to take me off on this trip). Steve was horrified when I told him I earned only £5 a week, and so he paid for everything – my room, my food and the beer.

During the filming of *Nevada Smith*, Steve planned to attend the premiere of *The Cincinnati Kid* in New Orleans in October. But he had to cancel that when Neile called him with the news that his mother had been admitted to Mount Zion hospital in San Francisco with a cerebral haemorrhage. He flew to San Francisco and kept vigil by her bedside. He had never stopped resenting her and yet suddenly he felt helpless and wished he could do something to help her. He told Neile, 'I wish I could give her my energy so she can live.'

Perhaps he suddenly felt the need to say to her everything he had held back, or hoped that, if she survived, he would finally resolve his problems with her. But it was too late. She died in her sleep on 15 October, and when she passed, Steve cried.

Neile went with him to Julian's apartment, where they found a dress on the sewing machine she had been making for Terry. Neile made all the arrangements for the funeral, and Steve asked that donations be sent to the Boys Republic.

On 20 October, Julian was buried in the Gardens of Ascension at the Forest Lawn Memorial Park in Glendale, California, in a plot under a tree which Steve bought. Apart from him and Neile, the only others there were Chad and Terry, David Foster (Steve's publicist and friend) and his wife, Jackie. There was no minister. Steve gave the brief eulogy. 'She would have liked this spot,' he said. 'Shady with no sun,' and then he broke down.

He told me, 'I looked down at her coffin in the open grave. I wanted to yell and curse her. I was suddenly overcome with . . . I dunno, some kind of emotion. I knelt down and cried, and all I could say was "Why?"'

He retuned to the *Nevada Smith* location and, according to Suzanne Pleshette, didn't say a word about his mother or the funeral. 'It was a long time before he opened up,' she said. 'I think he felt he'd lost the chance to ask her about so many things, and he was kind of lost. Like a child who'd become an orphan. But he never really had a mother or a father. He was always an orphan.'

Martin Landau, who played one of the killers Nevada Smith is hunting, recalled, 'I think he was different after his mother died. He argued more with Henry Hathaway, which is never a good idea. He was very good at knowing what he could do, and the kind of things he could say, and he wanted to change lines to fit his style, but Hathaway never changed a word in a script. So there was some tension between them.'

Hathaway recalled, 'Steve didn't like to show his grief, but I sensed it. I said to him, "You're behaving like a child. Pull yourself together and make this goddamn movie, and you'll feel better." We had a few run-ins, but when I was tough with him, he began to get in line again.'

Steve had mixed feeling about the picture. On one level he liked it. 'I think there was something about the moral code of men back then which appealed to me. In the same position, I'd have done the same as Nevada.' But he was dissatisfied with it overall, mainly, I think, because he was unable to make the changes to the script he thought were necessary. 'It could have been better if I hadn't had so much [dialogue] to say. Too much dialogue and too much length,' he said, meaning the length of the film, which came in at 131 minutes. And he had a point.

Hathaway disagreed with McQueen's judgement. 'He wanted to be so laconic that he'd hardly ever say a word. Sometimes it's too much to say too little. The audience can be left puzzled and then you lose them.' It was an old-fashioned approach to movie making.

Vincent Canby, the film critic of the *New York Times*, obviously agreed with McQueen and dismissed the film as 'an overstuffed Western drama. It is just too long. It is also too episodic.' But he did think McQueen was 'tight-lipped, craggy and believable'.

Wanda Hale of the *New York Daily Times* was disappointed the film didn't cover the story of the Harold Robbins character in *The Carpetbaggers*. 'You cannot connect the current Nevada with the one played by the late Alan Ladd. Everybody has missed the point which could have stimulated curiosity: how Nevada Smith got to Hollywood and into the movies.' She found it a 'tedious Western with too little suspense and too much talk'.

Variety agreed. 'Henry Hathaway's uneven direction alternates jarring, overbearing fisticuffs with exterior footage as spectacular in some cases as it is dull in others.'

However, Archer Winsten of the *New York Post* thought the film 'the real old thing, uncut, unwatered, undiluted'.

Steve had millions of fans waiting to see it, despite what the critics said, and it grossed $12 million domestic, and maybe as much again overseas. Many stars would never dare take a year's break, because the public, which is fickle, easily forgets, especially if someone new comes along to take their place. But McQueen's fans had been waiting faithfully, and he had two hits in a row with *The Cincinnati Kid* and *Nevada Smith* (though only the former is now considered a classic). He had made a successful comeback.

After *Nevada Smith*, Steve and John Sturges made plans to make their beloved racing film, *Day of the Champion*. Warner Brothers were interested in it, but only if McQueen and Sturges could get production under way before MGM began a film on the same theme, *Grand Prix*, to be shot in Cinerama. Plans were made to start after Steve's next picture, which was to be *The Sand Pebbles*.

Initially McQueen had shown interest in another movie that Joseph E. Levine, producer of *Nevada Smith*, had in mind for him, *The Ski Bum*, from a novel by Romain Gary. It required an athletic star oozing sex appeal and box-office magic. Steve McQueen was the right man for the job, but he decided instead to go with *The Sand Pebbles*, which was based on a novel by Richard McKenna, about an American enlisted navy man in war-torn China in 1926. The novel spent 28 weeks on the *New York Times* best-seller list and 20th Century-Fox and director/producer Robert Wise thought a film of it would make a lot of money, so much so that Fox were pouring $8 million into it.

Wise had been trying to get Paul Newman to star, but when Wise finally gave up on him, he turned to the next natural choice – Steve McQueen. The fee of $650,000 plus a percentage of the profits interested Steve, and he invited Wise to the Castle to discuss things. Robert Wise told me, 'I hadn't seen McQueen since the days when he was being a pain in the ass on the set of the movie his wife was making for me [*This Could Be the Night*], and all I could think of when I was in his house, discussing really big money with him, was how he had gone from being broke to just about the biggest star in the world in hardly more than 10 years.'

The Sand Pebbles was a three-hour epic, made in a decade when three-hour epics could either make huge profits if the public were interested enough, as they did with *El Cid* and *Lawrence of Arabia*, or break a studio, as *Cleopatra* almost did to 20th Century-Fox and *The Fall of the Roman Empire* did to Samuel Bronston.

20th Century-Fox was eventually saved by the three-hour war epic *The Longest Day* and then the three-hour musical *The Sound of Music*, which made Wise a hero to that studio, and it was confident that, with Wise directing and McQueen starring, they could afford to spend $8 million on *The Sand Pebbles*. Actually, $8 million was not a huge amount for so vast a movie, but the movie would look more expensive thanks to unprecedented help from the government of Taiwan, where it was to be filmed.

To keep himself in shape, Steve had his home gym shipped to the rented villa where he, Neile and the children would be living. He had plenty of time to work out because filming was delayed when the $250,000 recreation of a 1920s gunboat, on which much of the film's action would take place, was unable to dock because the Keelung River was at low tide, and so the gunboat had to wait two weeks for the tide to rise before arriving.

Then it rained for three weeks. One delay piled onto another, and the original schedule of 80 days turned into seven months, the last two back at the Fox Studio in Hollywood. Steve and Neile took the opportunity to see Taiwan and discovered an orphanage for girls run by a Catholic priest, Father Edward Wojniak. Many of the girls being given shelter there had been forced into prostitution. Steve, known for not picking up the bill, donated $25,000 to the mission and continued to support it. He never boasted of this charitable act, preferring to keep it a secret. I found out about it, after Steve died, from Suzanne Pleshette.

Filming finally began on 22 November 1965. It didn't begin well. Wise recalled:

From the first day Steve was fighting with me. He wanted scenes to be shot differently. I couldn't get him to understand that there's only one director on a movie. He made it clear he'd walk if I didn't listen to his ideas. So I told him I'd shoot the scenes his way and then my way, and if he liked his version better when it was edited, we'd use his. It was a bad idea because it just added weeks to the schedule, which was already getting behind, and added to the budget. But I figured it was worth it because McQueen was such a big star, and he knew it. When the film was edited with only the scenes done my way and not his, he didn't argue about it.

He drove me mad. He really did. One time I was setting up a complicated dolly shot and he tapped me on the shoulder and said, 'Now about this wardrobe,' and I exploded. I told him 'I got other things to think of right now,' and that got him upset and he didn't speak to me for three days. He watched the dailies, which I don't like an actor to do, but I let him, and he liked what I'd shot so much he started talking to me again and wasn't any more trouble.

Steve was so immersed in what he had to do. To him the movie was built around him, and he wasn't concerned with anything else or anyone else, which is okay because he was perfect for the role – he actually learned all the things that character had to know about the boat's engine. He was wonderful with anything mechanical.

Steve's co-star, his friend from *The Great Escape*, Richard Attenborough, was vastly impressed with Steve's attention to detail when it came to the mechanics of running the gunboat. 'He really got to know that boat. He knew the engine, he knew the decks. He could have run that boat if he had to, and that added a wonderful credibility to his performance.'

Attenborough recalled the friendship he and McQueen enjoyed during the months they spent working on the movie. 'We were in Taiwan for five months so we spent a lot of time together. My wife and children came over for part of the time and so did Neile and their kids. I saw how very precious his children were to him. He was so very proud of them.'

Steve had a lot of respect for Richard Attenborough. 'He's from that great English tradition of actors in the theatre. You know he's going to be good [in the scene], always ready, and a nice guy. Yeah, I liked him. We had a lot more time together on that than when we did *The Great Escape*.'

While there was camaraderie between the two men, there was little between Steve and his leading lady, Candice Bergen. She felt that he was trying to get her to 'get it on with some of his buddies', as she wrote in her autobiography. She described his buddies as 'a commando unit of six stuntmen', which she didn't find appealing. I've no idea if that's true, but I suspect that Steve was kidding around with her, the way he would with his buddies. He had no finesse when it came to women, and since Bergen was only 19 at the time, he might well have been at a loss as to how to treat her.

He admitted he could be intimidating to some women. 'They don't know how to take me. I know how to talk to my buddies, but some girls are maybe a little more delicate. They take what I say the wrong way. Or they don't get the gag.'

She was unable to relax around him. She said he was 'handsome and hypnotic, powerful and unpredictable, and he could turn on you in a flash'.

Steve told me he tried to help Candice Bergen, who had made

only one previous movie, *The Group*. 'Neile and me had her over to our house to eat with us and the kids. I wanted her to relax.' It obviously didn't work.

The film's other major co-star was Mako, a Japanese actor who had appeared in many American television dramas and comedy shows but hadn't made a film before (except for a brief appearance as an extra in *Never So Few*). During a rehearsal in the engine room, Mako scratched his head. Steve asked him, 'Are you going to scratch your head in the scene?'

Mako replied, 'I don't know.'

'Well don't.' Steve wasn't having Mako upstage him.

Despite the location and sometimes difficult conditions in Taiwan, it was the best time in the McQueen marriage. Neile called it 'our happiest period ever'. She put it down to 'no temptations'.

It would never be that good again.

Steve's greatest frustration was the delays that were holding up his racing picture, *Day of the Champion*, as its start date kept getting pushed back. John Sturges decided he ought to get out to Taiwan to meet with Steve and find out 'what the hell was going on', as Sturges put it. 'I wasn't there long. An earthquake hit, and I went home again to work on the screenplay with Edward Anhalt.'

Some time after that, still stuck in Taiwan, still making *The Sand Pebbles*, Steve read that the other racing film, *Grand Prix*, was under way and starring his friend James Garner.

Garner had tried to let McQueen know he was doing it. He said, 'I knew how passionate Steve was about his picture, and I thought it only right that I personally call him and tell him I was in *Grand Prix*. Turned out he already knew, but he said he appreciated me calling him personally, and after that he didn't talk to me for a year.'

Steve told me, 'I didn't think Jim had betrayed me, but I thought he wasn't a real racer, just an actor playing the part.'

I told Steve, 'But, Steve, you are *both* actors playing the part.'

'No, man. Not me. I'm the real deal.'

He felt that no other actor had earned the right to play a

racing-car driver. He and Sturges didn't give up, and pressed on with their search for a studio now that Warner Brothers, feeling there wasn't room for two pictures about motorcar racing, had pulled out.

The Sand Pebbles finally wrapped at the Fox studios in Hollywood in May 1966, $3 million over budget. The picture did not turn out to be as good as it should have been. Judith Crist, writing in the *World Journal Tribune*, thought it was 'over three hours of tedium, interspersed with a blood-spattered schmaltz-spangled compendium of screenplay clichés'.

Variety pinpointed the film's flaw: 'The major drawback: . . . is a surfeit of exposition, mainly in the second half. Every scene is in itself excellent, but unfortunately the overall dramatic flow of the pic [sic] suffers in the end.' It did, however, like what McQueen did. 'Steve McQueen looks and acts the part he plays so well – that of a machinist's mate with nine years of navy service.'

At last Steve gave Bosley Crowther of the *New York Times* something to praise, 'with the most restrained, honest, heartfelt acting he has ever done'.

Arthur Knight of the *Saturday Review* thought that while co-star Richard Crenna was 'outstanding', Candice Bergen 'attractive', and Richard Attenborough 'effective', 'all of them were dominated by Steve McQueen who is nothing short of wonderful in the pivotal role'.

The picture did very well, a third hit in a row since his comeback, perhaps thanks in part to Steve's quite uncharacteristic participation in promoting it over a 10-day period in New York. But he wasn't really enthusiastic about the movie – or rather about the character he played. After completing *The Sand Pebbles* he felt somehow dissatisfied with it, and he found it hard to explain exactly why. He took his family on a fishing vacation to Alaska to try to clear his head. He was never able to comprehend fully what was wrong about his role in the picture. He told me, 'He [the character] didn't do what I would do.'

'But that's what acting is all about, playing other people,' I suggested.

'Not for me. The characters I play have to become me or I can't do it well.'

He was wrong. As meandering as *The Sand Pebbles* is at times – it takes some stamina to sit through it in one go – Steve was excellent in it. And it earned him his first Academy Award nomination, although he lost to Paul Schofield in *A Man for All Seasons*. There were eight nominations in all for *The Sand Pebbles*, including Best Picture and Best Supporting Actor for Mako. Ultimately the film won none, but eight nominations is still a considerable achievement, although Steve disagreed with that. 'Nobody remembers the losers, only the winners,' he said. I think *he* remembered losing more than anyone else would.

Perhaps because he failed to win the Oscar, or because he was bothered at not being able to put his finger on what was wrong with his work in *The Sand Pebbles* – or both – he decided to take another break for at least a year. It was always a gamble for an actor at the top of his profession to take a break. Steve had taken a long break before and successfully returned. Perhaps he felt he could do it again and still win. Eventually, he would make one comeback too many.

CHAPTER 12

—

Top of the World

With the release of *The Sand Pebbles* came plaudits that weren't quite as glamorous as the Oscar, but it was still worth a lot to Steve to be voted favourite actor by the Hollywood Foreign Press Association. He also won the Photoplay Gold Medal Award, while in Japan he was voted the most popular foreign star for a second year running. On 21 March 1967, he became the 153rd star to put his footprints and signature in cement outside Grauman's Chinese Theater, watched by two thousand fans.

His year off was spent doing pretty much as before – racing cars and motorcycles, drinking beer and taking drugs, and just generally hanging around his house with his family. By the time the year was up, he was restless to get back before the cameras. He didn't seem to worry about whether or not he would still be welcomed by his fans, especially as he had spent the year collecting honours for his work. He saw no reason to suppose that his latest comeback would not be just as triumphant as the one before. But he knew he needed the right script.

Alan Trustman had written a very good script called *The Crown Caper*, about an investment banker, Thomas Crown, who, looking for new challenges in life, masterminds a bank robbery. Investigating the robbery on behalf of an insurance company is the glamorous Vicky Anderson. The script was eventually renamed *The Thomas Crown Affair*. Norman Jewison was already set to direct it, and it was being produced by the Mirisch Brothers and United Artists.

Alan Trustman had written the screenplay with Sean Connery in mind, so Jewison and Walter Mirisch made every effort to get Connery, and when he finally turned it down, they tried Rock Hudson. The idea of Steve McQueen playing the part never even occurred to Mirisch, who said, 'Steve McQueen just didn't fit the character, who wore three-piece suits especially tailored for him, and played polo. Steve was a guy in a T-shirt and blue jeans on a motorbike. Steve McQueen tailored all his roles to fit him, and there was no way I could see he was going to play Thomas Crown in a T-shirt on a motorcycle. Sean Connery and Rock Hudson looked at home in a suit.'

As far as Norman Jewison was concerned, he never wanted to work with McQueen again after the megrims of *The Cincinnati Kid*.

Steve's agent, Stan Kamen, thought it would be great to get Steve out of cowboy and navy uniforms and into something modern and sophisticated, playing an executive in a suit and tie who plays polo, and tried to get Steve to read the script, but he wouldn't even glance at it. Neile thought it would be a great part for Steve to play, so one morning, over breakfast, she told him, 'Norman Jewison doesn't want you for this film.'

Steve said, 'Who told you that?'

'Everyone knows it and everyone's got the script. Rock Hudson, Sean Connery . . .'

Steve called Norman Jewison and asked for the role. Jewison was reluctant to give it to him, but eventually he and Walter Mirisch decided that since the two actors they wanted to do the film didn't want to do it, and McQueen did, they would give him the part. But they had to allow his Solar company to become a part of the producing process, although it had minimal input. Mostly it meant Steve could call some of the shots, and it also meant that the screenplay needed rewriting to better suit McQueen. This infuriated Alan Trustman, who, knowing he had no choice in the matter, demanded that United Artists provide him with every piece of footage of Steve McQueen they could get their hands on so he could make a checklist of what McQueen could and couldn't do. Using his checklist, Trustman rewrote the screenplay to better suit McQueen's various traits. But he didn't change the concept of Thomas Crown as an executive in a suit and tie who played polo.

Steve found in Thomas Crown an element of social rebellion that he felt suited his own true nature. As he put it, 'He's my kind of cat.' He became dedicated to playing the part to the extent that he learned to play polo, spending hours playing until his hands bled. 'I had to show those cats who played I could do it *and* beat them.'

Steve sat in with Jewison, Mirisch and Trustman on all their script meetings, making himself ever more unpopular, so Jewison asked a Russian-born actor, Nikita Knatz, to take McQueen off their hands. Knatz was actually hired by Jewison more for his drawing abilities than his acting – he became Jewison's image designer – but he also had another talent which Jewison knew would intrigue Steve. He was accomplished in numerous forms of martial arts and, after filming began in June 1967, Steve began training with Knatz on Sundays.

Steve knew he was not what director, writer and producer had wanted for the role, and he worked hard to make himself as close to the original concept of Thomas Crown as possible. He was always pedantic about small details in regard to the characters he played. He felt Thomas Crown had to have the right kind of watch but he didn't know what that was, so on the set, on the first day, with everyone waiting, he tried on watches for more than 25 minutes until he finally said, 'My own watch is better than any of these.'

If people thought he was being difficult – and some of them did – Steve insisted he was just taking his work seriously. 'I always do a lot of preparation. It takes a lot of study. I find the right clothes. The details are important.' What Steve somehow couldn't understand was that he needed to do those things *before* filming began.

Jim Coburn thought this behaviour was 'the child that he really was. He didn't think to himself, "I'm going to screw up everyone's day by holding up the shoot while I decide what to wear." He probably just turned up and suddenly realised he wasn't going to play unless he had the right toy. So he stopped to get it right. It was, "I'm not playing till I got my toys." Trouble is, *everyone* had to stop too. But it was always worth it. Look what he brought to every role he played. Every one had something distinctive about it. That guy in the cooler had the baseball. When he was the bounty hunter he had that sawn-off shotgun. When he was Nevada Smith he had to have the right gun. That's what actors do. You just do it *before* you start shooting. Sometimes Steve waited until they began.'

Norman Jewison recalled, 'It was hard for him to settle into the part. He had to wear a tie and Steve McQueen had never worn a tie. Or a suit. He wouldn't wear a shirt unless he really had to. So I worked with him on his style, and he really made the part his own.'

Steve liked his tailor-made suits so much that he was allowed to keep them. He was also given the dune buggy that he drives over the beach and sand dunes in the movie. And he got paid $750,000 and was worth it, thought Walter Mirisch. 'Once you had Steve McQueen, and you worked out how he was going to fit this character, you knew you had a real star who was going to attract an audience, so you pay him what he's worth. I have to admit, Steve McQueen was worth every dime.

'He brought those good looks, that great smile, his genuine playfulness to Thomas Crown. He made that character himself. Thomas Crown was Steve McQueen in a suit.'

What McQueen didn't want to reveal to everyone when he began the film was that he was anxious and insecure about the part, which is probably why he took time to pick a watch. Coburn may have been right about him being a child picking the right toy, but I think Steve was also like the child standing at the edge of the swimming pool, about to dive in for the first time, who says, 'Don't push me in. I'll go when I'm ready.'

He told me, 'I wasn't so sure I could do it. I was nervous about it. Then I did a scene where I've done the first robbery and I'm a success, so I get home, get a drink – a martini not a beer – and I just start laughing to myself coz I *did* it. I robbed the bank and didn't need the money, but I was saying, "Screw you" to that kind of society. And that was *me*, because that's what *I* did.'

I asked him, 'Do you mean in your life or in Hollywood?'

'Both, man. I'm always looked down on.' That's how Steve saw himself in Hollywood – as the outsider, the delinquent nobody wanted to have at their party. But then, Steve had always *put* himself on the outside. However, there were times he just wanted Hollywood to open up and fully embrace him. 'I'd like some of the so-called elite to say, "You've done good, Steve." Frank Sinatra's about the only one who's said that. John Wayne too.'

I said, 'But, Steve, who else do you want to get approval from? Nobody's bigger than Sinatra and Wayne.'

And to that he replied, with something close to a pout, '*I'm* bigger than them.'

That was the child. And I think that aspect of him prevented him from ever becoming fully integrated into Hollywood, because part of him wanted approval and another part of him was saying, 'Screw your approval.' To some, that made him impossible. To me, it made him rather endearing. I'm lucky because I never saw the rage in him that could explode, sometimes into violence, that alienated him from some. Maybe that would have altered my perspective.

Even Norman Jewison, who didn't relish the idea of working with McQueen that second time, admitted, 'There's something about him I like. He was like the kid brother who didn't go to school, or who got hurt. He drives you crazy but you feel he needs something and you try to give it to him.

'There's no question he was dedicated to that movie. He worked so hard, and enjoyed the challenge, I think, but was also very insecure about it. He seemed to want to be somewhere else at times, even though he talked me into giving him the part. Maybe that's why he did it in the end, because I'd turned him down and then he won. I told Steve, "This guy is elegant. He plays polo, and that kind of part is going to be very hard for you." And he said, "That's why I want to do it." So I gave in.'

Jewison liked McQueen's offbeat charm, but his leading lady, Faye Dunaway, didn't fall for it. 'They were both very strong personalities,' said Jewison about McQueen and Dunaway. 'I don't know if he tried to seduce her, but she wouldn't have gone for it. Actually, he didn't want Faye in the movie. He felt she wasn't a star. She'd only been in *Bonnie and Clyde*. She hadn't proved she was a star. But they were explosive together on screen. That chess scene and the big kiss scene are classics. He actually held us up because he went riding in his dune buggy. We spent hours setting it up, waiting for the sun to be where we wanted it for the shot, so we could shoot it in silhouette. And we missed it. Steve came in and said, "Sorry, I didn't know you were ready."

'But when we did the scene and they began to kiss – they *kissed*. It was something! They made that scene so memorable and sexy.'

The moon buggy ride over the sand was another memorable scene, and one in which Steve was perfectly at home as he drove the buggy at high speed, with Faye Dunaway next to him expressing a mixture of both exhilaration and terror.

'He loved the dune buggy,' said Jewison. 'He had his mechanics put this big engine in. We shot on a beach and the camera was in the back, and Steve saw this flock of seagulls on the sand and he just drove straight at them and they took off, and he was so happy, just like a child. He loved the freedom. Scared the hell out of Faye though.'

The Thomas Crown Affair became another huge hit for Steve, bringing in $14 million – it had cost just $4 million.

Proving again how wrong critics can be about a film's eventual destiny, Archer Winsten wrote in the *New York Post*, 'McQueen, dashing around with verve, unlimited energy and bright, inquiring eyes, makes you wonder if he knows he's hatching something almost akin to a turkey.'

'There is a long soon-to-be-famous kissing scene that is so misdirected one thinks of Edsels on a summer's night,' wrote Renata Adler in the *New York Times*. 'McQueen is always special, and although his role is too indoors and formal, he does get a chance to race across the desert or fly a glider or lie on a beach, in the casual-intense work he is best at.'

Kathleen Carroll, writing in the *New York Daily News*, liked the film and McQueen. 'A polished McQueen, minus his motorcyclist's mumble, shows a whole new facet of his active personality. He is cast most successfully.'

Steve was in a suit again, with black tie, for the film's premiere at Boston's Sack Music Hall on 18 June 1968. He made sure he was the last celebrity to arrive, and when the crowd rushed at him, he had to be protected by the police, who virtually lifted him onto their shoulders to get him into the theatre.

Steve McQueen had made his second comeback and was on top of the world. He also decided he would become more of a film-maker, inspired by Clint Eastwood, whose Malpaso Company actively produced his films. Steve decided to make Solar Productions a more powerful company by buying scripts, so he could make the kinds of films he wanted and, above all else, be the boss.

He needed men to help him run the business and called on Robert Relyea, John Sturges's assistant director on *Never So Few*, *The Magnificent Seven* and *The Great Escape*, to be Solar's vice president and executive producer. A friend, Jack Reddish, became staff production manager. Steve would be president of Solar.

On 23 August 1967, Solar agreed a six-picture deal with Warner Brothers. Two of the pictures were to star McQueen and would be budgeted at $6–7 million each. The other four pictures would be without him and budgeted at $3 million each. The title of the six movies were *Bullitt*, *The Man on a Nylon String*, *The Cold War Swap*, *Day of the Champion*, *Adam at 6:00 A.M.* and *Suddenly Single*.

'I felt like I'd really achieved something for a kid from the streets,' Steve told me. 'I even wore a suit and tie each day to the office.' His office was at the Warner Brothers studio.

Bullitt was the first of the six pictures to go before the cameras. Steve was to star in this, although at first he wasn't keen on the project at all because he balked at the idea of playing a police detective, Lieutenant Frank Bullitt. 'Everyone called cops "pigs" and I didn't want anyone calling me a pig,' he said.

He changed his mind about the police after he was stopped for speeding his Ferrari through the hills of Brentwood. The patrolman who pulled him over filled out the ticket before realising it was for Steve McQueen, then apologised and said, 'Wait till I get out of here before you open that thing up again.' Suddenly Steve didn't think cops were so bad after all.

Alan Trustman, who wrote *The Thomas Crown Affair*, was tasked to write the screenplay. When Steve read it, he didn't understand the somewhat jumbled plot and again had misgivings. Neile persuaded him he had to do it.

Others who McQueen approached about the picture were also unimpressed with the script. Director Peter Yates said, 'When I first read the *Bullitt* script I couldn't believe how terrible it was. I thought, I can't do this. It's impossible.'

Robert Vaughn, who hadn't worked with Steve since *The Magnificent Seven*, said, 'Steve sent me the *Bullitt* script and I sent it back saying, "It doesn't make any sense. I don't understand the plot. Why are you doing this?" He kept sending it back, offering me more money. That made the script seem a lot clearer to me!'

Steve and Robert Relyea chose Peter Yates to direct because they had seen a British film he made, *Robbery*, which featured a car chase that Steve particularly liked. 'He shot it differently to any car chase I'd seen,' said Steve. 'It really kept you on the edge of your seat.' *Bullitt* was to feature a car chase, and Steve based his choice of Yates on his car chase sequence.

Peter Yates had only directed two films, both of them British – *Robbery* and the Cliff Richard musical *Summer Holiday* – but had directed many British TV shows, such as episodes of *Danger Man* and *The Saint*, and had learned his craft in major British feature films as assistant director on *The Guns of Navarone* and *A Taste of Honey*. Although he was unimpressed with the script of *Bullitt*, he knew that it was his chance to break into American movies. He said, 'I was happy to become a director working in Hollywood.

Who was I to say no to that? But I knew the screenplay needed another rewrite, so we got the best we could out of it.'

As Robert Vaughn noted, 'Of course, it was an enormous success but still very hard to follow the story, but that's not important.'

A British actress, Jacqueline Bisset, was cast as Bullitt's girlfriend. Bisset had played a number of small roles in British films of the 1960s but had her first Hollywood break when cast alongside Frank Sinatra in *The Detective*. She would go on to become a favourite leading lady in American films, and also enjoyed a huge success in prestigious European movies. But when she was cast in *Bullitt*, she was chosen not just for her beauty and acting skills, but because she was a lot less expensive than other leading Hollywood actresses of the time. The same was true of Peter Yates when it came to directors. Steve told me, 'Two of the best breaks we got for *Bullitt* were getting Peter Yates and Jackie Bisset, because both were as good as anyone in Hollywood but they cost a lot less.'

Steve's long-time friend Don Gordon was cast in a major supporting role, but when he tried to thank Steve for getting him the part, Steve told him, 'What are you talking about? I didn't do you any favours.' But Don Gordon knew that wasn't true. 'He wouldn't admit he did you a favour, and he never asked for a favour in return,' he said.

The film was to be shot in San Francisco. Usually Neile went with Steve on location, but he told her, 'It's going to be a heavy location, baby.'

To get a flavour of real police work, Steve suggested he and Don Gordon accompany San Francisco detectives. The two cops whom Steve shadowed thought they would shake him up by telling him to meet them at the morgue. 'I knew they were testing me,' said Steve. 'I like to test people too. So I turned up eating an apple and there were these dead bodies, and I said, "So what gives, guys?" They kind of accepted me after that.'

Then they drove him to a hospital to see actual crime victims. Steve found himself standing over a patient in intensive care who had been in a motorcycle accident. As McQueen was about to leave, the patient managed to say, 'Take it slow, Steve.' Steve told me he was very moved by that experience.

Steve gained tremendous insight into police work by riding with his assigned detectives. He recalled, 'They could get so frustrated and obsessed [with a case]. They had been tracking the killer of a woman who had been on her way to get married when she was murdered. I went with them to get him, and they put him in a cell. They thought he was going to the electric chair for sure. What was important to them wasn't that they were going to kill the guy but that their work paid off and the dead girl would get justice. But the night they arrested him, he hanged himself in his cell. I saw how that affected them. They were like . . . *I can't believe this is happening*. That told me a lot about these guys.'

Just as *Bullitt* was about to go into production, Warner Brothers was taken over by Kenneth Hyman and Seven Arts, which led to a change in the original agreement with Solar. Now Warners would make just the one Solar picture, which was *Bullitt*, with the option to make further Solar pictures. Also, the budget for *Bullitt* was reduced from up to $7 million down to $4 million. All this, as well as being in overall charge, even with Robert Relyea taking on the major production responsibilities along with producer Philip D'Antoni, took its toll on Steve. There were no practical jokes, and little sign of the humour he usually displayed. 'He wasn't depressed,' said Don Gordon. 'He just cared more than he normally would. I guess he snapped a little more. He was a great boss, I thought. If you were loyal to him, he was loyal to you. He only asked you to do your job.'

Steve was probably at his most professional on this film, never keeping people waiting, always knowing his lines, always setting the example. 'He wanted everyone to do the best they could so *he* did the best he could,' said Don Gordon.

He was often plagued by self-doubt, coming out of a take and telling Peter Yates, 'I could have done a lot better.' While the director noted Steve's insecurity, few others did and most everyone else thought he was giving nothing less than his very best. Robert Vaughn said, 'He was very sure of himself as an actor in *Bullitt*. He had captured by then the vision that he and Neile had about Steve McQueen the movie-star. He was very secure at being that character. Every move he made in that film, whether it was getting in and out of a car, every movement, every piece of physicality, was a demonstration of his instinct for what the camera would capture. He made anything look cool.'

This film, perhaps more than any other, demonstrated Steve's intense skill acting with a camera. He told me, 'The camera can do so much. It can do a lot of the work for you. So long as you know how to use the camera. I'll go through a script and cut lines because I know I can do it without words. I just need the camera.'

Don Gordon said, 'He didn't like a lot of dialogue. He liked it when somebody else talked, and then he would nod or say, "Yes," or "Hmmm." He'd look at the script and say, "I think Don should say that," and it would be three or four paragraphs, and I'd say, "McQueen, you're giving me all these lines and I know the camera is going to be on you." He said, "Hey, I'm the star. What are you gonna do?"'

Said Peter Yates, 'Steve said to me, "I'm not an actor, I'm a re-actor," but that's not true. He's a very good actor. He always thought he was at his best when he didn't have to speak. He was *always* at his best.'

Yates encouraged his cast to ad-lib at moments. Don Gordon recalled, 'We had a scene where we discover a trunk and don't know what's in it but we think it's important. And we really didn't know what was in it, and we ad-libbed that whole scene, and did it in one take. Peter Yates was very good like that.'

Neile, who only saw Steve when he was able to return at weekends, thought she noticed a change in him. Then she discovered he was having an affair. The rumour was that this affair was with Jacqueline Bisset, but he never confirmed that to me. But there was definitely someone he was involved with, and his friends warned him that he was in danger of wrecking his marriage. It seems he thought that Neile would simply stick by him – and she did.

Shortly after filming began, in February 1968, executives from Warner Brothers began turning up in San Francisco, concerned about the money being spent as the budget rose from four to five million, which wasn't a huge amount of money, and still a million or two less than originally agreed. All this added to Steve's stress, which was finally released in a rush of adrenalin when it came to shooting the famous car chase. Steve was busting to get behind a wheel and drive at high speed.

'Steve wanted to do *all* the driving,' recalled Robert Vaughn, 'but the studio and the insurance people wouldn't let him do all the driving, so he did all the driving he was allowed to do and *some* of the driving he wasn't allowed to do.'

From the outset Steve had wanted a different kind of car chase. He said, 'I wanted it to be real. Usually they crank the film to make the cars look like they're going fast. I wanted real speed. Up to 120, 130 miles an hour.'

Because of his experience shooting *Robbery*, Peter Yates understood, saying, 'Back then the idea of a car chase was of tipping cars over, and how can you have a chase where everyone crashes the whole time? You don't get anywhere. But what I wanted, and Steve also, was to see the skill of the drivers. We both admired drivers.'

Steve told me he got the idea of how the scene should be shot from the chariot race in *Ben-Hur*. 'They had the cameras close up to those chariots, and they cut from one angle to another, which is what made it so exciting. I wanted to do the same, and Peter Yates had done that kind of thing in that British picture (*Robbery*) he made.'

McQueen's good friend, Bud Ekins, now working regularly in movies, usually with Steve, took on the more dangerous stunts. He doubled for McQueen in the hill-jumping scenes, which Steve had hoped to do himself. Neile, anxious for her husband's safety, begged Peter Yates to prevent Steve from doing those stunts, so Yates arranged for Steve to have a late wake-up call the morning they were shooting the most dangerous stunts. When McQueen arrived, he saw Ekins doing the hill jumps, and then ran to Ekins's car and asked, 'Where did you learn to drive like that?'

'I don't know, Steve,' replied Ekins.

'Bud's a genius on a motorcycle or in a car,' Steve told me. 'I told him, "You fucker, you're doing it to me again." He said,

A scene from the 1957 TV drama *The Defender* in which McQueen made his first impact on screen. To his right is a young William Shatner.

McQueen with his two leading ladies, Paula Prentiss (left) and Brigid Bazlen, on the set of *The Honeymoon Machine*; McQueen had a tempestuous affair with 16-year-old Brigid.

The next big break in McQueen's career was the starring role in the TV Western series *Wanted: Dead or Alive* in 1958.

McQueen and Frank Sinatra in a scene from *Never So Few* for MGM; the two became friends by throwing cherry bombs at their colleagues.

McQueen and Yul Brynner had a well-publicised feud when making *The Magnificent Seven* in 1960, but McQueen later thanked Brynner for the part he played in helping Steve find stardom.

Trying to find success in a 1962 British film, *The War Lover*, with co-stars Shirley Anne Field and Robert Wagner.

McQueen dirt-biking, a favourite pastime.

McQueen with his mentor John Sturges while making *The Great Escape*; looks like McQueen is proving to be quite a headache for Sturges yet again.

Steve and wife Neile at the premiere of *The Great Escape*.

McQueen and two of his lifelong friends, James Garner and James Coburn at the premiere of *The Great Escape*.

In between scenes of *The Sand Pebbles*, Steve preferred his motorbike to a rickshaw.

Proving tough with adversaries as well as tough at poker, McQueen was *The Cincinnati Kid* in 1965.

On the set of *Nevada Smith*, Steve with leading lady Suzanne Pleshette; she was his surrogate 'baby sister' whom he always looked out for.

At the premiere of *The Sand Pebbles*, from left, director Robert Wise, his wife Patricia, Neile, and Steve who looks uncomfortable being on show at a Hollywood event.

McQueen filming *Le Mans* in 1970; it was his dream project which became a nightmare that drove him over the edge.

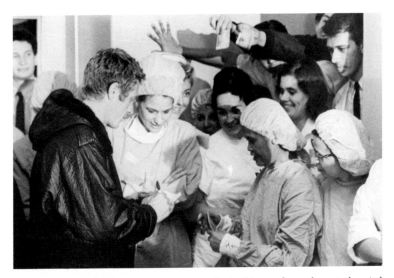

A very rare event – McQueen signing autographs, in this case for workers at a hospital where scenes for *Bullitt* were filmed.

McQueen found favour with the critics playing the middle-aged rodeo star *Junior Bonner* in 1972, but the picture didn't find an audience.

In between scenes of *Love with the Proper Stranger*, co-stars Natalie Wood and Steve McQueen were mutually attracted but remained just good friends; they later had a brief affair when Steve's first marriage ended.

In search of a hit, McQueen had his biggest success since *Bullitt* in the violent and action-packed *The Getaway* in 1972, with Ali MacGraw as his partner in crime; she became the second Mrs Steve McQueen.

Steve and director Sam Peckinpah, the man he had tried to turn to in his time of crisis in 1970, two years later finding friendship while making *The Getaway*.

McQueen, Ali MacGraw and director Sam Peckinpah between scenes of *The Getaway*. Ironically, Peckinpah united Steve and Ali, but would later separate them by casting Ali in *Convoy* against McQueen's wishes.

Behind bars, knowing how it felt, always trying to escape, Steve McQueen understood something of real-life convict Henri Charriere whom he portrayed in *Papillon* in 1973.

Never a conventional Hollywood star, McQueen put on pounds, grew a beard and his hair long, looking ever more out of place in black tie and dinner suit beside glamorous wife Ali MacGraw at a Hollywood event in 1977.

Shaving off the beard for his penultimate film *Tom Horn* in 1979, the excesses of life etched deep into McQueen's face were revealed, as well as the disease waiting to take his life at fifty, the age he always believed he would die at.

"Doing what?" I said, "After you did the jump in *The Great Escape* I had to explain on television that I didn't do it, and now I'm gonna have to do it all over again.'"

But Steve did get to do some of the dangerous driving. There's a scene where Bud Ekins comes off a motorbike as Bullitt's car is coming straight at him. Steve actually drove the car, aiming right for Ekins, and then swerved around him. It was the kind of stunt only experienced stunt drivers usually do. But, as Yates said, 'Steve was an experienced stunt driver.'

Yates also recalled, 'I was shooting close-ups of Steve in the Mustang, and we were going up a hill at over a hundred miles an hour, and I tapped him on the shoulder and said, "We're out of film," and he said, "That's nothing. We're out of brakes." He started to swerve the car side to side and revved the engine to get the gears down, and he managed to get the car to stop.'

There is some disagreement over when the car chase was actually thought of, or even scripted. Peter Yates told me, 'The chase scene wasn't in the first draft of the script that I saw. It was the producer, Philip D'Antoni, who wanted the scene because he'd seen the one I did in *Robbery*, and I really didn't want to do another car chase.'

Robert Vaughn said, 'All it said in the script was "car case" and nothing more.'

Alan Trustman said he wrote the car chase in detail into the script once Steve McQueen had committed to it.

Steve told me, 'I wanted that scene from the get-go.'

Which just shows that no matter who tells what to whom, people always have different memories. (In my experience, actors always have their own versions of any given experience or event.)

Filming wrapped in May 1968, ending with a scene in which a car crashes into gas pumps, causing the whole gas station to blow up. It was done in one take, although the car overshot the gas pumps. Clever editing fixed that problem. Yates brought the film in on schedule and a million over budget (although apparently, so I'm told, Warner Brothers said the budget came in at $6 million, a claim Steve strongly denied).

Warner Brothers inexplicably thought they had a box-office

flop on their hands and were surprised when Radio City Music Hall in Los Angeles requested the film be premiered there. It was shown on 17 October 1968.

The critics loved it. 'A terrific movie,' wrote Renata Adler in the *New York Times*. 'Just right for Steve McQueen – fast, well-acted, written the way people talk.'

The term 'cool' became a much used description for McQueen. 'McQueen joins the ranks of top movie detectives. His portrayal is cool, calm, casual, and convincing,' wrote Ann Guarino in the *New York Daily News*. The *New York Post*'s Archer Winsten wrote, 'McQueen keeps his cool as only he can, now that Bogart's long gone. The best, most exciting car chase the movies have ever put on film.'

Tom Milne of the *Observer* in London thought it 'a curiously exhilarating mixture of reality and fantasy, so actual that at times one could almost swear that the fictional adventures must have been shot with concealed cameras'.

Bullitt was an instant smash hit, grossing $18 million in America and another $35 million worldwide. It was quickly re-released on a double bill with *Bonnie and Clyde* and gave the film's gross an extra boost, coming in at around £80 million in its first year.

Steve McQueen was now the biggest star in the world. From there, it was going to be hard to know where to go. He hoped that *Day of the Champion* would top even *Bullitt*.

CHAPTER 13

—

Kung Fu, Drugs and Murder

Solar Productions sought a new partner after its deal with Warner Brothers was changed and, in April 1969, they signed a deal with Cinema Center Films, the newly formed movie arm of CBS, which invested $20 million into Solar.

Steve's only professional concern now was what to follow *Bullitt* with, while *Day of the Champion* was still being prepared by John Sturges. He liked William Faulkner's Pulitzer Prize-winning book *The Reivers*, about a road trip taken by four very different people in the early 1900s: a man with the outlook of a child, a Negro, an 11-year-old boy and a prostitute. He decided to film it, and hired husband-and-wife team Irving and Harriet Ravetch to write the screenplay.

Steve went into the project with a certain amount of trepidation because he knew it would be unlike any of the recent hit films which had established him as an action star. He told Robert Relyea, 'After *The Reivers*, I'll probably never be hired again.'

Mark Rydell, who knew Steve and Neile in the early days in New York, was assigned to direct. Rydell had been well known as an actor in an American soap, *As the World Turns*, for six years, and when the company arrived in Carrollton, Mississippi, to begin filming, women mobbed Rydell, not McQueen. That hurt Steve's ego and after that he and Rydell didn't get on.

Rydell was in for a rough time because McQueen was his boss, and Steve made sure Rydell knew exactly what he wanted from the script and on film, challenging many of Rydell's decisions. Things came to a head during a scene in which Steve and co-star Rupert Cross had to push a 1905 Winton Flyer through mud. The conditions were so difficult that the actors kept slipping and the car was impossible to shift.

Steve yelled Rydell's name and the director, convinced he was about to be fired, went over to face the music. Steve told him, 'There's only room for one boss on this picture,' to which Rydell replied, 'Yeah, and that's me.'

Steve paused, nodded, and backed off, but then tried to get Rydell fired by going to Bill Paley, the head of CBS films. When Paley saw the dailies, he told McQueen, 'Rydell's the director so shut up and get back to the set.'

Steve seemed to be on a quest to flex his muscles as head of Solar, so he turned on the director of photography, Richard Moore, and fired him. Moore went to Paley, who overturned McQueen's decision.

Something was eating at Steve, and it was more than just rivalry with Rydell or dissatisfaction with the cinematographer. Part of it was to do with drugs. He was smoking too much dope, and taking cocaine. He was extremely anxious much of the time. He told me that was because he had become so successful, and that Cinema Center was investing a great deal of money – not so much into his company but in *him* – that he was 'scared as hell with so much expected of me'.

I think it's likely that the drugs played a large part in Steve's paranoia. Jim Coburn agreed. 'You get to using any narcotic too much and it gets to you. I'm pretty damn sure that's what happened to Steve.'

A stabilising factor came into his life at that time. Bruce Lee, the yet to be proclaimed king of kung fu, was training a number of Hollywood stars, including James Coburn. McQueen began training with him too. 'Bruce Lee tried to teach Steve a mental and spiritual discipline which would have got him off drugs as well as teach him the martial arts,' said Coburn. 'So Steve had

Bruce with him on location when he was down in Mississippi and then at the studio.' The studio was actually the Disney Ranch, where much of *The Reivers* was shot. 'I know that Bruce worked Steve hard every day because that's the way he works,' said Coburn.

Steve told me about Bruce Lee before I'd ever heard of him. Lee hadn't yet become a star in Hong Kong-made kung fu pictures and the American-made *Enter the Dragon*. 'I like guys who are the best at what they do, and Bruce Lee was the best at what he did,' Steve told me. 'He kind of liked what I had . . . which was stardom. He told me he's going to be a bigger star than me. I hope he's wrong.' By 1973, Lee was a bigger star than McQueen, and just about everyone else, becoming a star/director like Clint Eastwood. But his stardom was short-lived. He died of a brain haemorrhage that year.

James Coburn told me, 'Steve and Bruce had enormous respect for each other but they were also very competitive with each other. Bruce wanted stardom and Steve wanted to be able to put a man down with one blow. They were two enormous egos that wanted what the other had.'

Even though Bruce Lee was trying to instil discipline into him, Steve couldn't help but use drugs to get him through the day and night.

While filming continued at the Disney Ranch, McQueen's name came up again on an FBI file. It was pretty innocuous and was about someone trying to contact Steve about a hunting trip to Canada. The FBI concluded that McQueen was fully occupied making *The Reivers* and had no plans to go to Canada.

Either the FBI had precious little else to concern itself with or they were keeping a close eye on Steve's activities for reasons best known to themselves.

Because of the huge success of *Bullitt*, Steve was voted, along with Joanne Woodward, 'Star of the Year' in November 1969 by the National Association of Theater Owners, which meant that he and Joanne Woodward brought more people into cinemas that year than anybody else.

Steve was concerned that *The Reivers*, his first 'family film', would get the wrong kind of marketing. He insisted that Cinema Center didn't push the movie as a 'Steve McQueen action film', and he promised to accommodate them any way he could to get the marketing right. He agreed to be photographed for the poster, wearing overalls and chewing on a straw. The final choice of photo had him with one eye closed. The tag on the poster read, 'You'll LOVE him as Boon!'

It wasn't inspired marketing, and Steve hated the photo, saying it made him look like 'a village idiot', but the film opened on Christmas Day 1969 and did well, earning $20 million domestically, a very respectable amount. The only problem was, it did virtually no business outside of America, where usually the box-office would double the domestic gross. Nevertheless, $20 million was a good return.

It's a rarely seen film, but one worth watching. It has its heart in the right place, and Steve gives one of his best non-action performances. Most of the critics liked his work in it, and found the film passable. 'It's fortunate McQueen is one of those rare modern actors whose presence carries the right kind of familiarity,' wrote Kathleen Carroll in the *New York Daily News*. 'He's ingratiating, and that's enough.'

Variety noted, 'McQueen gives a lively, ribald characterisation that suggests he will have a long career as a character actor after his sexy allure thins.'

Straight after filming, Steve spent time at his Palm Springs home to relax and consider what his next picture might be. He was determined it would be *Day of the Champion*. He also considered his whole future. He figured his marriage to Neile would survive, despite his philandering ways, and he saw no reason to give up using drugs.

He told me, in 1980, 'I wasted a lot of my life on dope and women.'

He liked to be alone when he could be, and often wandered into the Palm Springs desert by himself. He told me how one night he came across two young women by a camp fire. They were chanting and had strange objects about them which Steve said seemed 'somehow satanic'. He said that after that night, he suffered terrible migraines which would conjure up an image of the Devil in his mind.

Steve was so scared that he went to see a psychic in Los Angeles, who told him that the witches of England were gathering on Friday nights praying for him to die. They were trying to get him deeper into drugs and were cursing him to die in a racing car. The psychic told him not to get into a red and black car, and to pray to God for strength.

McQueen confided this to his friend Jay Sebring, who was into satanism, hosting satanic parties which were basically an excuse for sex, drugs and rock 'n' roll. Steve insisted that he never went to these parties. However, Sebring did provide Steve with hard drugs and plenty of women.

By this time, their one-time sex partner, Sharon Tate, was married to director Roman Polanski, and was carrying his child. Tate and Polanski lived in a house that had previously been owned by Doris Day's son, Terry Melcher, a music producer. He had met with a would-be-music star, Charles Manson, who had dreams of being famous. But Melcher wasn't impressed with Manson's music.

Manson also thought he could be a screenwriter, and had sent a script to Solar Productions which was rejected.

On 8 August 1969, Jay Sebring came to the Castle to cut Steve's hair. They agreed to go over to see Sharon Tate the next evening to keep her company while Roman Polanski was out of the country.

By a sheer stroke of luck, Steve didn't get to the Polanski house, but four of Charles Manson's 'disciples' did, and butchered her, Jay Sebring and two friends, Abigail Folger and Voytek Frykowski. There would have been another if Steve had arrived. Steve told me, 'I would have been there the night they were all killed but I ran into someone who kind of . . . was more . . . I liked her.'

Whoever she was, and Steve probably never remembered her name, that encounter, which was just a one-night stand, saved Steve McQueen's life. But, though he didn't know it then, he was still a target of Manson.

When the news broke of the massacre, much of Hollywood

went into lockdown. Stars who previously didn't have electric gates had them hastily installed. Guard dogs were bought. So were guns. Steve, who kept a gun by his bed at all times, took to carrying a loaded handgun about. He also installed a camera on the gate so he could watch for intruders on a monitor.

The first theory about the killings was that it was a drug deal that went wrong and resulted in a bloodbath. That scared Steve even more, because he thought there might be evidence in the house that could be linked to him, so he asked some 'special friends' to get into the house and find anything that could lead back to him. 'Sebring got me a lot of shit,' he told me, meaning drugs. 'I didn't want to be a suspect, so I had to do something.'

If what Steve said was true, then his friends had to be in the police force, because they were the only ones who had access to the crime scene. Somehow, his friends managed to clear the house of drugs, but not from Jay Sebring's car, which is where investigators discovered narcotics including hashish, marijuana and cocaine in the glove compartment. None of it led to Steve though. His friends had done a good job.

It took two months and further murders for the police to round up the Charles Manson Family, a commune of hippies who were high on drugs and willing to do anything their new Messiah, Charles Manson, told them to, including brutally murdering people.

Manson wasn't set upon a random murder spree. The police found he had a list of people whom he was going to have killed. Top of the list were Frank Sinatra, Richard Burton, Elizabeth Taylor and Steve McQueen. Sinatra was to be castrated while having sex with one of Manson's teenage disciples. The Burtons were to be boiled alive. Steve was to die 'at his own hand'.

Steve was in a cold sweat when he told me about all this, and I felt rather alarmed as well. 'Those two girls in the desert,' he said, 'they were Manson's girls. I was warned by this psychic. I'd die in a car while racing. I understood it all.'

Until then Steve had rather liked the whole hippie idealism of free love and peace, drugs and sex. 'They only ever seemed to be happy people,' he said. 'They didn't bother me. I think I could have been a hippie in another life. They gave good vibes. I would talk to some. Smoke a little weed with them. I thought they might be the great hope for us all. End violence and the war. But that Manson Family turned it all around for me.'

By 1970, he looked upon hippies as a generation who, as he put it, 'blew the chance to change the world. They were just tripping out and didn't care about anyone or anything. It was just hip to say they did.'

The 1960s had come to an end in the most shocking way, and so did Steve's perception of the peace and love movement which he thought might improve all mankind. Disillusioned, he lost himself in a world of drugs and sex.

James Coburn tried to help him. 'He was going to self-destruct,' he told me. 'I tried to help him but he wouldn't be helped. He said, "I got to do it all now, man, before it's too late." He seemed to think he was going to die.'

And that's what he did think. He told me three or four times, over those four days in 1970, and later in 1977, that he would die when he was 50. 'I have to live my life the way I want it,' he said in 1970. 'I got another 10 years.'

He was on the edge, about to tip over into the abyss.

CHAPTER 14

—

Over the Edge

In 1969 Steve made a cameo appearance in a documentary about motorcycle racing called *On Any Sunday*. It wasn't a cameo appearance in the conventional sense, because it wasn't an acting part. He just happened to be one of the racers. Solar invested $300,000 in the project. It was directed, written and produced by Bruce Brown, who had made a documentary about surfing, *Endless Summer*, which had proved so successful that it made Brown a millionaire.

McQueen had just one line in the picture: 'Every time I start thinking of the world as all bad, then I start seeing some people out here having a good time on motorcycles – it makes me take another look.' It wasn't scripted; that was McQueen talking from the heart.

Curiously, although everyone knew it was Steve McQueen, he raced under the pseudonym 'Harvey Mushman'.

His part in the documentary over with, he and Sturges felt ready to go with *Day of the Champion*. Cinema Center was happy to back McQueen's long-held dream to make what he considered would be the ultimate movie about motorcar racing. Somewhere along the way, Edward Anhalt's screenplay had been dumped, probably by McQueen, who really wanted to make a film that had no story and was just about racing. So now there was no script, just Steve McQueen, director John Sturges, a $6 million budget and a lot of racing cars.

Sturges recalled, 'We were going to develop the script, which isn't unusual. We barely had a screenplay to begin *The Great Escape*. It's how it works sometimes in movies, but it's not ideal.'

The title of the picture had changed to *Le Mans* because Steve felt that Le Mans was the *only* race to make a movie about. Said Sturges, 'It had to about Le Mans because John Frankenheimer had already made *Grand Prix*.'

Steve insisted, 'It was always going to be about Le Mans.'

John Sturges now had misgivings. 'McQueen ran Solar, and Solar was paying my salary, and that meant McQueen was going to tell me what to do.' He knew it didn't bode well.

Steve hadn't finished *Le Mans* when I ran into him in 1970. He was despondent over just about everything in his life, including the movie. He told me, 'I went into it feeling like I was like a real filmmaker. I didn't want to compromise any of what I'd been thinking about all those years. When we started it, I didn't have any studio fucking my head. And I had a director I trusted.'

John Sturges felt that he should have worked on a screenplay, but his time was taken up with a once-only chance to film the actual 1969 Le Mans race, so he had to leave McQueen to work on the script with whatever writers he came up with.

'I'd made my feelings clear that *Le Mans* had to have a good story with the race as the background,' said Sturges. 'Steve and I agreed that the picture had to be about what makes drivers tick. They are like Edmund Hillary. They have to climb mountains. Those guys drove at their absolute limit. They talked about ten-tenths driving. Noting less.' But there was one aspect he and Steve disagreed on. 'I'm old-fashioned, but a love story would be good,' said Sturges. 'Every man falls in love. Even those drivers. And a picture has to have appeal to women.'

Steve said to me, 'They did all that shit on *Grand Prix* and it was dullsville. The picture had to be *the race*.' (I don't believe I'd ever heard anyone say 'dullsville' before, or since.)

The story they did have was about a Porsche driver, played by Steve. He had survived a serious crash in the race a year before but his nemesis had been killed. A year on and he meets up with the dead driver's widow, then crashes again, then returns to the race and develops a rivalry with another driver. Sturges was adamant that Steve and the widow should fall in love. McQueen was adamant he shouldn't.

When Sturges completed his filming of the actual race, he returned to find that the story still had 'no backbone', as he put it. 'It was just the race and a few minor characters with little to do.'

McQueen continued to insist, 'That's all we need.'

Feeling he could still manage to get a decent script to pull the structure of the plot, such as it was, together, John Sturges began principal photography in June 1970 in France. Fifty-two world class drivers were employed to race the cars, and because they were filming in France, Solar had to hire a French crew to work with the American crew.

'We got thousands of props and all the equipment, and the crews, and Steve turns up with his leg in a cast,' recalled Sturges. Steve had broken his foot in a motorcycle race near San Diego. 'He said to me, "Don't worry, John, nobody'll know about it when I'm in the car." I said, "But what about when you're *not* in the car." He said, "That's not gonna happen much." I *knew* we were in trouble.'

Porsche mechanic Haig Alltounian was personally hired by Steve to maintain the Porsche 917 Steve would be driving as well as to act as his technical adviser. After a number of tests involving other drivers, Steve suggested they actually race at Sebring, which is a 12-hour race that uses the same cars as Le Mans. 'I thought it was a lousy idea,' said John Sturges. 'We didn't need Steve getting injured or even killed. But it was clear he was going to have as much fun as he could.'

Steve personally asked Formula One driver Peter Revson to team with him in a three-litre engine car. Steve drove with his broken foot in the cast. Towards the end of the race, Mario Andretti, in a five-litre engine car, was leading. His car broke down, putting Revson in the lead, but then Andretti caught up on the last lap and just beat Revson. Steve was still over the moon, because he and Revson won in their three-litre class, as well as coming second in the race.

'It was bad enough Steve racing,' said Sturges, 'but then the crowd went crazy and mobbed him and the car. There were tens of thousands trying to touch him. They almost tore the car to pieces and we all thought he was going to get killed by the goddamn fans, but then Steve climbed onto the car and shouted, "Stop!" And Jesus Christ, everyone did. There was silence. He was up there, in control, and they loved him and just calmed down. I'd never seen him so happy.'

Halfway through the race Steve's cast had literally fallen apart, and he was in terrible pain, but that didn't stop him finishing the race or getting up on the car to command his audience and take a bow.

'What I did admire about Steve was the way he prepared *everything*,' said Sturges. 'He always practised every bit of movement so it would look natural. He spent one whole evening just getting in and out of the Porsche so it looked like he did it all the time.'

Steve told me, 'I couldn't have the audience thinking I looked like an amateur.'

I said, 'How would anyone know?'

He replied, 'The drivers would know. The racing fans. I couldn't have them say, "He's a fake."'

To Steve it was a matter of being totally professional as an actor, but also a matter of not being thought of as just an actor pretending to be a racer.

According to Sturges, they were well into filming – most of it the race – but they still hadn't cast the leading lady. And they still didn't have a solid script. Three different screenplays had been written. 'I never got to work with them,' complained Sturges. 'I *always* work with my writers, but Steve had three writers working separately in different trailers. I said, "Steve, this isn't the way to get a script together." He got mad and told me to direct the movie and not interfere. I said, "You don't know how to put a movie together." But you couldn't tell him.'

Steve was stubborn, ignoring all the advice given by his mentor.

'I wanted to be an artist,' Steve told me. 'I didn't want to have to work by rules. I wanted to *break* the rules. I thought I could do it.'

On the set, with camera ready to roll on any given scene, Steve would almost throw the script, such as it was, away. Sturges said:

I'd tell him, 'Read the line, please, Steve,' and he'd say, 'We don't need the line.' I said, 'If you don't say just that one line the audience aren't going to have a clue what's going on.' He said, 'You have to show it. You're the director.' But I didn't feel like I was directing. I was just saying 'Action!' and 'Cut!' Steve was calling the shots. And I decided I'd have to have it out with him, and if things didn't change, I was going to quit.

Even [Robert] Relyea was having enough. He'd been my assistant director and was now working with McQueen at Solar and was executive producer of all Solar's films, and he was damn good at his job. But he said, 'Nobody's in charge. No one's in control,' and what he said got back to Cinema Center, and they got nervous and sent an important executive over. I thought Steve would throw him off the set, and that would be the end of our picture, but he greeted him warmly and then treated him to a ride through the countryside at over a hundred miles an hour in his Porsche. That guy was so scared, and that was what was so engaging about Steve.

Engaging or not, that executive closed down production for two weeks. Finally they told Solar that for the film to continue McQueen had to forgo his salary of $750,000 as well as any points he would have earned from the gross, and that Cinema Center would have complete creative control. Either that, or they'd shut down the unfinished film and cut their losses. Steve didn't want to lose his dream project and agreed to all the conditions.

Said Sturges:

Cinema Center told Steve to get the movie made and finished. I was relieved, and so was everyone else I think. But then Steve said that he was going to take a holiday with Neile to Monaco while I worked on the script. I knew that was a mistake because you can't work on a Steve McQueen script without Steve McQueen, but what really got my goat was there he was, taking a holiday, while the rest of us had to clean up the mess *he'd* made.

I got steaming mad and did what I hardly ever do. I lost my temper, and Steve squared up to me. I knew he could do karate or whatever the hell it was and could probably deck me, but I said to him, 'Lay a hand or a foot on me and, so help me God, I'll flatten you.' He started kicking wildly, out of control, knocking over the chair and a waste-paper basket, and he missed me every time. I said, 'Look at yourself, Steve. You've lost control of yourself.'

His foot was still in a bad way, which is why he probably couldn't kick me, but he landed a punch. I picked up a chair and threw it at him, and he punched it away. I suddenly felt very sad that it had come to this. I'd never seen Steve with a temper like that. I had never seen him violent. I told him, 'I'm done here.' And I walked away.

That was it for me. I went straight to Robert Relyea and told him I was going home. He just said, 'Oh, okay. Well, good night.' I said, 'I mean, I'm going *home*.' I had a car drive me to Paris and got the first flight back to the States.

Steve told me that he was devastated to lose his good friend and mentor. 'I screwed that up. That's what I'm good at right now. Screwing up.'

He was also screwing up his marriage, but he felt that saving his marriage was more important than the movie – to some extent, anyway. 'I need to get away with Neile to save my marriage. It's in deep shit. I thought I could count on Sturges to save the movie while I saved my marriage.'

The state of his marriage was almost a kind of limbo. Before he set off for France, with Neile to follow shortly after, he suddenly announced to her, 'Half my life is over and I wanna fly! I wanna go!'

Neile asked him if he meant he wanted a divorce, to which he replied emphatically, 'No!' But as much as she tried, she couldn't get him to explain what he did mean.

She did him one more favour while there was the merest spark of life in their marriage; she gave him a copy of a book called *Papillon*, the true story of Henri Charrière, who was incarcerated on Devil's Island, from where he made several escape attempts. The story appealed to McQueen, who was forever trying to escape his own past.

In France, before Neile arrived, Steve carried on an affair with an actress. One night, high on dope, Steve drove his girlfriend, a young man called Mario Iscovich who worked for Solar, and a member of the *La Mans* film crew, and crashed the car. The actress was knocked unconscious and Steve feared she was dead. Mario Iscovich broke his arm, and the crew member was seriously injured. Steve stole a farmer's car to drive them all to Loué, by which time the girl was conscious, so they left Iscovich and the crew member to find their own way to a hospital.

Steve's womanising didn't just stop with his affair with the actress. He picked any girl who was interested, and there was no shortage of them. Some days after Neile and the children arrived at the Château Lornay, a huge place built like a castle near the vineyards of Vire-en-Champagne, Steve told her that there would be women coming to visit him.

She demanded to know what women he was talking about. All he could tell her was, 'They're friends of mine.' Then he said, 'We are kind of separated, right?'

That evening he tried to persuade her to try some dope and even coke. She had never taken drugs and refused. He kept pressing her to admit that she had had an affair. Finally, she did.

'I went crazy,' said Steve. 'The thought of her with another man! I had a gun. I'd got it over [to France] with the props. I got the gun and was crazy. I pointed it at her and asked who the motherfucker was. Turned out she'd met him on a plane from New York to Los Angeles. I felt I coulda pulled the trigger. I slapped her instead. Again and again.'

Neile's fling had been with Viennese actor Maxmilian Schell, and was something she did out of revenge for all of Steve's womanising.

Steve really was crazy. He had lost all control of himself, and even Mario Iscovich, all of 19 years old, came in for rough treatment when he gave one of Steve's girlfriends a T-shirt worn by all the crew to promote *Le Mans* while it was in production. Steve grabbed him, accused him of playing up to the girl, and complained about the T-shirt he had given her, which Steve claimed he had paid for with his own hard-earned money.

Mario, 19, overweight, his arm broken, an employee of Solar and someone who had kept Steve's secret about the night he crashed, was thrown against the wall. The terrified teenager announced he was quitting. Steve seemed unable to understand why and asked, 'What did I ever do to you?'

John Sturges didn't witness any of this but he knew that Steve had become extremely unstable. 'I heard he was screwing other women and didn't seem to care if Neile knew. I told him he was ruining a perfectly good marriage, but he didn't seem to realise it. I wouldn't say he didn't care – he just didn't seem to know it. Then he started turning on people whom he looked on as friends and confidants. He just pushed everyone away. It wasn't the same guy I'd known. It's like he was just out of his mind. I think he was doped up so much – just drugged out of his mind. He was a runaway train. You knew it wasn't going to end well.'

In this drugged-out-of-his-mind state, Steve took off with Neile to Monaco to salvage an unsalvageable marriage, while Relyea and Solar's production manager, Jack Reddish, sought another director. Cinema Center picked one for them. Lee Katzin had directed a lot of shows for CBS, which ran Cinema Center, such as *Mission: Impossible* and *The Rat Patrol*, and had directed a few movies but without distinction. He was assigned the unenviable task of directing *Le Mans*.

Ironically, Neile passed on another book to Steve. It had come from Steve's publicist, David Foster, who thought Steve might like it as a future film project. It was called *The Getaway*, a thrilling heist story which Steve loved. He encouraged Foster not only to try and secure the film rights but also to become a film producer in the process. But Neile had failed to make her own getaway, and Steve continued to confront her about her brief fling, even though he was involved with at least one actress and God knows how many other women.

They returned to France from Monaco, and Steve got back to work under the direction of Lee Katzin, who insisted that the film should have a proper storyline, which Steve was still against. For the next six weeks there were arguments between director and star, and often Steve would storm off the set.

A leading actress still hadn't been found. Steve wanted Diana Rigg but she was unavailable. Statuesque Maud Adams arrived, but when Steve saw that she was taller than he was she was rejected. German-born Elga Andersen was chosen.

Two weeks after returning from Monaco, Neile discovered she was pregnant. She was so fearful of how Steve would react, along with the continual mental and physical abuse she was suffering from him, that she tried in secret to find out if she could have an abortion in France. The French doctor she saw said it was illegal in France, but not in England.

It was three more weeks before Neile found the courage to tell Steve. His only thought was that it couldn't be his. She was adamant it *was* his. She suggested an abortion.

Steve wasn't convinced. He told me, 'She screws some other guy, gets pregnant and wants an abortion. What am I gonna do – say, sure, yeah, that's all okay?'

But I got the impression that he did believe her, and that he felt intense guilt about the abortion, which she had in London. He wasn't able to go with her to London because of the movie – or he simply didn't want to be around while she was having their baby aborted.

In September, Neile returned to California with Chad and Terry. Filming in France continued uneasily, with accidents occurring, largely because of the hurry Katzin was in to finish the picture. During a rehearsal, driver Derek Bell's Porsche caught fire and his face and hands were treated for minor burns. During a race shot by the second unit, driver David Piper hit a guard rail at 200 miles an hour in his Porsche, which virtually disintegrated.

Piper suffered a triple compound fracture and his right leg had to be amputated from the knee down.

Haig Alltounian, the technical adviser McQueen had hired, insisted that the racing cars and their tyres needed to be warmed up properly before racing but Katzin and his second unit were eager to get all the footage they needed before Cinema Center pulled the plug.

Steve did most of his own driving, of course, and managed to avoid a possibly fatal crash when a Solar Productions truck pulled out onto the track as he was passing a car at 200 miles an hour. He managed to keep control, missing the other car and the truck. But he was convinced if he hadn't, he would have been killed for sure.

During one of his spats with Katzin, and with Neile in California, Steve decided to escape the nightmare that had begun as his dream project. For reasons best known to himself – probably because it was across the Channel and not too far away from France – he went to London, where he heard that Sam Peckinpah was in Cornwall. He told me, 'I had to escape from that madness.'

Katzin concentrated on second-unit footage of the professional drivers, and I can't be sure that he even knew where Steve was.

I think the time I spent with Steve gave him a much-needed respite from his work, his life and his marriage. He had this 'juvenile delinquent' to take under his wing. I think the Steve McQueen I saw, away from Hollywood, away from the pressures of making a film he had lost all control over, and away from a marriage he knew he had wrecked and couldn't find a way to repair, was the more natural McQueen. In England, he was virtually unrecognisable, although you could tell that people were scratching their heads trying to place him.

A funny thing happened on the day before we returned to Penzance. As we were driving along, we passed a car that had broken down. The elderly driver was standing by the roadside, his wife sat inside. Steve turned the bike around and drove up to the man, asking, 'Can I help?'

'Only if you think you can fix it,' said the old man.

'I might be able to,' said Steve, getting off the bike and walking over to the car. 'Pop the hood,' he said to the driver.

The old man looked perplexed, so I said, 'Lift the bonnet.'

He released the catch inside the car so Steve could lift the bonnet and look under it. I wandered away with the driver who said, 'He's an American, isn't he?' I confirmed he was. 'He looks familiar.'

It wasn't long before Steve closed the bonnet and said, 'Try it.' The driver got in, turned on the ignition, and it started straight away. Steve gave an explanation as to what was wrong, which neither I nor the driver understood. The old man expressed his gratitude, and Steve smiled and walked back towards his motorbike. Then the driver suddenly snapped his fingers and said to me, 'I got it. He's one of those film stars, isn't he?'

I said, 'Yes.'

'That's it. Paul Newman!'

People often mixed up Paul Newman and Steve McQueen. Paul Newman was once asked to sign an autograph by someone who thought he was Steve McQueen, so Newman signed it, 'Fuck you, Steve McQueen.'

When I climbed on the back of the bike, Steve said, 'What did he say?'

'He said he thought he recognised you.'

'I hope he didn't. I don't want it getting in the news that I was even here.'

I thought that was odd, because for the past four days we had openly ridden all over this part of England. But maybe having some stubble – and just the fact that nobody expected to see Steve McQueen in England – was all the disguise he needed.

I said, 'He thought you were Paul Newman.'

He shook his head, then chuckled. 'For once I'm glad about that.'

When we got back to Peckinpah's house, Steve thanked me and I thanked him, and we talked of getting together again some time in the future, although that seemed unlikely to me. I don't think he ever knew how scared I had been when we set off four days earlier, riding on the back of that bike at high speed. But I stood high in his estimation, probably because I didn't fall off the bike.

He obviously didn't believe in long goodbyes. He said, 'I'm glad you were able to open up to me. I hope I helped.' That was odd, because I hadn't opened up much about anything – not that there was much to open up about. He had done most of the talking; I did most of the listening.

I told James Coburn what had happened, and he said, 'He didn't want you thinking he needed someone to talk to, but you must have been the right man at the right time. He wouldn't let you know that though.'

I can't claim that our road trip was a life-changing experience for Steve McQueen, but I think it changed some of his perspective. He returned to the Le Mans location, where, apparently, he went to Lee Katzin and said, 'I'm going to work with you and not against you,' and there was no further trouble.

Nobody had any explanation for Steve's turnaround.

But there were still others Steve was gunning for. His good friend and associate Robert Relyea came in for a rough time for what Steve considered a betrayal; Relyea had said that nobody was in charge, which got back to Cinema Center, which was why they took over the production. Relyea tried talking it through with him, but Steve remained hostile and they rarely spoke after that.

Filming should have been completed in September, but it spilled over into November 1970, and went $1.5 million over budget. As far as Steve was concerned, all he wanted to achieve was gaining the respect of professional racing drivers, and he did that. But he had little respect from anyone else. He wanted to be involved in post-production, but he was banned by Cinema Center, who hoped they could find a story in the 450,000 feet of film, most of which showed little but cars racing. John Sturges later learned that all his footage was left on the cutting-room floor. He said to me, 'It didn't make any difference. It was just film of racing cars. They had more than they needed of that. There wasn't a story. Nobody can say what the picture is about. It was just Steve McQueen wanting to be a racing driver.'

I think Steve actually wanted the film to be more than just that. He wanted it to be a new kind of motion picture that broke the rules of story-telling on screen. 'I liked what they did with *Easy Rider*,' he told me. 'It didn't have structure. It was loose. They made it real. I wanted to do that.' I think Steve might have achieved that more easily making a smaller film and not an epic, which *Le Mans* was. *Easy Rider* was about people who just happened to ride bikes. It was the journey they took that was important. Motorbikes weren't their obsession.

There's no doubt that McQueen's intentions were noble, but they were extremely flawed, and I think that's because he had reached a stage where he thought he was such a big star he could do anything. But his knowledge of the movie business was shaky. The people who pay for the film to be made will always end up with the movie they want, not what the star wants, or often what even the director wants. Cinema Center wanted a big movie with Steve McQueen as a racing driver. They obviously hoped for more than that, but although they did get Steve McQueen racing cars unfortunately, there was nothing else to it.

It took six months to complete post-production. When Steve saw it, he admitted that John Sturges had been right, according to Sturges. 'He [Steve] called me and said he'd been a jerk. He was right. We had been good friends for many years, but he thought he knew my job better than me, which he didn't.'

The breakdown between McQueen and Sturges was one of those macho things where two very masculine men found it hard just to set aside their differences, although for Sturges, it was a matter of bitter disappointment that the actor he had made into a star and had mentored had turned on him with violence.

For Steve, it was a blow that probably caused him sadness for the rest of his life. At least he was the one who called Sturges and tried to make amends by admitting he had been wrong, but I gather Sturges didn't accept what was Steve's form of an apology. And as far as I know, they never spoke again. I do know that both men deeply regretted their falling out, but neither of them knew how to fix things, so they just didn't try.

Determined to get all they could in revenues, Cinema Center

hyped the film so much that it proved to be a disappointment. They should have just sold it as a semi-documentary with a lot of racing and Steve McQueen at the wheel. The film couldn't hope to live up to its hype when it opened in June 1971, and the critics savaged it.

'The picture is a bore,' wrote Howard Thompson in the *New York Times*. Kathleen Carroll of the *New York Daily News* thought the film 'appears to be an excuse for Steve McQueen to indulge his passion for auto racing. There is no attempt at characterisation. The dialogue is dreadful.'

Jay Cocks of *Time* noted, '[McQueen] only stands in front of the camera and allows himself to be photographed. Occasionally, his lips will twitch into that shy, strong, ironic half-smile he had made his trademark. In really grandiose scenes he may make a gesture. He might even wave. He has surrounded himself with the sort of second-rate production talent that offers no protest to his rampant self-indulgence.'

Apart from *Grand Prix*, which had already ready come and gone, there was another racing picture to compete with *Le Mans*. Paul Newman, also a fanatical racer, had made a racing picture for Warner Brothers – presumably after they pulled out of Steve's dream project – called *Winning*. It went too far in the other direction from *Le Mans* by not having enough action on the track.

Those who wanted little more than to see lots of cars racing were not disappointed by *Le Mans*. But there weren't enough of those to make the picture a winner, and it took just $19 million worldwide, a decidedly unimpressive amount for a picture of that size. Steve never made a penny from it, having given up his salary and any profits he would have earned. He could have used some money, because the IRS presented him with an order to pay $2 million back-tax. He was declared bankrupt. Steve had frittered away much of his fortune buying as many motorcycles as he could find room for, very expensive fast cars and antiques that ranged from toys to 1950s jukeboxes. He rarely spent money on other people, but he loved to spend it on anything he could play with.

Robert Relyea and Jack Reddish left Solar Productions shortly after the film wrapped. The company returned to what it was originally intended to be – just a tax shelter – and all its staff were laid off. Profits that Solar earned from previous films went straight to the government to pay Steve's tax bill. And his marriage was now a sham neither Neile nor Steve seemed to be able to find the motivation to call it a day, officially, even though it was well and truly over.

One of the biggest stars in Hollywood of the 1960s had lost everything he had ever wanted. Now that he was powerless and broke, so-called friends abandoned him, driving him ever deeper into a state of paranoia. He had, finally, gone over the edge.

CHAPTER 15

—

Friendly Divorce

Having gone over the edge, Steve had only two choices – stay down and out, or climb back up. He did the latter. And he knew it wouldn't be easy. He knew there had to be changes, and only he could make them.

Suzanne Pleshette told me, 'He just adjusted after the failure of *Le Mans*, and of his marriage and his company. He said, "Suzy, it all got too big, too complicated. That's not me. I'm a simple country boy. I got to make it all simple again." He was determined to start again and this time do it right.

'But I don't think he really had the drive any more. He kept saying, "Suzy, I'm going to settle in Australia and run a farm. I just want a quiet life, with a wife and kids, and animals. Drive my cars. Fly a plane if I can. That's what I'm going to look for. I just want peace."

'And that's what he spent the rest of his life looking for. That's all that mattered to him.'

The motorcycle-racing documentary *On Any Sunday* hit the screen in 1971, and was no doubt helped by the fact that Steve McQueen was in it. As Gary Arnold of the *Washington Post* noted, 'The last time an actor's athletic feat thrilled audiences for a sustained length of time was probably McQueen's motorcycle ride in *The Great Escape*.'

Variety thought it 'an exciting documentary of one of the most dangerous of all sports. McQueen's prowess as a racer is demonstrated time and again and his name should spark interest in a film that alone stands as a spectacular piece of filmmaking.'

Not every critic was as enthralled. Jay Cocks of *Time*, for example, called it 'a distinctly unconvincing celebration of motorcycle racing'.

Nevertheless, the picture was an outstanding success for a documentary and raked in a staggering $24 million worldwide. All of the money that should have gone to Solar went, instead, to the taxman.

In need of money, Steve agreed to star in a Honda commercial for a fee of $1 million, but only for Japanese television. It was never to be shown anywhere else in the world.

Although he was still living with Neile and the children, Steve considered this arrangement to be one purely of mutual convenience, especially for his convenience. Curiously, he still expected Neile to sleep in his bed, yet he was seen publicly with a variety of women.

'I never understood Neile's compliance with his demands,' said James Coburn. 'Maybe she still wanted to keep the family together even though she and Steve were separated. And yet they weren't. They still lived in the same house. I think she's a remarkable woman to have put up with all that shit.'

There didn't seem to be an actual legal separation. It was more a case of Steve saying he wanted to be free, and her letting him have his freedom. But to all intents the marriage was over. 'I think she hoped they could survive,' said Coburn. 'But she must have known that there wasn't a chance.'

In many ways Steve was wiping the slate clean. Solar was an inactive force, and he didn't care, just so long as he could act. He no longer had partners, and he got rid of the lawyers and public relations people. He stopped wearing suits and went back into T-shirt and jeans. He was more the old Steve McQueen. As he told me in 1974, 'I had lost myself, and then I found myself again.'

What didn't change was his womanising and the drug taking.

And the paranoia. Steve made it policy never to do interviews or to sign autographs. When he told me that, I said, 'Steve, there are millions of fans out there who would give their eye teeth for an autograph.'

He replied, 'They need to get lives. I had to get one.'

I didn't agree, but his point almost seemed valid.

Steve had a new agent, Freddie Fields, who had formed a new production company, First Artists. He already had Paul Newman, Barbra Streisand and Sidney Poitier signed up, and would soon get Dustin Hoffman. Fields's idea was to guarantee those stars almost complete creative control provided they took no upfront salary, accepted 10 per cent of the gross, and the movie of their choice could be made for no more than $3 million. Steve signed up to make three pictures with them.

For the most part, it was to prove an exercise in illustrating that a star name did not guarantee box-office. Newman made a modern Western called *Pocket Money*, which nobody went to see. Streisand did her most obscure film, *Up the Sandbox*, which went unnoticed. Poitier did *A Warm December*, his most unmemorable picture. Meanwhile, Steve went to work for ABC pictures and Cinerama Releasing (the company I worked for) to star in *Junior Bonner*. He was to play an ageing rodeo champion who wants to win a contest in his hometown just one last time. It's also the story of a man who lives in the past and sees the modern world changing everything he knew.

The author of the screenplay, Jeb Rosebroo, thought Robert Redford would be ideal to play Bonner, but producer Joe Wizan wanted McQueen, so he sent the script to Steve, who liked it and signed to do it in April 1971. A month later Sam Peckinpah, to the amazement of just about everyone in the business, was signed to direct.

Peckinpah had made his name making graphically violent pictures, notably *The Wild Bunch* and *Straw Dogs*. But he had also proved himself to be an intelligent director with his first few movies, which included *The Deadly Companions* and more especially *Ride the High Country*, a 1962 Western which, he told me, 'was the picture which had a lot in common with *Junior*

Bonner'. Both films were about men of the past living in a changing world.

Peckinpah was a maverick who refused to be tied down by studio rules, but he was given a free hand to make *Junior Bonner*, a film without violence, although the scenes of cowboys riding on ferocious bulls had a sense of violence about them. 'I wanted to show that these beasts could kill anyone,' said Peckinpah. 'They were deadly weapons if you fell under their hooves.'

Peckinpah shot a scene in which an old house, where Junior Bonner had lived, is demolished by modern bulldozers in slow motion, a technique he usually saved for more violent blood-splattered moments. 'It was still violence,' he told me. 'Junior Bonner looks on as they murder his home by these huge vehicles, which were literally giant mechanical bulls. Violence comes in many forms.'

Filming began on 30 June 1971, in Prescott, Arizona, which held an annual rodeo in July. Peckinpah shot the film around the event, capturing the sounds and sights of the holiday atmosphere and the rodeo itself, complete with extras and parades that could otherwise have proved prohibitively expensive.

Ben Johnson, a great character actor in Westerns since the days of John Ford, was among a small but solid cast that included veterans Robert Preston and Ida Lupino, and newcomer Joe Don Baker. Johnson told me, 'I figured we were in for a rough time when we started, because McQueen and Peckinpah didn't get on.'

Peckinpah told me he didn't think there was any great problem between him and McQueen. 'I've known Steve for years. Things didn't work out on *The Cincinnati Kid*. But I knew Steve always kind of liked me. That's why he came to see me that time in Cornwall, but I'm no help to someone with demons because I got plenty of my own.

'So I figured [on *Junior Bonner*] Steve came with all his own demons, and we were like a couple of rattlesnakes, jumping and biting at each other. But behind all that was a lot of respect. I had it for him or I wouldn't have done the picture, and he had it for me because he kept calling me "Mr Peckinpah", until I finally said, "Shit, Steve, do you want me to call you Mr McQueen?

Then stop calling me Mr Peckinpah." He said, "I wondered when you were going to say that. I was getting sick of it." And then we got along okay. Not all the time. I don't work so good with someone who can't think. I want an actor who can think, and that's what I got with McQueen.'

It was a complicated relationship that I think neither Peckinpah nor McQueen ever really understood. Steve said to me, 'He's one of the best film-makers around. I knew I had to have my guard up or he could have walked over me, but he knew I wasn't going to do anything I thought was wrong for me, and between us we got it right. I think we really did. I think he got one of my best performances out of me. If I hadn't thought that, I'd never have made *The Getaway* with him.' *The Getaway* would be the film that Peckinpah directed and McQueen starred in following *Junior Bonner*.

Peckinpah helped Steve in a scene he had with Robert Preston playing his father. It was a reconciliation between father and son. It obviously struck a chord in Steve, who, having failed to find his own father and with highly mixed emotions about his dad, found it hard to express emotions for another man no matter who he was. 'McQueen just wasn't cutting it,' Peckinpah told me. 'I said, "Steve, this is your father, and you're playing it like he was the storekeeper." Steve took me aside and said, "I don't know if I can do this. I'm not used to this 'feelings' crap. And I can't find a way to play it because of my own dad."

'So I said, "Don't try to play for anything. Don't let your emotions through. I don't want to see them. If you can't do it, just say the damn lines and then move on." I don't know why I thought that would work in any way, but I hoped it would, and it did, because he realised he could express so much with hardly showing anything. The camera just captured it, and he gave more than he thought he could, probably to show me he could when I said he couldn't do it. And he had Robert Preston, a really good actor, and Steve and he played off one another. That's how acting works. Forget being the star. Just work with the other actor. I don't think I ever saw McQueen so sincere in any scene in any film as he was in that.'

When it came to money, Steve had always been tight, and things hadn't changed. Maybe at this time it was because he was having to crawl back from bankruptcy. But I think there was always something of the scam artist in him from his days as a juvenile delinquent, and he used that skill when filming the last scene of the film in which he needed real money to buy a ticket to Australia. He was handed several hundred dollars by the props man. After the scene, Steve handed back the money, and the props man realised it wasn't as much as he had given him. He decided it was best not to ask for the rest back.

Typically, Steve wanted to do as many of the stunts as he could. He wasn't a rodeo rider, and he could easily have been killed. 'I saw what mean motherfuckers those bulls were and decided I'd rather not try and show how brave I am,' he told me.

I always thought Steve craved danger, but in 1974 (after another hair-raising motorcycle ride which I'll get to later) he told me, 'I will do dangerous things that other people won't do. But I'm not courageous. I'm really a coward, so I am always trying to prove myself. Just happens that there are some things I take right to the limit.'

I asked him why he thought he was a coward.

'I just want to prove I'm better than I think I am,' he replied. 'I was always doing that when I was a kid. I had to be better than I thought I was. And I had to be better than everyone else. I wasn't brave, I was scared shitless. But I couldn't show it.'

But I was sure there was more to Steve's often reckless behaviour, such as driving cars at high speed on the way to *The Great Escape* set, than proving he wasn't a coward. He said, 'That's because I was always late.'

I pressed him further because, as far as I could tell, he definitely enjoyed the thrill of speed. 'Speed is something I don't equate with danger,' he said. 'Speed is when I relax. Racing is something different to just driving at speed. Racing is competing and showing you can be as good as the best.'

I think McQueen liked to flirt with danger for many reasons – to prove he wasn't a coward, to feel the thrill, to defy death, and maybe even to dare death.

The one time he didn't want to prove he was as good as the best was when it came to riding bulls in *Junior Bonner*. He told me he was happy to leave all that to the professionals. 'Cars and bikes can be dangerous if you don't show them respect, but they don't kick and bite like bulls,' he said.

For his close-ups in the rodeo scenes, Steve rode a mechanical bull, which he found embarrassing. 'I hated that. It made me look like I was just chicken shit.' His macho image was bruised, but it was the only sensible way to shoot those scenes.

He may have admitted to me he didn't want to ride the bulls, but that's not what he told Sam Peckinpah. 'McQueen said he wanted to do all his stunts,' said Peckinpah. 'I knew that he knew he couldn't do them, but he said he wanted to do them anyway. It was all bravado.'

Ben Johnson recalled, 'McQueen was arguing with Peckinpah about riding those goddamn bulls. I knew Sam wouldn't let him do it, but Steve kept right on arguing with him. I thought he was crazy to want to do those stunts. It was only when we were working on *The Hunter* eight or nine years later that Steve said to me, "I never wanted to do those stunts. But I couldn't let the other cowboys and stuntmen think I was a coward." He'd argued only so he *had* to be told he couldn't do them and so he didn't lose face with everyone.'

Junior Bonner was a movie that pleased the critics but which the public stayed away from. Kathleen Carroll of the *New York Daily Times* called it 'a nice, loose, easy-going rodeo picture. McQueen had met with a role that fits him like a glove.'

Archer Winsten in the *New York Post* wrote, 'McQueen has a chance to do a lot of what he does so well: nothing much while he thinks about some action that has happened or will. He keeps it all in focus with those deadly blue eyes of his. A hero from the past.'

Critics delighted in pointing out that this was not one of Peckinpah's violent movies. 'For those of us who have come to expect (or fear) that each new Sam Peckinpah film will be a new bloodbath, this comes as a pleasant surprise, a reminder of milder, gentler films,' wrote John Russell Taylor in *The Times*.

And that was the kind of picture which audiences in 1971 didn't want to see. *Dirty Harry* and *The French Connection* were the crowd-pleasers; films about hardened cops. And yet there was a flurry of films about rodeo riders at that time – *The Honkers, J.W. Coop* and *When Legends Die* as well as *Junior Bonner*. None of them were hits. *Junior Bonner* earned a mere $2 million worldwide, but it won a new respect for McQueen from critics. Today is it well known by critics and students of film, but remains generally unknown to the public. Steve McQueen was suddenly no longer a box-office draw.

Things in Steve's private life took a sudden turn when, to his complete surprise, Neile finally filed for divorce. 'He couldn't quite believe that Neile wanted to actually divorce him,' said James Coburn. 'I said to him, "Steve, what did you expect?" He said, "Not a divorce." He just didn't get it. He was so angry about it. He said, "She didn't need to divorce me. We could have stayed happy. We were doing okay." He was the only one who thought that.'

He didn't contest the million-dollar settlement Neile was awarded, or the $500,000 a year alimony and child support he was to pay for the next 10 years – alimony he would never stop paying because his life expired before the period of alimony ended.

Steve moved out of the matrimonial home and into a rented guest house on Coldwater Canyon.

Despite his anger at being divorced, he said at the time, 'She deserves every penny of it. Without my old lady, there wouldn't have been any me in the first place.' The money he had to pay was never an issue. He wasn't going to leave his children without financial support, like his father had done to him. And he wasn't going to leave them without a father's love, as his father had done to him. I don't think in the annals of Hollywood history there was ever a more amicable divorce than that of Steve and Neile McQueen, nor a more friendly divorced couple. After an initial cooling-off period, they remained good friends for the rest of his life.

'It's incredible that they could get along so well,' said James Coburn. 'But they are both good people, and great parents, and they really liked each other, even if the love had gone. Though to tell you the truth, I don't think Steve ever stopped loving Neile, and maybe she didn't stop loving him either. Not deep down. That's a really precious kind of love. And he really loved his kids. I mean *really* loved them.'

When I saw Steve in 1974, he told me, 'The important thing in any situation [like divorce] is never argue in front of the kids. Neile and me never did. We didn't need to. We didn't argue at all [after the divorce]. Not like before, but then we never did [argue] when the kids were around. Don't be bitter. That's where it's at. Don't hate.'

Through two more marriages, Steve and Neile (who also remarried) managed to keep their family unit together, which was quite a feat in the world of Hollywood. That isn't to say there weren't problems. When Neile's boyfriend, David Ross, a surgeon, moved in with her and the children, Steve was jealous. 'He couldn't bear to think of her having another man in her life,' said Coburn. 'He had to get used to it. And then he got Ali MacGraw and it didn't matter any more.'

But before Ali MacGraw, there was, for a brief time, Natalie Wood. When they had worked together on *Love with the Proper Stranger* in 1962, they had been mutually attracted, but Natalie was married to Robert Wagner and was faithful to him, even though she teasingly flirted with Steve.

A year after I met Steve, I met Natalie Wood, who mentioned how much she liked Steve's 'vulnerability because it reminds me of me'. She had thought that, if things had been different, the two of them 'might have made a good match.'

She discovered she was wrong in October 1971, when Steve called her and invited her for dinner. She had just come out of a marriage to producer Richard Gregson, and was, as I well knew from a week I'd spent with her a month or so earlier, a deeply vulnerable woman who, I think, was ready to fall in love with the first man who showed interest.

Steve later told me, 'I was *always* interested in Natalie. She is a warm, caring and very funny girl. She's kind of nutty. She's also insecure.'

Steve was also insecure, and kind of nutty, and funny. And, of course, they had both come out of a divorce. I don't think he was all that caring, at least when it came to women, but I think he did actually care about Natalie. Almost in the same way he cared about Suzanne Pleshette.

Natalie was only too happy to accept Steve's invitation to dinner, and he took her to a discreet restaurant. 'I knew it wasn't going to be a big-time thing,' Steve told me. 'We discovered we were different people. She liked going to Hollywood. Big parties and premieres. That's not my thing.'

Natalie wasn't disappointed to discover it was never going to be serious. 'I just needed some fun,' she later told me in 1976. 'So did Steve. He could get a girl any time, anywhere. But we liked each other, and we could tell each other our sad stories.' They could also share something more physical. 'We went to bed and we had some happiness for a while,' she said.

Steve admitted to me, 'Yeah, we got it on a few times.'

They went out a few more times, daring even to be seen in public going to high-class restaurants, and even buying his and hers solid-gold sunglasses that cost $800 each.

When it dawned on them that they were not suited, they agreed they would just 'hang out' and enjoy a brief fling. It lasted about two weeks. 'There was no bust-up,' said Natalie.

'We just called it a day,' said Steve.

They had become very fond of each other, and they could easily have fallen in love, according to each of them, but they knew it was never to be. Besides, Steve was aware of something I also realised when I was with Natalie: the only man she really needed in her life was Robert Wagner.

In January 1972 Natalie and Wagner finally got back together. Steve called them in Palm Springs and said, 'You're back together again. That's great.'

'I was really happy for them,' Steve said. 'If Hollywood ever had a perfect couple, it was Natalie and Robert. I knew they should be married again.'

This was all staggered information I slowly gathered from Natalie and Steve, without searching for it, over several years, meeting Steve in 1970, 1974 and 1977, and Natalie in 1971, 1976 and 1980, the year Steve died and a year before Natalie drowned.

The brief affair Steve and Natalie had was good for them both because, I think, they both knew it was temporary. They put no pressure on each other. I know that they remained fond of each other, but they rarely met up. They moved in different circles, Natalie inside Hollywood, Steve outside of it.

Both had career problems. Natalie actually wasn't too bothered about her career when she and Wagner remarried, and only later tried to resurrect it, without success, proving that the biggest of stars can stay away too long. Steve wasn't intending to stay away any longer from his career, needing a sure-fire hit after the disappointing returns from *Junior Bonner*.

He also wanted a woman in his life. He admitted to me, 'After Natalie I felt I needed someone . . . a woman who was mine.' He was about to have both wishes come true.

CHAPTER 16

McQueen and MacGraw

Steve suddenly found he wasn't quite as employable as he had once been. He hadn't had a hit movie since *Bullitt*, which was followed by three commercial duds, the biggest of which was *Junior Bonner*.

He wanted to do *Butch Cassidy and the Sundance Kid*, which his publicist, David Foster, had tried to buy in his first attempt at becoming a movie producer. He and his partner Ben Sherman thought that with McQueen willing to star in it as the Sundance Kid, they would win what turned into a bidding war for the screenplay, which was written by William Goldman.

Ironically, Steve suggested Paul Newman for the role of Butch, and so Bob Sherman called Newman. The actor was in the middle of filming *Harper*, written by William Goldman, who had already told Newman about the Butch Cassidy project. But he hadn't mentioned to Newman that Steve McQueen was interested in it. When Newman found out, he was furious with Goldman.

The rivalry between Steve McQueen and Paul Newman had never abated. I met Newman a few times and found him to be a charming, amiable man who was very secure in his own success and was not known for throwing his weight around. Steve was also charming and, when in the right mood, amiable, but he was never quite secure in his own success, always looking over his shoulder to see what the competition was.

It was a clash of tremendous egos. Newman knew that McQueen was *always* the star, and nobody else could share equal screen time with him. What he didn't know was that, having gone over the edge and survived, Steve had changed – or was in the process of changing. He had discovered he wasn't Hollywood's golden boy any longer. He also knew he had a terrible reputation as a troublemaker on the set, arguing with directors and storming off to his dressing room or trailer. All that had come to a head with *Le Mans*. He was trying hard to change and just wanted a chance to prove it.

On *Junior Bonner* he had come face to face with just about the toughest director the movies had ever known in Sam Peckinpah, and although sparks flew from time to time, there was a mutual respect as well as a real fondness between the two men. Steve McQueen was literally mellowing and was willing to share billing and equal screen time with Paul Newman in *Butch Cassidy and the Sundance Kid*.

Two things occurred to stop that happening. The first was when David Foster and Bob Sherman were outbid for the Goldman script by 20th Century-Fox, which was able to go as high as a record-breaking $400,000. The second was when Paul Newman told Fox president, Richard Zanuck, that he wanted Marlon Brando to play Sundance.

Steve, who saw himself as the first star actor who had declared an interest in the script and had asked for Paul Newman, saw this move by Fox and Newman as an act akin to professional assassination. Paranoia was taking over again, and peaked when he accused Foster of betraying him by producing *McCabe and Mrs Miller* and casting Warren Beatty in the star role. 'So you think Beatty's a fucking better actor than me?' he yelled at Foster.

But Foster had something else in mind for Steve. Something he thought would be ideal for him. While Steve was filming *Le Mans*, Foster had managed to buy the screen rights to *The Getaway*, and now urged him, '*This* is the movie for you. Not *McCabe and Mrs Miller*. This is the big one you've been looking for.'

I don't think Steve had any idea how big it would be. It would herald his screen comeback – his third – as a top box-office star. And it would change his life in more ways than one. It would introduce him to his second wife, Ali MacGraw.

'I loved the idea of playing Doc McCoy,' Steve told me in 1974. 'I loved [Humphrey] Bogart for playing those good guy/bad guy roles. I wanted to do something like that coz he was one of my greatest heroes.'

The story of *The Getaway* begins with Doc McCoy's release from prison after serving four years for armed robbery, to be met by his wife. Together they plan a bank heist and a dash for the Mexican border. Somewhere in the middle of this simple premise were scenes of extreme violence, political corruption, double-crosses and car chases. It had all the elements of a box-office hit for the early 1970s.

But McQueen wasn't box-office gold any more, and it was difficult to find a major studio to back it. They looked first for a director, and agent Jeff Berg suggested a client of his, Peter Bogdanovich, who was fresh from his success with *The Last Picture Show*, which had earned him an Oscar nomination. That film had been nominated as Best Picture, and it brought Ben Johnson a Best Supporting Actor award. It had also received almost unanimous praise from the critics.

Steve had his doubts about Bogdanovich. He told me, 'I thought *The Last Picture Show* was a beautiful picture. But I wasn't sure he was the kind of director we were looking for.'

Nevertheless, McQueen and Foster decided to go with Bogdanovich, forcing him to sign a contract with them even though they had no studio backing as yet. There was a clause which said that if Bogdanovich was unable to start the picture when McQueen and Foster were ready to go, the contract was void. I think McQueen felt sure that this would happen.

Meanwhile, Jeff Berg, determined to get his clients in on Steve McQueen's comeback, got Foster and McQueen to meet with a talented young writer, Walter Hill. They asked him to adapt the book into a screenplay.

Bogdanovich was hired by Warner Brothers to direct *What's*

Up, Doc? with Barbra Streisand and Ryan O'Neal. It was an offer the director couldn't turn down, but it meant he might not be available to make *The Getaway*. When Bogdanovich, out of professional courtesy, advised Foster and McQueen of the situation, Steve said, 'So Streisand's more important to you than I am, right? Fuck it, we'll get another director.' He could still pout and take umbrage when none was meant.

Steve didn't hesitate to suggest Sam Peckinpah, who was also reeling from the failure of *Junior Bonner*. He told me, 'I'd wanted to do *The Getaway* for years. I read it when it was published [in 1958]. I thought it was very nice of Steve to bring it to me when he had it.'

I think it was obvious that there had been discussions going on between Peckinpah and McQueen for some time, though neither would admit to it.

Walter Hill was initially alarmed with the choice of new director. He said, '[Peckinpah] scared the hell out of me because he had such a reputation. And he drank so much. I had been writing the screenplay before he got involved and had a pretty free hand, but he had his input, and Steve had his input, but I have to say they were both great to work with. A few sections got trimmed down and they put in more action. I actually liked Sam, and when I wanted to become a director he was very encouraging.'

In search of an actress to play McQueen's screen wife, Peckinpah wanted Stella Stevens, but when she wasn't available, David Foster, thinking like a producer *and* a publicist, came up with the idea of Ali MacGraw, fresh from her success in *Love Story*, the biggest box-office hit of 1971 – proving not everyone wanted action movies after all. *Love Story* was a favourite with women who wanted a good old-fashioned weepy. The critics didn't like *Love Story* but the women of the world did. And men liked Ali MacGraw because she was beautiful and sexy, but not out of a mould.

Foster announced, 'Wouldn't it be great if we could get Ali MacGraw? I can see it now on the marquee, "McQueen and MacGraw".' It definitely had a ring to it.

Foster was very canny, because he knew that, apart from the

potential marquee value of McQueen and MacGraw, Ali was married to Paramount's production chief, Robert Evans. If Evans liked the idea of Ali being in *The Getaway*, then Paramount would back the movie. That would be two major problems solved.

But Ali didn't want to do *The Getaway*. She had her heart set on playing Daisy in *The Great Gatsby*. Evans, however, thought that *The Getaway* was a perfect vehicle for Ali to break away from her sugar and spice image, and persuaded her to go for it before playing Daisy. He set up a meeting at his mansion for Ali to talk to David Foster, Steve McQueen and Sam Peckinpah.

Ali had met McQueen before, briefly, at the Academy Awards that year in March. Ben Johnson told me, 'She knew I'd worked with Steve and she asked me to introduce her to him. He was there to present an Oscar. So I introduced them, and she was obviously a big fan of McQueen's. It was all very cordial. Nothing extraordinary.'

Ali had no reservations about working with McQueen, and agreed to the meeting because she hoped to talk Steve into playing the part of Jay in *The Great Gatsby*. But she had no desire to work with wild man Sam Peckinpah (although she would go on to make two movies with him, the other being *Convoy*).

Steve remembered that meeting with some amusement: 'Poor Ali was presented with the sight of Peckinpah having a [B12] shot in his ass. He had a lot of them, on the hour, so he had to have one when she met him.'

Peckinpah recalled that meeting: 'She came in like someone who was going to the dentist to have teeth pulled. She hated it. But when Steve set eyes on her . . . ka-boom!'

Steve told me, 'I never saw such a nice ass.'

And it seems she was likewise struck by him. Ben Johnson told me, 'Ali said to me she had to leave the room at one point to compose herself.'

It was instant sexual attraction. But it scared Ali, who knew that Steve was now free and extraordinarily attractive. She knew she was not going to be able to resist him.

Problems arose with Paramount that caused complications which even Steve didn't understand, but the upshot was that

Paramount would have complete control over *The Getaway*. However, the studio agreed that Freddie Fields could set up a deal with another studio within 30 days, otherwise Paramount would own *The Getaway* outright.

Because Fields had signed McQueen to a three-picture deal to First Artists, it was decided to make *The Getaway* as Steve's first picture with that company, which wasn't in itself a studio, although it was a major production company. First Artists had a deal with National General, which would finance their movies up to $3 million. That wasn't a huge amount by 1971 standards, but Fields and Peckinpah thought they could manage with that budget.

To the surprise of McQueen, Peckinpah and Foster, Robert Evans still urged them to cast Ali MacGraw. She had remained their first choice but her price was a fee of $300,000, which the film's budget couldn't meet. Freddie Fields had the idea of giving Ali all the profits from Germany instead. She accepted and, according to Peckinpah, she made a whole lot more than $300,000.

The cast and crew gathered in Huntsville, Texas, to begin filming in early February 1972. Ali MacGraw arrived on location to be met by McQueen and Peckinpah, and driven, with Steve at the wheel, to the condominiums where the cast and crew were staying. En route, Steve showed off and spun the car across four lanes of the freeway. Ali MacGraw said, 'It was a prophetic start to our relationship.'

The first scene, set in the local penitentiary, was shot on 7 February. Steve recalled, 'They were real cons – real guards. We did our first scene, and I was in prison clothes. And we finished and I was heading out of the yard where we shot, and suddenly I got these hounds snapping at my ass and I'm running like hell because they were trained to go after anyone in convict clothes. I just made it outta that place.'

It wasn't too long before something was happening between Steve and Ali, which surprised him because, he said, apart from having a great ass, 'She thinks too much for a woman.' She was a woman of intellect, which was at odds with his chauvinistic expectations of a woman. Physically, she excited him, and the physical attraction he had for her overcame his reservations, and he fell for her.

Ali found his rough-hewn manner refreshingly different from the more controlled air of her film-executive husband, who insisted that everything had to be just right so she could be presented as a movie-star. McQueen's macho charm was suddenly preferable to the smooth charm she was exposed to in Hollywood. She rebelled and fell for him.

It was a classic Hollywood love affair, probably the biggest of its type since Elizabeth Taylor and Richard Burton caused such a scandal when they made *Cleopatra* 10 years before. Peckinpah told me, 'I don't know when it happened. It kind of snuck into the movie. There they were just falling in love and not all of us knew until it was too obvious not to notice.

'I had to keep Robert Evans away, so I told him if he ever came to the set I'd kick his ass off, and he was a true gentleman and stayed away. So Ali's husband wasn't around to know what was happening or stop it.

'I thought it would be great for the picture. Our producer [David Foster] blew a gasket when he realised. He went to McQueen and told him to leave Ali alone. McQueen told him to forget about that.'

Ben Johnson, who co-starred in the film, told me:

Ali had this life with Bob Evans where she couldn't do anything for herself. And she hated it. She couldn't get anything for herself. Someone else would always do that. With Steve she not only did everything herself, she could do it for *him*, and she liked that. She could cook him eggs. She was never allowed to cook her own eggs when she was married [to Robert Evans].

Steve was wild. I mean *wild*. You never knew what he would do. And he loved to show off in front of Ali. Like a kid. He rented a station wagon, and he and Ali were in it, and suddenly he drives it into this big waterhole. The damn car almost sank. There was just the back end sticking out. I jumped in – a lot of us did – and they were sticking their heads out of the back window so they wouldn't drown. I helped them out, and they were okay. It was just a crazy stunt to show off for Ali. I thought she would take off from him after that, but she stuck with him. He was a breath of fresh air to her because she never knew anyone like him.

While he may have been a breath of fresh air, it was hardly a good foundation on which to build a full-time relationship, let alone a marriage, but that's what seemed to happen. Ali and Steve had a great time during the courtship, but eventually the marriage would be fraught with arguments as Ali demonstrated that she was a woman who had a brain.

'What Steve wanted was a woman who just did what he wanted her to do,' said Johnson. 'Ali was never going to be that kind of wife.'

One of the supporting actors, Sally Struthers, said that she thought the romance between Steve and Ali was 'romantic'. 'Ali was suddenly very happy with Steve. I know she was married but a lot of married people aren't happy. But I thought it was sweet and romantic when they fell in love. Falling in love happens. It doesn't mean people should get married.'

The wild side of McQueen spilled over into his acting. In a scene in which he had to hit Ali, he surprised everyone, not least Ali, by slapping her more than he should have. 'I thought, *this is great acting*, although I don't know what drove him to do it,' said Peckinpah.

It certainly shook Ali, and the shock on her face is real. But it didn't harm their blossoming love affair.

Steve also had to slap Sally Struthers in a scene. She said, 'He hit me with the flat of his hand. He had to. I could have used a stunt girl but it always shows, so I said, "Okay, Steve, do it." And he didn't do the kind of side-swipe you see in movies where the other actor just snaps his head like he's been hit. That's so fake. Steve likes it to look real, and I wanted it to look real. You bet it hurt, but it looked great in the movie. He was really sorry for hurting me. I liked Steve a lot.'

As has been told to me by a number of actors, working on a Sam Peckinpah movie was always eventful and surprising. You never knew what was going to happen, and this was partly because his creativity was sometimes questionable. Steve said, 'I think Peckinpah is one of the greatest directors. We did two movies and they are two of my best. But he can have the wildest, craziest ideas. He thought Ali and me should get it on for real – a sex scene – real sex. I never told Ali. She would have left the picture. So would I. But I fought it out with him. He was drunk. I was stoned. My God, everyone was stoned on that picture. He had a crew who were all smoking grass. But I wasn't too stoned to know he was wrong. I was offended. The next day he was sorry for it.'

Peckinpah credited McQueen with coming up with ideas of his own which were too good not to use. One of them was a scene in which McQueen held two police officers at bay and unloaded a pump-action shotgun into their car. 'That car was pumped full of holes and it looked great,' said Peckinpah. 'All McQueen's idea.'

Steve also did his usual line-cutting. Walter Hill recalled, 'The great thing about Steve McQueen is he can do a lot without dialogue and find something physical to expand his character. He handled guns better than anyone I ever saw, and he made all that a part of his character. Then he would just take out lines of dialogue because he could show it all in his face, which you couldn't see on the set but you saw it on the screen. He was wonderful at doing that.'

Peckinpah recalled, 'Steve would say, "I got too many words. I don't want all these words. Let me give it to you in a close-up," and he did that.'

Although McQueen and Peckinpah managed to make two good movies – only one of which, *The Getaway*, was a success – they never had an easy working relationship. But then no actor ever did with Peckinpah. 'He had so many demons and drank far too much,' said James Coburn, who made two Peckinpah movies. 'But then out of his demonic state could come something that was close to genius.'

McQueen said he thought Peckinpah had great ideas but also some really lousy ones. 'I fought with him on every lousy idea he came up with. But I was right behind him on every one of his best ideas. He could also have some really fucking awful ideas that were brilliant.'

When I asked Steve to clarify that, he told me how Peckinpah brought in an Italian-American actor, Al Lettieri, to play the film's heavy (a part originally intended for Jack Palance, who proved too expensive). Peckinpah had seen some footage of Lettieri from *The Godfather*, in which he had a brief role, and decided he looked mean and ugly enough for the role Palance had rejected. Lettieri had connections to the Mafia – his brother was in the mob, or, as Peckinpah put it, 'he was an honest-to-God Mafiosi'.

Steve said, 'Lettieri was a psycho. He scared even me.'

Lettieri and Sally Struthers struck up a love affair. 'Al was a sweet guy when he was sober, but drunk he was a very scary guy,' said Struthers.

Not knowing at first that she and Lettieri were an item, Steve and Ali took her to dinner, hoping to match her with a single friend of his. 'I didn't know she was seeing that mob freak,' Steve told me in 1977. 'So when he found out we tried to pair her off, he threatened to kill me. People can say, "I'll kill you if you do that again," but he really meant it, coz after Sally dumped him he turned up with a fucking gun, and I admit, I hid. I could take him in a fight, but not against a gun. So I got myself a couple of bodyguards, and I packed a gun. Couldn't let anyone know I had it. But I would have shot him before he shot me. I was scared he'd kill Ali, and I wasn't going to let that happen. Thank God the freak is dead.'

Lettieri died from a heart attack in 1975.

Although Steve was divorced from Neile and now in love with Ali, he couldn't help but keep in touch with Neile, and it wasn't just for the sake of their children. 'She was the best friend I ever had and will ever have,' he told me in 1977.

He often telephoned Neile from the location in Texas and El Paso, and it was during those conversations that she noticed a hoarseness in his voice and he was always clearing his throat. She asked him what was wrong. He said it felt as though he constantly had something at the back of his throat which wouldn't clear. She begged him to stop smoking cigarettes and grass, and he told her, 'Don't be silly, woman! I need to wind down at night.'

He did, however, agree to undergo tests when the picture was complete.

During the last week of filming, Robert Evans arrived in El Paso to collect Ali, which was when she finally broke the news to him that she was in love with Steve. In an effort to keep her away from McQueen, Evans demanded that Peckinpah assign someone to escort Ali and fly with her to Los Angeles, where a car would drive her to a home Evans owned in Palm Springs for a two-week vacation. Then she would be flown back to Los Angeles.

Peckinpah gave his property man, Bobby Visciglia, the task of accompanying Ali. Then Peckinpah tipped Steve off about the plan and, disguised with a hat and sunglasses, Steve got a ticket on the plane and sat right behind Ali and Visciglia. Only when they were in the air did Steve let them know he was on board. Then he sent Visciglia back into economy so he could be alone with Ali in first class.

When they landed, Steve disappeared as Ali got into the waiting car that drove her to join Evans at his Palm Springs house.

McQueen enlisted the help of Peckinpah's long-time companion, Katy Haber, to join him in Palm Springs so she could pass messages to Ali. But he was unable to meet with her. He told me, 'I thought I was going to lose her back to Evans. I even drove to Palm Springs to try and see her, but he was watching her like a hawk.' He admitted, 'I was scared I'd lose her. It drove me nuts. I was freaking out. It almost hurt, like real pain.'

After the two-week vacation, Ali returned to Los Angeles, resigned to giving her marriage to Evans a second try. But her love for Steve was too strong, and she moved out and into a rented house on Mulholland Drive that looked down on Steve's house in Coldwater Canyon. They were within easy reach of each other, and although they officially had their own separate homes, they were, in essence, living together.

Their love affair was back on but it was interrupted by a series of fights. Ali was a woman who had her own opinions and wasn't afraid to express them, leading to arguments, leading in turn to passionate reconciliations as they would each leave their home and cross the field that separated their houses to meet in the middle. Added to the pressure was a threat from Robert Evans to have Ali declared an unfit mother to their son, Joshua, because she was essentially living in sin with Steve McQueen – something that, back then, was still frowned upon in law. Steve was convinced he was bluffing.

Steve took Ali and Joshua to the Castle to become acquainted with Neile, Terry and Chad, a rather bizarre situation to some, but perfectly normal to Steve, who wanted to ensure that his family – all of it – remained as close as it could be.

Steve at last had his throat checked out and polyps were discovered, the result, doctors suggested, of too much smoking. He checked into Mount Sinai Hospital. Few people knew. Ali sent flowers but didn't dare visit as she didn't want to make any public acknowledgement yet that she was anything other than the wife of Robert Evans. The surgery was relatively minor, and Steve's was advised to remain in hospital for a few days' observation. But he was irritable, cranky and downright bad-tempered being kept in hospital unable to speak, so, the morning after his surgery, he discharged himself.

Meanwhile, Peckinpah was fighting with McQueen over the final edit of *The Getaway*. Because it was a First Artists picture, Steve had control of the final cut. Peckinpah finished the film the way he wanted it, complete with a great music score by Jerry Fielding. This was the first version I saw at the London office of Cinerama, where we were told that this was only a 'rough cut'. It was the slickest-looking rough cut I ever saw – but this was told to us because McQueen had already decided that it was not to be the version that would be released.

Steve made sure that his version had a lot more of his close-ups, showing him reacting to dialogue from other actors. As Peckinpah put it, 'He wanted all these pretty-boy shots because he wanted to play it safe for his face.'

McQueen also replaced Fielding's score with one by Quincy Jones. It gave the film a more modern feel to it. Fielding had scored Peckinpah's *The Wild Bunch* and, like that score, his music for *The Getaway* emphasised the film's drama and violence. I saw both versions, and I can't honestly say that one was better than the other, although I preferred Fielding's score.

Because *The Getaway* – in McQueen's version – was such a commercial success, earning a domestic gross of $18 million and $35 million worldwide, it has to be said that Steve had learned from his mistakes on *Le Mans*, and gave his public what they wanted – McQueen in action. It is still very much a Sam Peckinpah movie and he deserved to take credit for its success, although he virtually disowned the picture. It also salvaged his career, as well as McQueen's, making Steve the year's highest-paid movie-star in the world; his 10 per cent of the gross netted him a cool $3.5 million.

The film split the critics. Jay Cocks of *Time* declared, 'If *The Getaway* had just rolled off the studio assembly line, the work of a competent craftsman, it could easily have been passed over and forgotten. It is, however, the work of a major American film artist.'

Pauline Kael wrote in the *New Yorker*, 'The picture's bewildering con is that it makes the pair such lovely, decent gangsters that they can stroll off into the sunset with their satchel stuffed with money as if they'd just met over a malted at the corner drugstore. As for McQueen and MacGraw, they strike no sparks on the screen.'

It's true that the film ended with the pair of gangsters getting away – hence the film's title – but in some quarters there was outrage that a movie should allow villains to escape justice. In fact, one of the golden rules of film censorship was that crime should never be seen to pay. So for some territories, where local councils objected to the film's ending, a caption was included at the end, explaining that the couple were captured. I doubt any version with that caption exists today.

While McQueen was the highest-paid actor in the world, it is debatable that he was the most popular. Clint Eastwood was having huge success in films like *Dirty Harry* and was, I thought then, someone McQueen felt was his biggest competition. Steve told me in 1974, 'I've competed with the best and even beaten John Wayne, but Eastwood just won't go away. But I could take him down in a one-on-one.' He was boasting of his martial arts prowess, which he continued to progress in.

After finishing *The Getaway*, Steve started learning karate from Chuck Norris on the recommendation of Bruce Lee, but when Norris began appearing in films, thanks to Bruce Lee, he recommended Pat Johnson.

For the rest of his life, Steve McQueen counted Pat Johnson, his karate instructor, among his greatest friends. James Coburn told me, 'I think Steve finally found someone he could call a mentor. He'd lost John Sturges, but he had Pat Johnson, and I think he told Pat Johnson just about everything he had on his mind.'

Karate offered a way for Steve to expel all his pent-up energy, and he became so proficient that he reached red belt, just one level below black belt. 'I could be a black belt,' he told me, not an idle boast, I think. 'But if I ever cracked someone's skull and you go to court, you're better being a red belt than a black belt, coz you're not supposed to use your skills as a black belt. I only use karate if I *really* have to.'

CHAPTER 17

I Am Papillon

It was Neile who had urged Steve to read Henri Charrière's account of his years on Devil's Island in his memoir *Papillon*, and it proved to be a story which struck a chord in Steve. Happily for him, producer Robert Dorfman, who bought the rights to the book for $600,000, never had anyone other than McQueen in mind for the role of Charrière.

The screenplay passed through the hands of a number of talented writers, including William Goldman and Lorenzo Semple Jr, but the final screenplay was largely the effort of Dalton Trumbo. Even when the film got the green light from Allied Artists, which was willing to spend $7 million on a Steve McQueen picture, the screenplay was still being written by Trumbo.

McQueen's name might have got Allied Artists' interest, but it's doubtful that the film would have gone ahead with his name alone above the title. He was a risk, albeit a good one. What the production company really needed was a second star name. They got Dustin Hoffman.

But there wasn't an obvious character for him to play, so one, Dega, was created for him. Said Hoffman, 'That character wasn't really in the book but was a composite of different characters, and I kind of worked on it with Dalton Trumbo to create that character. I wanted Dega to have integrity and a vigorous strength which came from Trumbo.'

With McQueen and Hoffman, Allied Artists, which had once been a small-time company making low-budget movies like *Never Love a Stranger* with McQueen in 1958, hoped for a huge return. They paid McQueen $1.75 million and Hoffman $1.25 million. The director, Franklin Schaffner, got a mere $750,000.

Then McQueen's salary went up to $2 million after he expressed misgivings which had him threatening to pull out. I think he just wanted to be the first movie-star to earn $2 million.

Other costs kept creeping in until the film's budget rose to $14 million. Money was wasted, according to Don Gordon, who had a small role. 'They shot it in sequence because Dalton Trumbo was out there on location in Jamaica and Spain the whole time, writing the screenplay day by day, and that meant that actors were being kept on location and being paid when they didn't need to be. I was in the first couple of scenes and then my character died. Several scenes later they find my body, so I had to stay there in Jamaica at full pay so they could shoot me looking dead, instead of shooting all my scenes in one go. I had a great time for two months, but it cost a lot of money doing it that way.'

According to Don Gordon, Allied Artists tried to keep costs to a minimum simply by not paying people. 'They had a crew that didn't get paid for over a month. Now, McQueen had already been paid, but he went to the producer and said, "If you don't pay the crew, I don't work."'

McQueen didn't work for the next five days until Allied Artists came up with the money to pay the crew.

Ali went with Steve to Jamaica. Chad could have gone but, according to Neile, he felt he couldn't leave his mommy behind. Thirteen-year-old Terry, however, initially loved the idea, movie-star Ali MacGraw being her new best friend, and she also loved being with Daddy, who was, said Neile, the love of her life. But she had changed her mind by the end of the first week in Jamaica, finding that she was competing for her dad with the new woman in his life. 'We had to work on that,' Steve said laconically, adding, 'Teenage girls!' and clicking his tongue.

Steve had some anxiety about working with Hoffman, knowing him to be a theatre-trained actor with a whole different approach to acting. He wondered how they would work together, and at first there were problems, because Steve would get his work in one or two takes and then became impatient waiting for Hoffman, who wanted to try things different ways. So Schaffner shot McQueen's coverage first, and Hoffman's coverage second, and that method kept both actors happy.

Hoffman respected McQueen as a screen actor and told me, 'He gave me advice, which I took. He'd just say, "Less, Dusty," or "Just throw that out, you don't need it." He knew a lot more then about screen technique than I did.'

Don Gordon laughed when he recalled the first time Hoffman came onto the set wearing Coke bottle glasses and his teeth coloured. 'We had a great time on *Papillon* because of Dustin Hoffman, because he would show up on the set and you never knew what he was going to be wearing. He'd always have a different hat, and he looked so quirky. McQueen said to me, "What's he doing?" I said, "He's got glasses today." When Steve saw those glasses he had to think, "Now what am I going to do?" Dustin really kept him on this toes. Those two guys really brought out the best in each other.'

Henri Charrière visited the set in Spain, where a huge replica of the prison had been built. McQueen found Charrière's sense of restlessness and obsession with escape something he identified with. 'I *am* Papillon,' Steve told me.

He believed the whole Charrière story, but, according to Don Gordon, Franklin Schaffner didn't. 'Frank Schaffner told me that Charrière was a lying son of a bitch and he didn't believe half the things he wrote about,' said Gordon.

Charrière died before *Papillon* was completed. 'I wish he could have seen what we did with his story, and how it affected me,' said Steve. He had become interested in the penal system, especially as he had experienced it for himself as a boy and considered himself lucky. Some time during the early 1970s, he read in a newspaper a story about two teenagers in Florida who were caught breaking and entering and sentenced to three years in a maximum-security prison. Outraged, Steve called officials in Florida and told them in no uncertain terms, 'Those kids don't belong in that place.' He was told the boys would have to wait for an appeal, which could take several months, so he got in touch with James Bax, Florida's state health secretary, who sympathised with Steve but told him that the boys had been moved to the Lake Butler prison for adults and could not be contacted. Bax suggested Steve talk directly to Governor Claude Kirk, which he did, guaranteeing that he would take personal responsibility for the boys if they were transferred to Boys Republic in Chino. The governor considered Steve's proposal and compromised, transferring the boys to a juvenile rehabilitation home in Florida. Steve kept his part of the bargain.

He also began corresponding with prisoners. He didn't write to hardened criminals but to young people he thought could be rehabilitated. He secretly got involved with a church programme which invited anyone who wanted to become pen pals with inmates. He never wrote under his real name, preferring to remain anonymous. When he knew one of his correspondents was about to be freed, Steve sent them money and helped them find work through second and third parties. But I don't think they ever knew that it was Steve McQueen who had helped to give them a second chance in life.

That was the kind of effect his personal experiences and *Papillon* had on him. 'I believe in reformation,' he told me. He'd reformed as an angry young man, and now he reformed again, in a more conventional way. He had reduced his drinking and cut out the drugs since being with Ali. Or so he claimed. In 1977 he admitted to me, 'I did cut out the coke and other hard stuff, but I was secretly smoking weed. But hey, that was progress.'

Steve decided to give Hoffman advice about the pitfalls of drugs, to which Hoffman replied, 'It's none of your business.' Steve recoiled, and the first chink appeared in their relationship.

Further damage occurred when Hoffman allowed guests to come on the set and take photographs. Steve had them removed and told Hoffman, 'You should have run that by me first.' Hoffman saw no reason to run it by McQueen, and after that the two never spoke except in their scenes, which they did with complete professionalism. But the friendship was over.

This affected Steve deeply and, for years after, he wished he could call Hoffman and make amends. 'I just want to tell him what a great actor he is, and that I was sorry,' he told me. 'But that ain't easy for me.'

When I interviewed Hoffman in 1979, he had little to say about McQueen, apart from how he helped him on his screen technique. My impression was that Hoffman had great respect for McQueen as a screen actor and I would guess that while they never did become friends, had Steve survived the illness that killed him in 1980, he and Hoffman might well have eventually shaken hands and buried the past. Steve liked to choose his enemies, and I don't think he ever chose Dustin Hoffman as one.

Don Gordon knew how difficult McQueen could be but never held it against him. He said:

People don't know what it's like being a movie-star, and I only know because I'm around a lot of them. I watched what went on during *Papillon*. And it's tough being a movie-star because you're carrying the whole movie. Okay, on that picture McQueen was sharing the load with Hoffman to some degree, but it was really on McQueen that the movie rested. He was the main character, and the money people depended on *him* to attract people to see a multi-million-dollar picture. They're saying to him, 'We think you attract people to see a multi-million-dollar picture.' They're saying to him, 'We think *you* are the guy to draw people to see this,' and that's a hell of a load to carry. So, sometimes you have to forgive the temperamental star because it's a bitch, and I know that. That's how it was with Steve.

On *Papillon* you had these two guys – Steve and Dustin – and they are both talented. McQueen was the older guy and he sees this younger guy coming up quickly as a star, and there's a little competition going on. Dustin would sit with his stand-in. I'd sit with McQueen. And he didn't care what Hoffman thought of him. He never talked about other actors. He never had time for gossip. The only important thing to him was the movie and that takes precedence over anything. Personalities don't mean anything. Just the movie. Steve never bitched about Dustin. I don't know what Dustin said about Steve.

Despite the problems with the script and two star actors who no longer got on, Schaffner succeeded in bringing *Papillon* in a week ahead of schedule and within the $14 million budget.

Papillon is one of those films that isn't as brilliant as it should be, nor anywhere near as bad as might be thought by its virtual disappearance into obscurity. Critics at the time were baffled by it. *Variety* criticised the script for 'insufficient identification with the main characters'. Pointing out that McQueen's character has been framed for a murder, it complained, 'we do not see the injustice occur, hence have insufficient empathy'. Noting that 'for 150 uninterrupted minutes, the mood is of despair, brutality, and little hope', it felt that 'the oppressive atmosphere is so absolutely established within the first hour of the film that, in a sense, it has nowhere to go for the rest of the film'.

Vincent Canby of the *New York Times* called it a 'sometimes silly melodrama'. Pauline Kael acknowledged in the *New Yorker*, 'McQueen is an amazing actor whose expressive resources are very small,' but added, 'If ever there was a wrong actor for a man of great spirit, it's McQueen.'

However, *box-office* magazine declared, 'McQueen has never done finer work and will doubtless be remembered come Oscar time.'

Perhaps the draw of McQueen and Hoffman was enough in itself to overcome the bad reviews, and the picture went on to gross $25 million domestic and $50 million worldwide. Somehow, over time, it has become a lost classic, just waiting to be rediscovered.

Steve didn't get an Oscar nomination after all, but he was nominated for a Golden Globe. He might even have won it, but when he was asked by someone representing the Golden Globes if he would appear at the ceremony, he said, 'You can send the award to me at my address.'

He lost and it went to Robert Redford for *The Sting*.

McQueen told me, 'All I was saying to them was that if they thought I deserved the award then I'd be proud, but I wasn't going to a fancy Hollywood party. That's not my scene. Doing that shouldn't have anything to do with how good your performance is.'

Dustin Hoffman was nominated for an Oscar in the Best Supporting Actor category and, despite falling out with McQueen during filming, he thought it an outrage that Steve was overlooked for an Oscar, complaining to newspapers, 'Not only should Steve McQueen have been nominated for *Papillon*, he should have won.'

James Coburn was of the opinion that McQueen was snubbed by his peers – since it is the actors who vote for the Oscars in the acting categories – saying, 'They just didn't think he was one of them. And neither did he.'

I once talked to Charlton Heston about this kind of attitude among actors, and he said, 'I guess it's all down to George C. Scott and Marlon Brando.' Both actors failed to show up to collect their Oscars. 'It *shouldn't* have anything to do with being best, but what's being best got to do with acting anyway? All I can say is, when you win an Oscar, you *love* it, and think you deserve it more than anyone else. But acting isn't a competition. As for the Oscars show, it is important because it's not just the industry slapping itself on the back but it's entertainment to keep the public *caring*, and if *you* don't care enough as an actor to turn up, then you *seem* not to care about the industry.'

I think it may well be true that McQueen didn't actually care about the industry. He cared about his films, and no one else's. I never heard Steve talk about other movies or other actors. He was caught up in his own world, and anything outside of it didn't affect him. And that's no great sin. He cared about things that he considered far more important than the film business. He was interested in disadvantaged young people and children, and he worked, often in secret, to help them. Making movies just happened to be the way he could make the most money and take care of his family, indulge himself in his own pleasures, like collecting old and rare cars and motorbikes, as well as a whole range of antique toys and models and even jukeboxes.

He was coming to a point in his life when making movies was even less important. He had taken breaks from acting before, and he thought constantly about retiring from acting altogether. 'I might make one more movie,' he told me in 1974, 'then call it a day.'

He was finding too much happiness in his private life to want to sacrifice a moment of it just to make movies.

CHAPTER 18

One Comeback Too Many

By June 1973, Steve concluded that he had to marry Ali, for her sake and for the sake of Joshua. If Robert Evans was to carry out his threat of having Ali declared an unfit mother, then being married would solve that problem.

Steve confided to Neile that he had asked Ali to give up her career to be a wife and mother. Neile told him frankly that that was a big mistake. He said that Ali had promised she would give up her career. Steve still respected Neile for her advice and she felt that the time would come when Ali would want to resume her career. Steve was convinced Ali would be the wife that he wanted – compliant and unemployed. Neile was right.

Steve was shocked by the news that, on 30 July, Bruce Lee died from a brain haemorrhage. Lee had just become an international movie-star, and his first American film, *Enter the Dragon*, not yet released, earned him $3 million, a million more than McQueen had earned for *Papillon*. 'It was almost a private competition between Lee and McQueen,' said James Coburn. 'Who could earn more money?'

Both Coburn and McQueen were among the pallbearers, along with Chuck Norris, at Lee's American funeral – he also had one in Hong Kong. 'I had the privilege of delivering the eulogy,' said Coburn, 'and we were all in tears. All these grown men, crying over the friend we loved and lost. All except Steve. I don't know why. Was he just an unemotional guy? Did he hide it? That's a side to Steve I never discovered. I think probably he just didn't feel things the way most everyone else does because he was desensitised to emotion as a kid.'

I didn't hear this story from Coburn until after I had last spoken to Steve so didn't challenge him on it, but Steve did once tell me, 'People sometimes think I don't care because I don't show my feelings. I don't show them because I don't know what my feelings are sometimes. But I care about a lot of things. Caring and feeling aren't the same.'

He certainly didn't care so much about work any more and was having serious thoughts about permanent retirement, and so he told his agent, Freddie Fields, to find a deal – Steve called it a 'sweetheart deal' – that would pay him a fortune, earn him a percentage of the gross, be based in California, and then he could call it a day. That 'sweetheart deal' came with *The Towering Inferno*.

Producer Irwin Allen, who began the short cycle of expensive disaster epics with the phenomenally successful *The Poseidon Adventure* in 1972, wanted to follow up with the biggest and most ambitious disaster movie of them all, *The Towering Inferno*. The project was so massive that, for what I think is the first time ever, two major studios co-operatively produced it, Warner Brothers and 20th Century-Fox. Warners had the rights to a book called *The Tower*, about a fire in a skyscraper, and Fox had the rights to *The Glass Inferno*, about the same subject. It was Irwin Allen who suggested they join forces, and an agreement was signed between the two studios in October 1973.

The deal that Freddie Fields got for Steve was $1 million up front, with 7.5 per cent of the gross. The film took over $100 million worldwide, and Steve's earnings grew to around $12 million.

A big-name cast was assembled, including William Holden, Faye Dunaway, Fred Astaire, Richard Chamberlain, Jennifer Jones, O. J. Simpson, Robert Vaughn and Robert Wagner.

And Paul Newman. For years McQueen and Newman had

failed to become friends. Now they were to work together for the first time since Steve's debut in a tiny role in *Somebody Up There Likes Me*. The question now was, which was the bigger star? McQueen was determined to prove he was. It all came down to a matter of billing.

Four of the movie's stars were to be billed above the title – McQueen, Newman, Holden and Dunaway. But who would be first – McQueen or Newman? Freddie Fields suggested the second name along should be slightly higher than the name on the far left in all the advertising – whether it be McQueen or Newman – the next one (which was Holden) slightly lower than the one on the left and then Dunaway's on the far right, lower than all of them. It was left to McQueen and Newman to decide whose name would be on the far left and which one would be slightly higher.

McQueen decided he wanted to be on the far left, leaving Newman's name to be placed second but slightly higher. McQueen made his choice because people read from left to right and so would see his name first, even if Newman's name was high up on the poster. In fact, when looking at the poster, neither McQueen's nor Newman's name looks the most prominent. It was a stroke of genius on Fields's part.

Steve had initially been offered the role of the architect, the part Newman played, but, unsure if the role was right for him, he sought Neile's advice. He told her he thought the role of the fire chief was more suited to him but was concerned because that character didn't appear until halfway through the film. Neile persuaded Steve that he would still dominate the screen, provided he was in the movie through to the end. Not all the characters were. Some died in the inferno. The fire chief, being the hero, survived. That convinced McQueen, and he told Irwin Allen and the film's director, John Guillermin, that he wanted to play the fire chief. Paul Newman was offered the role of the architect and he accepted.

I'm sure that Steve had decided to play the fire chief before consulting Neile, since that was the most heroic part in the movie, but he still valued her opinion. She reinforced his decision, and also, I think, he needed her approval. It mattered to him what she thought.

Steve actually counted how many lines he had and how many Newman had. When he discovered that Paul had 12 more lines than he did, he demanded that 12 extra lines be written for him. That settled, McQueen and Newman worked well together, laughed and developed a camaraderie which I know Steve treasured for the rest of his life. 'Newman and me – we're never going to be best buddies, but we're finally comfortable with each other,' he told me in 1974.

Robert Vaughn recalled, 'They were like two old college buddies.'

McQueen and Newman even made a pact, and insisted on doing as many of their stunts as possible. Steve told me, 'We agreed together that we'd both do our stunts. It was an agreement. We were like a two-man fraternity. I love that guy.'

It was a friendship that was later reinforced when Paul's son, Scott, died from a drugs overdose and Steve was the first person to call.

For a scene in which the fire chief had to drop from a helicopter onto the top of the burning building and into the middle of the fire – to be shot on a studio sound stage – Steve put on a flame-resistant suit and leaped 15 feet from the prop helicopter into the flames.

The most dangerous scene was the one in which the rooftop water-storage tanks were blown to flood the building and douse the fire. All the surviving characters had to be tied down so the water would not sweep them away. McQueen and Newman were not the only actors to refuse to be doubled for that scene. William Holden and Fred Astaire also refused doubles, and Guillermin was able to get shots of them all being deluged.

The set was built 25 feet off the studio floor, so the water would have somewhere to go after being released. It was filmed under strict control, but it was a once-only event shot with multiple cameras, because the water would destroy the set. What no one wanted destroyed were the actors.

'It was scary as hell,' said Steve, insisting he wasn't being unnecessarily courageous. 'But we were all in it together. Shit, they wouldn't have done it if they thought any one of us would get killed or hurt bad.'

Robert Vaughn observed that McQueen was a lot less intense and far happier than he had been when they worked together on *Bullitt*. 'Steve was unusually happy because of Ali. He was starting on a new adventure in his life.'

Vaughn also believed that Steve was thinking of retiring. 'By the time of that picture I think he was planning on not working so much and just spending time in the sun and enjoying the money from *The Towering Inferno*.'

It's generally thought that straight after *The Towering Inferno* Steve went into retirement until he made *An Enemy of the People* in 1977. But in 1974 he was already thinking of making that movie. I only know this because that year I met up with him unexpectedly.

Myself and actor Jack Wild had been invited by Oliver Reed to his Victorian mansion in Surrey, England, where, to my great surprise, he had a house guest – Steve McQueen. His hair was shaggier than usual, and he hadn't shaved for a few days.

When Oli Reed had told McQueen that Jack and I were coming, Steve said, 'Yeah, Mike, I know him.'

Oli was surprised. 'You do?'

'Sure. We bummed around on a bike once.'

I had no idea he was going to be there but it seems he knew I was coming, and when I arrived he greeted me warmly like a long-lost friend. So maybe I really was his friend for life.

It turned out that Steve was there to discuss a project he had in mind for him and Oli Reed. Frankly, I thought Steve McQueen and Oliver Reed would make an unlikely screen pairing, but you never know. As someone once remarked about Hollywood, 'Nobody knows nothing in this business.'

Oli had recently come back from Spain, where he had made *The Three Musketeers*, and was at the peak of his career about then. I later discovered that Charlton Heston, one of the stars of *The Three Musketeers*, was very impressed with Oli's talent and had recommended him to Steve, who had approached Heston about *An Enemy of the People*, a play by Norwegian Henrik Ibsen.

The talk over lunch was largely Oli trying to get Steve to give Jack a role in whatever movie he had been thinking of. Jack Wild's reputation as a drunkard, which sadly he was, was known throughout Hollywood. Steve said, 'I hear he's trouble.'

Reed wanted me to back him up, but I had trouble doing that, and Steve, sensing my discomfort, suddenly changed the subject and asked where he could get a motorcycle from. He winked at me and my heart sank, as I feared I was in for another road trip.

A motorbike was secured, and we sped along Surrey country roads, through fields, along dry stream beds, up small hills and through villages, scattering sheep.

When we arrived back at Oli's mansion, Jack was smashed. He and Oli had been drinking and while Oli, though obviously not sober, was still standing and talking, Jack was completely incoherent. Steve took one look at him and said, 'Yep, like I heard – trouble.'

Steve then made a futile attempt to teach me to ride a motorbike. He didn't seem disappointed when I failed even to drive 20 yards. I said, 'I'm really more of a car man.'

He said, 'Great. Next time we'll go to Brands Hatch and burn up the track.' I hoped that day would never come and, in a sad way, it didn't. Maybe if Steve had lived longer, he might have managed to scare me in a fast sports car going 130 miles an hour.

We had dinner while Jack slept. Night fell, and Oli said he wanted to treat us to a night out at a favourite nightclub of his in London. I wasn't keen, and I don't think Steve was either, but he didn't want to offend Oli and said, 'Let's do it.'

We were driven into town and dropped off at a nightclub, where Oli proceeded to drink prolifically. Steve seemed to be merely tolerating the situation and I felt pretty sure that he was beginning to think twice about working with Reed. The music was so loud we could barely speak, but when a moment came while Oli was in the men's room, I asked Steve, at the top of my voice, 'What is this film you have in mind for you and Oli?'

He yelled back, 'Ibsen.'

That meant nothing to me at the time and, deciding I'd had enough of booze and loud music, I told Steve, happily dancing with a pretty girl, that I was leaving. 'Say goodbye to Oli for me,' I yelled.

'He won't even notice you've gone.'

I later heard that some time after I left Oli threw up all over Steve. The staff managed to find him some clean clothes but couldn't find him any shoes, so they cleaned his shoes as best they could, but apparently he could smell Oli's vomit for the rest of the night. I don't know what happened after that, and I never did find out what the project was that Steve had in mind.

Jack could never remember being at Oli's mansion, let alone meeting Steve, so he never felt bad about screwing up his chance to work with McQueen.

Apart from what now seemed to be his aborted Henrik Ibsen movie project, Steve did essentially retire from movies. He and Ali retreated to a secluded house they had in Trancas Beach in Malibu, where he did little but ride his dirt bikes, drink beer, watch television, smoke weed, and fight and make up with Ali. She was never going to remain his compliant wife, and their arguments were often accompanied by flying crockery, which she hurled at him in frustration. Once, when he told her she needed to cool off, he made sure she did by throwing her into their swimming pool.

He put on weight, let his hair grow long and grew an untidy beard. When I saw him next, in 1977, complete with long hair and beard – which he intended to keep for his role in *An Enemy of the People* – he was barely recognisable. 'I can go almost anywhere and nobody knows it's me,' he said. He loved being anonymous.

One time when he was out with Ali a fan rushed up, asking Ali for her autograph, but failed to recognise Steve. She was happily going to sign but Steve said, 'We don't sign autographs.' Ali was still an actress at heart, Steve just a bum, which he happily conceded, telling me, 'I started life as a bum and I'll end it a bum.'

He was a bum who drank too much beer and smoked too much pot, making his behaviour more unpredictable than ever being with Ali, and so she turned to Steve's friend and karate trainer, Pat Johnson, asking him to try and talk Steve into giving up alcohol and dope. Johnson tried, and Steve admitted he knew what he was doing was bad for him, but he didn't want to give up any of his vices.

He had changed his tune by 1977, when I last saw him. He told me, 'I'm trying to stay clean. Before I was killing myself, because I figured I was going to die soon anyway so what the hell?'

He could do whatever he liked to his body and, for some irrational reason, still believed he would die at 50 and thought that nothing would change that, even if he took daily exercise, stopped drinking, stopped the drugs and drove carefully.

But he was taking chances on everything, almost as though he just didn't care about the consequences. He had once been temperamental and difficult, then after *Le Mans* had mellowed, but now in his retirement he became belligerent again.

Steve was still receiving offers of work, and got so fed up with the number of scripts arriving at his home that he removed his mailbox and arranged with a local gas station to take all his mail. He also told his agent, Freddie Fields, that he wouldn't even read a script unless he was paid a million dollars. He was determined to price himself out of the film market.

But despite his withdrawal from public life and playing games to put producers off trying to lure him back into movies, Steve still had it in mind to make Ibsen's *An Enemy of the People*, which he didn't reveal to Ali until her 37th birthday party at Le Bistro in Beverly Hills, on 1 April 1975.

He had arrived late and drunk on a motorbike, weaving in and out of the tables, holding a birthday cake. Unimpressed, Ali told him, 'Either straighten up, or I'm taking Josh and we're leaving. I'm tired of living with a drunken beach bum.'

That's when he told her he had grown the beard and the hair and had put on weight for a reason – he wanted to do Ibsen.

'You mean you want to do a classic play by Ibsen?' she asked incredulously.

'Yeah, but a movie. And not just act in it. I want to produce and direct it. The whole bag.'

Steve's plan may not have been altogether a purely artistic ambition. He had an outstanding obligation to First Artists to make two more pictures, and his plans to retire were essentially on hold until he had fulfilled his contract. First Artists were only prepared to spend up to $3 million on a film, and that was almost a shoestring by the standards of the late 1970s. It seemed that Steve would have to make low-budget films to fulfil his agreement with them.

I think his decision to do *An Enemy of the People* was not so much a double-edged sword as a triple-edged one. First, he simply had to fulfil his First Artists contract, so second, knowing that Ibsen would be the most non-commercial venture of his life, he hoped First Artists would simply cancel his contract. Third, he felt that if he had to make another movie, he wanted it to be something with artistic integrity which he might actually be proud of. And I believe he might have been thinking of making a picture to prove to himself that he could really act before retiring.

Charlton Heston, whom Steve had hoped would join him in his Ibsen project, told me, 'I think Steve McQueen had aspirations to prove he was more than just an action star, though God knows, he's one of the finest screen actors around. He had something in mind for us to do, but I felt he would do better with a good British actor. I don't think that worked out though.'

James Coburn had another theory about why Steve wanted to do Ibsen, although he said it with his tongue in his cheek. 'He was on something, man, and it came to him in a trip. It blew his mind and he thought it would blow everyone's mind.'

Well, who knows if it came to him while he was high – maybe it did – but he also wanted to overcome his fears as an artist and do something dangerous . . . but a different kind of dangerous to driving fast cars. As Steve was preparing to make the movie in 1977, he told me, 'I've never been so scared in my life. I'm not making this movie because I'm brave but because I'm scared. I'm doing it to prove something to *me*. And I can tell you now, it won't take a dime, and I don't care.'

Meanwhile, he was turning down other lucrative offers, like

one from Francis Ford Coppola to star in *Apocalypse Now*. 'I shot that down coz I didn't want to spend 16 fucking weeks in the fucking Philippines,' he said.

He didn't so much turn down the role as price himself out of it, demanding $1.5 million up front, then another $1.5 million deferred, knowing Coppola would not go for it. Coppola countered by offering him a smaller role, that of Colonel Kurtz, which would take just three weeks to film. McQueen made the same demands, and it was left to Coppola to reject and look elsewhere. McQueen was wanting to tell Hollywood that he came at a high price regardless of the role or the movie.

In June 1977 Steve's daughter, Terry, turned 18, and Neile threw a party at her house. As well as Terry's friends, the guests included James Garner and his wife, David Foster and his wife, and James Coburn. Steve brought Chad and Joshua, but Ali didn't go.

Neile observed that Steve had put on a great deal of weight and was suffering from a succession of flu-like symptoms. Steve balked at the idea of having a health check-up.

By this time, Steve's agent Freddie Fields had, with Steve's encouragement, set his sights on becoming a movie producer, and he sold his agency and its clients to Marvin Josephson's International Creative Management. McQueen's first demand to Josephson was to get the First Artists deal cancelled. It was put to Phil Feldman, the president of First Artists, who threatened to sue McQueen if he didn't complete his contract with two further movies.

Desperate to free himself from First Artists, McQueen offered Feldman 'a great Western', provided First Artists spent double the money on it and then freed him from his contract. But Feldman demanded *two* pictures from McQueen, of his own choice, budgeted at $3 million a piece. McQueen announced his penultimate movie for First Artists would be *An Enemy of the People*, which he knew would probably bomb at the box-office. But he still hoped to do good work in it.

Henrik Ibsen wrote his play *An Enemy of the People* in 1882. It had been adapted for the American stage by Arthur Miller, so

Miller's version was adapted into a screenplay. It was set in a small Scandinavian town where the local spring is the town's main attraction for visitors and therefore the major source of income for the townsfolk. But Dr Thomas Stockman discovers the spring is polluted and writes a report to his brother, the town mayor, who decides to bury the report. Stockman goes to the local newspaper with his findings but the townspeople try to drive him and his family from their town.

It was the most un-Steve McQueen movie of his career – and he wanted to look entirely different from the Steve McQueen of *The Great Escape* and *Bullitt*. He succeeded there, with his long hair, beard and extra pounds.

As executive producer, McQueen chose George Schaefer to direct. Schaefer was a good director of television dramas and had won 12 Emmy Awards, and also had a good record of Broadway productions. But he had made only four previous movies, and *An Enemy of the People* was to be his last. I think McQueen thought he was choosing someone with the class to take on his classic project because of Schaefer's theatrical career and all the Emmys, but while some fine movie directors had come from a background in theatre and television, Schaefer sadly was not among them. I think it's also likely that Steve was unable to afford a more established film director. Ultimately, *An Enemy of the People* looks like a prestigious TV movie rather than an artistic cinematic achievement.

McQueen threw his heart and soul into the movie, spending six months developing the screenplay with Schaefer. They considered making the film in Sweden or Norway, but ultimately it was simply cheaper to shoot on sound stages in Hollywood. I think it was after a trip to Scandinavia that Steve passed through London in early 1977 when I last saw him.

Determined to cast it with fine actors, McQueen, having failed to secure Charlton Heston and then deciding to drop Oliver Reed, sought British actor Nicol Williamson for the role of the mayor. Acclaimed Swedish actress Bibi Andersson was cast as Mrs Stockman. The rest of the cast were American.

For the duration of the production, Steve lived alone at the

Beverly Wilshire Hotel, and returned home to Ali at Trancas only for the weekends. This was clearly a sign that the marriage was in trouble, but it also indicated that McQueen was in need of time alone for this particular role.

Some suggested that Steve simply chose to be apart from Ali so he could have all the women he wanted, and that a constant stream of models and movie-star wannabes were in and out of his room. James Coburn refuted that idea:

Warren Beatty was almost next door to Steve and all the starlets and models that were seen going in and out were going in and out of *his* suite.

I went to visit Steve one evening, and he wasn't even up to a few beers. He was dog tired. He was working hard on his picture, and really the thing about Steve was he was at his most hyper in the morning. There was a time when he could keep going all morning, all day and all night, but he was older and fatter, and I guess he may even have begun to get sick by then, so by the middle of the evening all he wanted to do was go to bed and sleep.

Steve liked to be on his own. He liked to take off into the desert on his own. At most, he'd have one other pal with him. I spent a few evenings with him at the Beverly Wilshire, and I guess other nights he had a pal come visit, but a lot of the time he just wanted to be left alone. He had no time or energy for girls. All he wanted to do in the evening was smoke a joint and relax till he fell asleep.

Coburn had the impression that the McQueen marriage wasn't good, saying, 'At the start, Steve and Ali were a great pair because they were an adventure for each other. But as much as I love Steve, he's gonna wear any woman down. He was a caveman. Ali's too smart a lady to put up with that shit. It was gonna get to them, and I think it did before he made that Ibsen.

'I was surprised when Steve stayed faithful to Ali for the first year. That was some kind of record for Steve. But then he began playing the field. He couldn't help it. He met a beautiful model, Barbara.'

Barbara Minty was a model who later told Neile and Terry that Steve had seen her picture in a magazine, tracked her down and invited her to his suite at the Beverly Wilshire Hotel. She arrived to find him with two attractive blondes sitting either side of him on the couch. (If this version is true, then James Coburn was fooled by Steve's seeming desire to be left alone and get early nights.) Apparently, Steve and Barbara hit it off right away (despite the presence of two attractive blondes), and before long she was taking motorbike rides with him. She happened to own a property in Ketchum in Idaho, and before long Steve was making plans to have a log cabin built right next to hers.

I asked Coburn what he and Steve talked about during their evenings at the hotel, presumably before Barbara came into the picture. He said:

He liked to talk a lot about the past. He missed the early days when we did *The Magnificent Seven* and *The Great Escape*. I thought he always hated Yul Brynner but he said, 'You know, Jim, if it wasn't for Brynner I might never have made it.' I said, 'How do you mean, Steve?' I thought Steve would have made it with or without Brynner. So he said, 'Brynner could have had me fired.' That's true. Brynner approved all the casting. If he'd said to Sturges, 'It isn't working out with McQueen, get rid of him,' Sturges would have had to do it. Then Steve said to me, 'Brynner gave me good advice. He said to never back down, never be intimidated, never be anything less than *the big star* of the picture.' I guess Steve took that to heart, because that's the way he always was.

But those evenings . . . he was sad, you know. Maybe even bitter. He missed Neile, I can tell you that. He loved her. He loved Ali too. He said, 'Why can't a man love two women?' Neile was with him from the start, and she was his guiding light, and he knew it. He knew he'd blown it with her. You know, maybe it was because of all that that he ate so much . . . got depressed. In hindsight I'd say he was very depressed. He pined for Neile. I don't know if Ali knew that. She's a smart lady. She must have. I think she was a classy lady putting up with Steve.

He was only living for the work . . . for that picture [*An Enemy of the People*]. It meant everything to him. I think it kept him going.

Perhaps the five-day separations made the weekends seem good to both Steve and Ali.

Before the start of filming, Schaefer gave the cast three weeks of rehearsals, a rare thing in Hollywood. On the first day, Nicol Williamson failed to arrive. After frantic calls to his agent, it was discovered he was going through some kind of personal crisis and was drunk. He was immediately replaced with American actor Charles Durning, who had a distinguished theatrical record and had become a highly regarded character actor in films.

Steve gathered his cast about him and told them, 'This is your world, not mine. I'm a little out of my depth here, but I can promise you I'll give the best I have in me. If I fail, I won't blame anybody. The fault will be mine.'

Charles Durning said he came to the part with some trepidation, not because of the role, but because of McQueen. He said, 'I'd heard all these terrible stories about him being short-tempered and firing people. I don't know if that was true on his other pictures, but on this one he was nothing like that.' He became a friend of Steve's and was invited to spend some weekends with the McQueens. He said, 'I went with them to jazz concerts at the Hollywood Bowl. They were a lovely couple. I never saw them fight.'

I had certainly sensed a more mellow Steve McQueen when I saw him earlier in 1977. He'd learned from his mistakes as a film-maker on *Le Mans*, and was truly looking forward to a future living on a ranch and raising animals and just kicking back for the rest of his days, which he still felt were numbered.

There was something else that was different about him in 1977. He told me, 'I've done too much shit in my life.' That might have been a reference to drugs, or just the way he lived his life. 'Now I'm looking for something different. Something spiritual.'

I asked him if he meant religion, and he replied, 'Not necessarily, but who knows? I like the way Jim Coburn thinks.'

Coburn was interested in the Eastern philosophies. 'I just need a little peace,' he added, proving as laconic as he did on the screen, and also saying more with his eyes than a whole monologue could ever reveal.

After three weeks rehearsing *An Enemy of the People*, the cast were able to run the whole screenplay as though it were a play. Steve had begun the rehearsal period reluctantly. Charles Durning recalled, 'At the beginning of rehearsals Steve was saying, "Do we really have to rehearse? Let's just do it." And by the end of the second week, beginning of the third, he was saying, "Are we only gonna rehearse this one week more?" He wasn't in competition with anyone. He was so enthusiastic, he said to me, "For the first time in my life I feel like I'm acting."'

Coburn was aware of the new-found zeal Steve had for acting. 'Steve told me, "I'm actually acting, man. It's a gas to work with real actors." I said, "Steve, you already worked with some of the greatest actors." I was thinking of Dickie Attenborough and Eli Wallach, E. G. Robinson and Karl Malden.' He said, "Oh sure, they are the best, but we weren't doing Ibsen." He thought doing Ibsen made him into an act-*or*. But he loved it. He said he wanted to quit acting after this but he *had* to make another picture for First Artists, and then he thought that would be it. But I don't think he ever would have quit. He kept quitting. He made a career out of it.'

On this picture, Steve behaved. The only problem Schaefer had with him was when he realised Steve couldn't work late in the day, mainly because he would smoke pot in the afternoon, or would disappear somewhere for 20 minutes and hold up filming. Steve was always apologetic when he returned, but it didn't help Schaefer or the rest of the crew and cast. So Schaefer scheduled all of Steve's scenes before lunch, when he was at his best. From then on, filming went smoothly and McQueen was on his best behaviour. 'He had to toe the line,' said Charles Durning. 'It was his picture, and he wanted it to be really good. He wanted everyone to be really good.'

Steve wanted so much to surpass everything he had ever done as an actor that his insecurities suddenly kicked in towards the end of filming and he went off the rails, but only temporarily. It was because he had a monologue of over three pages to do. He had never delivered any kind of monologue, and it scared him so much that the night before the scene was scheduled, instead of staying in and learning his lines, he went out, drank beer, smoked dope, and turned up in the morning unable to deliver any of his dialogue.

Schaefer blew his top. He yelled at Steve in a way no director had ever done, and it shocked Steve. Schaefer rescheduled the scene for after lunch, the time when McQueen was never at his best. But it had to be done.

In the afternoon Schaefer had the scene already lit when Steve stepped onto his mark. The sound was running, the camera was running, Schaefer called for action, and Steve delivered the whole speech, word perfect.

After Schaefer finished the movie on time and on schedule, Steve and Ali threw a wrap party in a swanky restaurant in Malibu. Steve told Charles Durning, 'Keep in touch, because we'd really like to see you again.' Sadly, Durning never did see Steve again.

After the film was edited and scored, Arthur Miller asked to see it and was happy with the results. Warner Brothers, who were to distribute the film, tested it in an art house in San Francisco, but the preview audience were bemused by it. The publicity department at Warners had no idea how they were going to promote a Steve McQueen picture with no action in it. They came up with an ad campaign showing McQueen as Stockman surrounded by shots from previous McQueen films, and the tag:

In a time when people say there are no more heroes – there is still STEVE MCQUEEN. You cheered for him in *The Great Escape*, prayed for him in *The Cincinnati Kid* and held your breath for him in *Bullitt*.

Now Steve McQueen portrays the most striking hero of them all – the man they called *AN ENEMY OF THE PEOPLE*.

It was an ad drawn from desperation, not inspiration. It didn't help that some at Warner Brothers thought the film was, in the words of one executive, 'a piece of junk'.

Then the critics tore into Steve for daring to try to do an art house picture. 'The problem has nothing to do with the abandonment of a successful action-adventure image, but rather the unsuitability of this particular actor to this particular role,' said *Variety*.

Michael Stragow of the *Los Angeles Herald-Examiner* wrote, 'For McQueen to play Ibsen's volatile, idealistic intellectual Dr. Stockman is as unusual as it would be for Dr. Carl Sagan to try and play Darth Vader.'

Arthur Knight of the *Hollywood Reporter* was more positive: 'Steve McQueen lends a quiet dignity. Although lacking the voice and authority to sustain Ibsen's intense confrontation scenes, it is by no means a bad performance. It nevertheless lacks the sweep and stature to make it a memorable one.'

I saw the picture at a rare screening – since the film was withdrawn from distribution before it even reached the UK – and was impressed with McQueen's performance. I haven't seen it in years, but I think I was struck not so much by the quality of the acting, which did lack strength at times, but by the fact that McQueen actually did it and proved that he was much more than an action star. Some of his peers agreed. James Coburn said, 'Steve's no Laurence Olivier, that's for sure, but he put his neck on the line and did his best, and you have to admit that he did a good job. It takes courage to do what he did. I felt proud of him.'

Charlton Heston, who was Steve's first choice to play Stockman's brother, said, 'If you want to call yourself an actor you have to do the mankiller parts. It doesn't matter if you fail because we [actors] all fail at everything all the time. Critics like Steve McQueen as the POW or a cop or a cowboy. It made them uncomfortable to see Steve McQueen *trying*. The same happened to Gregory Peck when he played Ahab in *Moby Dick*. He might not have quite pulled it off but by God he did the bloody thing. And so did Steve McQueen. It's just that, in a classic, you have to be better than good. I'm glad he did it. Some day someone will watch it and go, "Hey, that guy who rode the motorcycle in *The Great Escape* was a pretty damn good actor too."'

Heston sent his congratulations to McQueen. Clint Eastwood personally told Steve, 'You have the guts and the courage that I don't. I would love to be able to leave a classic behind.'

Steve had said from the beginning that the picture wouldn't make a dime, but when it didn't even get a distribution, he was gutted. What he would never know was that, after he died, the Ibsen Society asked George Schaefer if they could screen the film in New York, and it finally found an appreciative audience.

But commercially Steve had made one comeback too many. His public, remembering the way he was, didn't want to see him as he was now. He would never again be the superstar who packed a box-office punch.

CHAPTER 19

—

Set for Retirement

After filming *An Enemy of the People*, Steve remained at the Beverly Wilshire Hotel instead of going home. He was at his lowest ebb, knowing his second marriage was a disaster but unsure how to fix it. It didn't seem to occur to him that having a new girlfriend, Barbara, had something to do with it.

He also had a second picture to deliver to First Artists. He and George Schaefer set about preparing Harold Pinter's *Old Times* with Audrey Hepburn and Faye Dunaway co-starring. But Phil Feldman decided that, after *An Enemy of the People*, the next and last McQueen picture for First Artists had to be an action movie. Feldman had previously told McQueen he could make pictures of his own choosing and, since Steve had spent $50,000 on pre-production for *Old Times*, he sued First Artists for that amount. The matter was settled out of court when First Artists agreed to allow Steve through Solar to make the film elsewhere. I think Steve had hoped First Artists would simply cancel his contract with them but they still demanded another film.

Steve came up with what he thought was a realistic and commercially viable movie, *Nothing in Common*, in which he was to play a kidnapper who takes a child for ransom but then develops a relationship with the child. A meeting was set up with Warner Brothers, First Artists and Tony Bill, who wrote the screenplay. It was agreed the picture could be made on a low budget and would be an entertaining and enjoyable movie, but Phil Feldman announced that First Artists wasn't interested.

The hatred McQueen had for Feldman grew.

Then Sam Peckinpah came asking Ali MacGraw to be in a picture he was making. She had been eager to get back to work, and Steve, knowing that, had promised to find something for them both to do, and came up with *Fancy Hardware*, the story of a pre-Word War Two pilot who flies across Texas selling bathroom fixtures. He meets women, loves them and leaves them, but then meets a girl, who would be played by Ali, and falls for her. It was a script First Artists liked. But Steve decided to hand the project over to Barbra Streisand, who could make it for First Artists herself.

I doubt Steve ever intended to make it with or without Ali, using it to keep her happy in the belief that she would work again. When it was obvious that the film wasn't going to happen, she accepted the offer from Sam Peckinpah. It was the beginning of the end of the McQueen marriage.

'Steve was sometimes his own worst enemy,' said James Coburn. 'He wanted to keep Ali as his "old woman", but when he was being screwed over by First Artists and he really needed her, she went and did *Convoy*, and that to Steve was a betrayal. He was like a child who couldn't get his own way. But I also think he loved her so much that he couldn't bear to be away from her. Or rather, she from him.'

Ali headed to New Mexico to work on *Convoy*, leaving Steve in a sulk. He called up Sam Peckinpah on the phone and told him, 'You're disrupting my marriage. What the hell do you think you're doing asking my wife to do a movie?'

Steve couldn't stand for Ali to be so far away from him, and much of that came from his insecurity. He was suspicious that she was having an affair, and that was simply because he knew that *he* would have had an affair if on location away from his wife. Not only that, he had his own affair going on with Barbara Minty. For him, what was good for the goose was never sauce for the gander.

And yet Steve was desperate to save his marriage, even though it was common knowledge among his friends, and to Ali, that he was spending time with Barbara. Steve and Joshua flew to New Mexico to be with Ali, and upon meeting her Steve presented her with a beer can full of daises.

'It was a bizarre situation,' said Jim Coburn. 'He wanted to keep Ali *and* Barbara. And he would have kept Neile too if he could. He said to me, "I just gotta save my marriage," and I said, "To which one?" He didn't think that was very funny. But I was trying to make a point. He had to decide which woman he wanted. He just wanted them all.'

Steve hung around the set while the film was being shot, for once staying in the background while his wife, whom he really would have preferred to be at home, cooking his meals, was the main attraction.

It turned out that Steve's suspicions, brought on by sheer paranoia and guilt rather than evidence, were right about Ali; she was having an affair (as she revealed in her autobiography but without mentioning with whom). Ali didn't do it out of revenge, but, as she wrote, 'as it was now common knowledge that Steve had been living a flagrantly free life for some months, I thought that if I did not go into my own escapade, the whole mess of our lives might blow over and offer us a fresh start.'

But there was to be no fresh start. As far as Steve was concerned, the marriage was over. In November 1977 he filed for divorce. He felt guilty, not about Ali, but about Joshua because he thought he was deserting the boy he had raised as his own son. Steve knew what it was like to be abandoned by his father, and he felt he was doing that to Joshua.

Once again McQueen was at a crisis point in his life. *An Enemy of the People* had failed, his marriage to Ali had failed, he had failed as a father to Joshua, and he was bogged down in a contract with First Artists which frustrated him at every turn. He was on the very edge once more.

The divorce was a bitter one. Steve moved Barbara into the house in Trancas, leaving Ali to fend for herself.

He suddenly had a desire to make a fresh start and vowed to give up smoking and to lose weight, no doubt due to the fact that

Barbara was much younger than he was – he was 49, she 22. Being older, overweight and in generally poor health, Steve wanted to try to rediscover the vitality of his youth. He enrolled in the Schick Center in Los Angeles and succeeded in losing many of the pounds he had gained in recent years.

He felt a lot more optimistic now, looking forward to the future in earnest, planning to quit the business once and for all and settle down, hoping to make one last big score before dropping out of acting altogether. He told his agent, Marvin Josephson, to find something that would make him a lot of money and put him back on top as a major movie-star. Josephson succeeded in landing a sensational deal for McQueen which would earn him $10 million – $1 million up front plus deferred payments of $9 million plus 15 per cent of the gross – to star in *Tai-Pan*, adapted from James Clavell's best-selling novel.

Steve actually complained that Josephson would himself earn a million dollars as his 10 per cent agent's fee from the deal, considering it too high and demanding he take only 5 per cent. When Josephson, who had just got McQueen the biggest deal in Hollywood history up till then, refused to cut his percentage, McQueen fired him. He later rehired him when he found he couldn't cope with all the scripts being sent his way.

Unfortunately the deal fell through – unsurprisingly for such an expensive project – when the producer, Georges-Alain Vuille, was unable to make the second of the million-dollar payments to McQueen. Happily for Steve, the contract Josephson had secured for him guaranteed that he would keep the first million if further payments could not be met, so Steve earned a cool million just for signing his name.

Steve's old friend Richard Attenborough came asking Steve to appear in a cameo in his World War Two epic *A Bridge Too Far*. Putting friendship aside, Steve demanded a $3 million fee, which producer Joseph E. Levine balked at, so the part went to Robert Redford. I think that Steve just didn't want to be a cameo star in a film heavy with some of the cinema's biggest names of that time. Redford's sequence, where he has to get his men across a river in small boats while his men are hopelessly and mercilessly killed, is one of the most memorable in the picture. McQueen would have done well in it, but as it was, Redford did equally well.

There was still a picture for First Artists to be made, and Steve set his sights on a Western, *Tom Horn*, based on the life of the gunman hired by the businessmen of Wyoming to chase off the local cattle rustlers; Horn shot one of the rustlers dead and was hanged for murder. This was a movie that Steve had actually wanted to make for some time, but he hoped not to have to make it for First Artists. He had producer Phil Parslow working on it for many months before announcing to the press that he would star in *Tom Horn*.

Almost immediately, Robert Redford announced that his own company, Wildwood Productions, was going to make a film about Tom Horn. Both McQueen's Solar office and Redford's Wildwood office were at Warner Brothers studios, just along the hall from one another. Steve confidently predicted, 'Redford won't take me on.' Redford dropped his Tom Horn project, but not, I think, because he was afraid to take on McQueen. I think he simply saw so sense in making a rival film, and instead went on to make other successful movies and direct *Ordinary People*.

Steve was hopeful that he could convince First Artists to spend more money on an action-packed Western, and planned for a $10 million epic, hoping he could produce something to surpass Clint Eastwood's monumental *The Outlaw Josey Wales* in 1976. The first screenplay draft, by Tom McGuane, was 450 pages long – an epic of some four hours. McQueen knew it had to be cut, but he particularly liked the dialogue, and made sure some of it ended up in the finished film, despite further rewrites.

Don Siegel was set to direct, but grew impatient with Steve because he was unable to articulate what it was he wanted the film to be. Siegel withdrew and Elliot Silverstein came on board, bringing with him Abe Polonsky to write the script. They came up with a story that included a famous episode in Horn's life when he tracked and caught Geronimo. Intimidated or just unwilling to share screen time with such a major character as Geronimo, Steve balked at the idea, as well as at the rather cerebral approach Silverstein and Polonsky had, and so Silverstein departed.

First Artists made it clear that they were only prepared to spend $3 million on *Tom Horn*, so suddenly it was no longer going to be the grand Western Steve envisaged. However, Warner Brothers thought it worth spending a little more on and they brought the budget up to $6 million. Phil Parslow expected Steve to fight for the extra $4 million they needed, but Steve was a tired man and, though he didn't want to admit it, in poor health. All he wanted to do was make the damn film and end his contract with First Artists.

To make sure the film was brought in on schedule, Warners hired producer Fred Weintraub to take over the movie, demoting Phil Parslow to executive producer. Weintraub had the reputation for getting successful action films made on tight budgets, like *Enter the Dragon*. Parslow, who was told all he had to do was sit in his office, quit, having worked for 18 months on pre-production. He felt betrayed by McQueen, but Steve really had no choice in the matter. Only McQueen was billed as executive producer.

Despite the disappointments and the setbacks, Steve felt he could still make a worthy picture. He wanted to explore the essence of Horn, and even spent an entire night at Horn's grave, where he believed he felt the spirit of the man, as though he were saying to him, 'Please tell my story.'

He also sensed his own mortality. Tom Horn had died at 50. Although Steve had once believed he would also die at 50, by this stage of his life he wasn't so willing to accept an early death, and he planned to defy his own prediction, make this film, move on and live in retirement with Barbara for many more years.

A director still had to be found, and one was, in Ketchum, Idaho, of all places, where Steve and Barbara took a short vacation. James William Guercuo, who had only directed one film, *Electra Glide in Blue*, joined them (he later claimed that he had originally pitched the idea of a film about Tom Horn to McQueen), and for some reason Steve gave him the job of directing the picture. Steve was in too much of a hurry to find the right director, and Guercuo came cheap. They worked together on a screenplay made up of one written by Bud Shrake and the original by Tom McGuane.

The screenplay came to 237 pages, which was still too long, making the film over three hours of running time. Weintraub had it cut to 110 pages – the film's final running time was 98 minutes. The whole Geronimo episode was cut, saving time and expense on the hundreds of extras that would have been needed. Weintraub told Steve frankly, 'This is not an epic film.'

Before filming began, Barbara went away on a modelling assignment, and so Steve took the opportunity to visit Neile in Las Vegas, where she was appearing in *Can-Can*. They had remained good friends and occasional lovers. During that visit they made love for the very last time. Then, to Neile's surprise, he asked her if they could actually get back together again. She told him, 'I couldn't put up with you any more.' It was a friendly rebuff, and he took it as such. He said he wondered what it would be like if he, Neile, Barbara and Ali could all live together.

As the start of filming approached, Weintraub insisted that Steve shave off the beard he had kept, and which he intended to use in the movie. Steve agreed only to trim it.

Filming began in January 1979, in Mescal, Arizona. Virtually everything was to be shot on location to maintain a realistic and gritty feel. The day before filming began, Gary Combs, Steve's double and sporting the same style of beard, was asked for his autograph by a fan who thought he was McQueen. Steve turned up the next day sans beard.

What was revealed was a face that was deeply lined and so much older than when it was last seen, in *The Towering Inferno*. The fat Steve had lost from his face left it looking gaunt, and the hard living had taken its toll on his appearance. As Horn, he wore chaps and suspenders (or what the British would call braces). Instead of a gun belt, he simply tucked his gun into his trousers. It was a gritty, unglamorous look, which was actually enhanced by Steve's weather-beaten face.

Conditions were tough on the cast and crew. It was a two-hour ride for most of them to and from the hotel each day. Steve chose to live on location in a trailer. The weather was unpredictable, sometimes hot, sometimes cold. When they filmed in Tucson, it snowed, a rare event for that town.

After three days of filming, Steve fired James William Guercuo after talking it over with the director of photography, John Alonzo, who agreed with Steve that their director knew nothing about the camera. Weintraub had already expressed his misgivings about Guercuo, having talked to the cameraman and first assistant director of *Electra Glide in Blue*.

Steve decided to take over the directing with Weintraub's approval. Despite being the man who kept a tight rein on his budget, Weintraub was very supportive about McQueen directing the picture. Steve felt that if Clint Eastwood could direct *The Outlaw Josey Wales*, he could direct *Tom Horn*. But the Directors' Guild had a rule that an actor or anyone else previously involved in a movie could not take on the role of director (which is odd, because Eastwood took over *The Outlaw Josey Wales* after firing its original director). Weintraub encouraged McQueen to fight the guild, but Steve just wanted to get the picture made and accepted his assistant director Cliff Coleman's suggestion that William Wiard, who had directed a good deal for TV, direct *Tom Horn*. Wiard had never directed a movie before, but an agreement was reached whereby McQueen and John Alonzo would do most of the directing and Wiard would take the credit. However, Wiard did make a contribution too.

Steve worked on the screenplay each day and each night. He became dedicated to making this a film he could be proud of. He also took care of the people he was essentially employing. When he saw a group of extras shivering in the cold, some of them quite elderly, he shut down production until heated tents and thermal underwear arrived for every one of them.

For the scene in which Tom Horn is hanged, stuntman Gary Combs built the gallows. McQueen was apprehensive about this particular stunt, so Combs tried it himself. The noose tore the skin on his neck, so he re-rigged the gallows to make it safe, but when Barbara had a dream that Steve would die doing the scene, Steve declined to do it himself. It was the only time he ever refused to do a stunt. Combs stood in for him, and the shot was safely performed.

Filming ended in late March, by which time Steve had already decided he would make *The Hunter*, which, he told a number of people, including John Alonzo, would be his last movie. He kept privately announcing his retirement after just one more film, and I think that he had really originally intended *Tom Horn* to be the very last picture, but he was aware that it was not going to turn out as he had hoped, and he still wanted to go out in a blaze of glory. His intended final films, *An Enemy of the People* and *Tom Horn*, were not, he felt, the films to bid farewell with.

Steve personally liked *Tom Horn*. 'I think it was different,' he told me in 1980. But it wasn't what the public wanted when the film was released in 1980, by which time Westerns were well and truly out of fashion. Ironically, the film Steve wanted to emulate, *The Outlaw Josey Wales*, was, in 1976, the last really successful Western of that decade – and the genre has still not made a true recovery, although there was Eastwood's masterpiece *Unforgiven* in 1992. *Tom Horn* took just $12 million. It didn't lose money (*An Enemy of the People* was the only Steve McQueen film actually to lose money) but it didn't make a big enough profit to be considered a success (films need to earn around more than twice their cost to make what is considered a realistic profit).

Shortly after *Tom Horn* finished filming, Steve and Barbara drove from Malibu to Santa Paula, a small town 50 miles northwest of Los Angeles. The town had largely remained untouched by modern life, with its groves of orange, lemon and avocado trees, and a population unimpressed by film stars, millionaires or businessmen. Steve was in search of an antique World War Two plane, a Stearman; he had once owned a Stearman, which he couldn't fly himself, but a friend flew it and crashed it. Steve was told that Santa Paula Airport was somewhere he might find what he wanted.

In an open hangar Steve and Barbara saw someone restoring an old Apache aeroplane, and Steve asked the man if he could help find him a Stearman. He was shown a magazine which listed companies that restored old planes and in it he saw what he wanted, a yellow PT-17 Stearman for $35,000. He ordered it and then found a local pilot, Sammy Mason, to teach him to fly. Mason was to change Steve's life radically, just in time for his death.

Steve also bought a hangar to store his plane and, deciding they wanted to live in Santa Paula, Steve and Barbara moved into the hangar while they looked for a suitable home. Into the hangar Steve also moved all his prize possessions – various antiques he had collected over the previous three years, including jukeboxes, slot machines, toys and what was said to be the second largest motorcycle collection – 170 in all – in the world.

'Some people buy art. I don't know art. I know what I know,' Steve said. He bought everything because it was an investment, knowing what he had would never lose value. 'A museum would pay a lot for what I got,' he said. 'But it's all for my kids when I go.'

Steve and Barbara finally moved out of the hangar and into an 1896 four-bedroom ranch with 15 acres, just a few miles from the airport. The place needed a lot of work, but it was, for Steve, the home he had sought since childhood. It was a place like his Uncle Claude had. He was all set for his retirement.

Or, if he knew he was ill, for his final days.

CHAPTER 20

Die to be Reborn

If Steve knew he was ill at that time, he chose to ignore it. He looked forward to the future now that he had the ranch he had dreamed of, and a beautiful young woman he hoped to spend many happy years with.

He settled into an idealic lifestyle, spending nights at his hangar, lighting a campfire outside and chatting to the locals. By now Steve's back hurt a lot of the time from various injuries he'd sustained over the years, so he often just lay down on the concrete and talked to those who came visiting. They were local people, or people who liked to fly. They became his friends. He earned their respect, and he respected them. It was a million miles away from Hollywood.

Steve had made it a policy never to sign autographs and usually nobody asked him, but whenever one of the locals did, he'd say, 'I don't sign autographs, but I'll shake your hand.' He made an exception for children.

When his neighbours, the Endicotts, who had become good friends with Steve and Barbara, found themselves in difficulties, Steve gave a hand. Mr Endicott had to undergo cancer treatment in hospital and his wife wanted to be with him, but they had seven children at home, so Steve volunteered to watch over them. He stayed with them for five days and fed them pizza.

When Mr Endicott, who ran an aircraft maintenance business, became more ill and had to give up work, the people at the airport began a fund so they could still make their house payments. Steve made regular contributions. He was now one of the community. Nobody thought of him as a movie star. He was just one of them. 'That's all I ever wanted,' he told me. He just wanted to belong.

Steve also did something nobody in Hollywood ever thought could happen. He began attending church. He had told me in 1977 he was looking for some kind of spiritual meaning in his life, and he began to find it in Christianity. It sprang from conversations he had with his flight instructor, Sammy Mason, who, Steve noticed, had an air of calm about him. When Steve asked him what it was that made him that way, Mason told him it was because he was a Christian. 'I wanted what he had,' Steve told me, 'so I asked him if I could go to church with him, which pleased Barbara.'

Barbara was pleased because she came from a church-going family and had begun to feel she wanted the church back in her life after giving up her modelling career to be Steve's wife.

'It all fell into place,' said Steve. 'It seems to be by design, all this happening.'

Some have said that Steve only became interested in religion because he was dying. I think he found it because he was looking for it, but it happened at a time when he probably did fear that he was seriously ill, even though, at the time of his conversion, which was not immediate, he hadn't had any tests that revealed he was terminally ill. I think he still feared that he might not make it past the age of 50. Steve always insisted he didn't become religious because he knew he was going to die. But I think he feared it. Fear of dying makes people turn to some kind of God. It's a natural process.

Steve said one thing to me, in 1980, that gave a different and more spiritual interpretation to what he always thought would be his passing at the age of 50. He said, 'You know, when you get baptised, you kind of die, coz you kill the old you and get reborn, and that's what I did.'

When he began going to church, at the Ventura Missionary Church, he didn't get baptised straight away. But he attended every Sunday, always smiling, always happy. From here on people who had known him from way back noticed a change in him. Eli Wallach, who would co-star in *The Hunter*, told me, 'He was not so wild. He was calmer. I got the feeling he was very happy.'

James Coburn said, 'He was happier than he'd ever been, as far as I could see. He said, "You should try it, man. It's a bigger high than weed."'

That summer of 1979 was to be the happiest time of Steve's life. He was content, courteous, gentle – and in a lot of pain. He would be in pain all through *The Hunter*, which was based on the life of modern-day bounty hunter Ralph Thorson. Bounty hunters went after bail jumpers rather than wanted outlaws, as in the old Westerns, such as the series that made McQueen a television star, *Wanted: Dead or Alive*. Thorson was a church minister, an astrologer, and an opera and classical music fan. He preferred to spend hours talking a bail jumper out rather than using force. His friends, and the people he arrested, called him 'Papa' Thorson.

Before filming, Steve met with Thorson and found that they shared many values, especially since both were Christians – or at least, Steve was a fledgling Christian. Steve admired the nobility and honesty in Thorson, and wanted to try to convey those aspects in his portrayal of the man, although he knew that *The Hunter* would have to be an action film with violence. But he was determined that in the movie the violence would never be perpetrated by Thorson, and it would never be gratuitous.

I think Steve had it in mind to compete again with Clint Eastwood, this time in a modern-day crime thriller. But he didn't want to be another Dirty Harry. When I suggested to Steve that he was almost being the opposite to Eastwood's Dirty Harry, he laughed and said, 'They shoulda called me Clean Harry.'

Paramount was eager to have a Steve McQueen action film and agreed to make it, paying him $3 million plus 15 per cent of the gross. The budget was to be $8 million, not a whole lot by the standards of the day, but enough to make a good contemporary crime thriller.

Steve wanted to have some old friends in the movie and, since nobody at Paramount objected, he called Ben Johnson, who had appeared in *Junior Bonner* and *The Getaway*. Johnson told me, 'He said there was a part of this older corrupt sheriff and hoped I'd play it. And then he said, "This is my last movie and I want you in it with me." I thought he was talking about retiring. Now I think maybe he knew he had cancer.'

I don't think he did know, but he must have known something was wrong. He had flu-like symptoms a lot of the time, but he still had not seen a doctor. When I last saw James Coburn, in 1986, he had had time to reflect on Steve's final year, and said, 'Steve was scared to find out what was wrong with him. He just hoped he'd get better. I don't think he knew he had cancer. But he had his religion, and he thought if anything was wrong with him, then maybe God would make him better.'

Steve certainly had no plans to die, just to live, and he and Barbara arranged to have their Santa Paula house remodelled while they were in Chicago for *The Hunter*. It was a 10-week schedule, starting in September, with five weeks in Chicago, one in Kankakee, Illinois, then four at Paramount in Los Angeles. Steve and Barbara were installed at Chicago's Drake Hotel. Their suite had a sauna, Jacuzzi, bar and plush furniture. When Steve discovered that the rest of the cast and crew were staying at the Holiday Inn, he moved himself and Barbara out of their luxury suite and into the Holiday Inn to be with everyone else.

Filming began on 10 September in a tenement block where only a week before someone had been murdered. Moved by the poverty of the people and the tragic crime they affected by all, Steve immediately gave a substantial donation to the local Catholic priest who was trying to improve the plight of his parishioners. He also paid for a hundred baseballs, a hundred mitts, a hundred bats and a hundred footballs, and had them taken to a local field for all the kids in the neighbourhood. He also signed autographs, handing out over two thousand signed 10 x 8-inch portraits.

There was still one element of the old Steve McQueen. He and his director, Peter Hyams, had 'creative differences'. Hyams left the project and McQueen planned to take over the direction. 'That would have been a terrible mistake in his condition,' said Ben Johnson. 'I don't know how good a director he would have been, but he wasn't well enough to direct a big movie, or any kind of movie.'

What stopped Steve from directing *The Hunter* was, once again, the Directors' Guild. Steve accepted Buzz Kulik, who had directed McQueen in television back in the 1950s, as the new director. It was a crucial mistake. Kulik was a very workmanlike director, a craftsman who could get a film made efficiently but not brilliantly. He did his best work in television, and made very few films, none of which were exceptional. In fact, *The Hunter* was his final theatrical movie.

No doubt, with a TV director at the helm, McQueen was able to maintain a degree of control over the filming, but not, apparently, in an aggressive way. Buzz Kulik told me, 'On *The Hunter* Steve was easy to work with. Not like before, when we worked on a TV drama' (the title of which Kulik couldn't remember, and neither did Steve – it was *Four Hours in White*, an episode of *Climax!* in 1958). 'Back then he was a real pain in the ass. He was undisciplined and very insecure and frankly a shit. He was trying too hard to be Marlon Brando and James Dean.

'But when we did *The Hunter* he was very different. He wasn't so driven. He knew what he wanted to do and I don't think any director at that time could have made him do things any better, but I never had a problem with him. He was very lovable, you know . . . a lovable kooky guy. He loved to kid around and make people laugh. I hated him when we first worked together, and loved him when we made *The Hunter*.'

Ben Johnson confirmed that McQueen wasn't a problem for Kulik. 'Steve knew what he wanted to do in the picture, as he always did, and he went about it as he usually did, but in a sort of less aggressive way than I remember him being before. He'd cut dialogue and do everything that was needed to be said [on screen] with just a look. I don't think he was a problem for the director . . . and I don't think he did anything he didn't want to do. That was just Steve McQueen.'

Kulik recalled that a lot of ideas for the film came from Steve, but Steve didn't reject the ideas that Kulik added. Steve was also aware of his failing health, said Kulik. 'I don't know if he thought he was dying then, but he wasn't well. He said, "I can't run any more and we got this long chase scene." I said, "Let's show you getting out of breath and having to take a break," and he loved that idea. It was his idea to send up his image with the cars. As Thorson, he couldn't drive a car properly. You see him trying to park a car, and he's just terrible at it and hitting all the other cars. I said, "When you do it, make it look as though you can't see that there's anything wrong with your driving," and he did it that way. He thought that was fun.

'And the scenes in his house with all those toys and the jukebox. That was all from his aeroplane hangar. All his own stuff. And he loved showing you how his antique toys worked.'

Making *The Hunter* may well have been a happy experience for all concerned, but the film was not destined to be a classic. Part of the problem is that it looks too much like a TV movie, perhaps because of Kulik's style of direction, but also because the film, while packed with action, was, unlike the thrillers of that time, quite tame. The violence often looks as if it's toned down. That was, said Kulik, McQueen's choice. 'He was getting into religion and didn't want to use bad language or have Sam Peckinpah-style violence. He thought it was time for a less violent kind of movie.'

Throughout filming, McQueen was plagued by a cough and shortness of breath, as well as pain in his back. Despite all that he still insisted on doing some of the dangerous stunts. During the long, 15-minute chase scene, he hangs onto the roof of an urban train going 55 miles an hour. He did the close-ups but allowed his stunt double, Loren Janes, to do the more dangerous long shots.

Shortly after Steve died, the debate started as to whether he knew he was dying while making *The Hunter*. Eli Wallach was cast as the bail bonder who often hires the bounty hunter at McQueen's request. He said, 'I didn't see any sign of him being ill. He was a lot *happier* than when we did *The Magnificent Seven*. And when I arrived at the studio and we met for the first time in years, he greeted me like a long-lost brother. He said, "I'm, so glad you're in this movie," and I felt really welcome. He was a lot . . . gentler.'

'Gentle' and 'kind' are the two words which came up a lot when talking to Ben Johnson, Buzz Kulik and Eli Wallach about McQueen on his last movie. When Steve noticed that his leading lady, Kathryn Harrold, needed a new set of tyres on her car, he simply went ahead and changed them.

When he asked a teenage girl who was recruited as an extra what she would spend her extra's fee on, she said it would go to her mother, who was dying from alcohol poisoning. Steve visited the lady in one of the slum areas of Chicago, and when she told Steve that all she wanted was for her daughter to go to school and escape from the slums, he promised that she would be taken care of.

Later, after *The Hunter* wrapped, Steve and Barbara took the girl back to Santa Paula with them and paid for her to attend a nearby private boarding school. At weekends she stayed with them. It was just one of many examples of McQueen's generosity that never received publicity. 'He had plenty of money,' said James Coburn, 'and he wanted to spend it on good causes, especially when it was about kids or young people. You couldn't get him to buy you a coffee, but he'd spend a fortune on a school or sports centre.'

In 1970, when Steve was making sure I would stay on the straight and narrow, he said, 'I think our young people are what's most important in the world. They're like . . . our tomorrow. Every kid deserves a chance.'

Despite his policy of not giving interviews (he hadn't done an interview of any kind in eight years), when filming took place at Alexander Hamilton High School in Los Angeles, Steve surprised everyone – especially the unit publicist, who had *Time* and *Newsweek* begging for an interview with McQueen – by agreeing to do an interview for a boy who was a reporter on that school's newspaper, *The Federalist*. It was the last published interview Steve McQueen did.

After returning to Santa Paula in November 1979, Steve finally saw a local doctor about his cough. An X-ray was taken which revealed a spot on his right lung. He was checked into the Cedars-Sinai Hospital in Los Angeles on 17 December 1979, where a new set of X-rays revealed that Steve had a massive tumour on his right lung. On 22 December, he underwent immediate exploratory surgery, which revealed that he was suffering from a very rare and terminal cancer called mesothelioma. It was in his lung and along the lining of his stomach, as well as in his neck. To that date there had only been 24 cases of mesothelioma and all had died.

This kind of cancer is usually associated with asbestos inhalation. Steve had been around asbestos much of his life. The ship he joined when in the merchant marines was a type where the ceilings were lined with asbestos. As a motorcar racer, he had often worn flameproof uniforms treated with asbestos. In addition, he wore asbestos-treated rags to cover his nose and mouth under his helmet.

He was also, and had always been, a heavy smoker. He told me in 1970, as we puffed our way through God knows how many cigarettes during a night's discussion, 'These things'll kill us. John Wayne told me to quit. He had the Big C – that's what he called it. He said smoking a hundred cigarettes a day gave it to him. We're probably getting it right now.' I stopped smoking for the next week. He didn't.

Steve chose to keep the news that he had mesothelioma from Chad and Terry because he didn't want them worrying. He told almost everyone that a rare fungal infection had been found on one of his lungs but that it wasn't serious. That was also the story he released to the press. He told only a few friends what the real problem was, and he assured them all that he was going to beat it.

There was a macho side to Steve's deception. He simply didn't want everyone knowing he had cancer, as if it were some kind of weakness. At least, that was his initial reaction. Later he recalled that John Wayne had immediately announced to the world that he had cancer when he was treated for it in 1964. He told me on the telephone in 1980 – because I reminded him what he had said in 1970 about John Wayne having cancer – that he now realised having cancer wasn't a weakness. Steve said it gave him strength. And he wasn't just referring to the strength of his spirit. During his last months of life, he was to tolerate unbearable pain, going without pain relief for much of the time because of questionable treatment he was undergoing.

Probably the biggest reason Steve kept his illness a secret was because he had trouble accepting it himself, which is what most people go through when they are told they have a terminal disease. They all ask themselves, 'Why me?'

Steve remained in hospital over Christmas 1979, and was discharged on 29 December. He returned to his ranch at Santa Paula and announced to the few friends who knew the truth, 'I've done my last film.'

He had a tremendous will to fight the disease. Steve's belief in God helped him. If he had turned to God for fear of dying, even before he knew he had cancer, his faith strengthened his resolve to overcome his death sentence.

Steve's announcement that he had made his last film shouldn't have come as a surprise to anyone, regardless of his cancer, as he had always intended to retire and live out the rest of his days on his ranch in peace and solitude. He rejected his agent's suggestion that he read the scripts still coming in, but instead he looked to a future and made plans that had nothing to do with making movies. He would just live the life of a rancher, with lots of animals, cars and aeroplanes around him. Steve told me he planned to tell people that he had been 'saved by the Lord Jesus', which he felt was an important mission for him regardless of whether he lived or died. He was going to help others, especially young people.

Steve had been recommended to have a series of chemotherapy treatments. He turned up for his first one and was told by the nurse that he had to stay completely still because if the chemicals in the chemo got on his skin it would burn and blister. He told her, 'If it does that to the outside of my body, what will it do to the inside?' She didn't answer, and he said, 'Forget it,' and left.

The plans he had been making were set in motion almost immediately. The first thing he had to do was marry Barbara. They had been together now for three years, and he knew that the church considered that they were 'living in sin'. He would probably have married her anyway, but it speeded things up. Steve didn't want to live in sin. He told me, 'I'm trying to be a good Christian.'

In 1977 he had told me, 'I've looked at a lot of religions and seen that they are on the make. They're a lot of scams. Eastern, Western, Christian, whatever – I've not been convinced by them. I've put some of their thoughts and ideals into my life for a time now and then, and found nothing at the end of it. I'd like to find something that's true . . . but I'll probably die with no reason to have anyone pray over me.'

Apart from worrying about his mortal soul, Steve also had a sincere desire to make sure Barbara was taken care of if he died, which is another reason he made her the third Mrs McQueen. (Steve never talked about 'when' he would die, but 'if' he died.) He hoped the pastor of his local church, Leonard DeWitt, would marry them, but DeWitt said he couldn't marry a divorced person. He did, however, recommend another pastor, Dr Leslie Miller, who would. Dr Miller agreed to marry them provided they both took Bible study lessons on marriage and living a Christian life. The couple agreed and started on a short but intense period of study.

On 16 January 1980, Steve and Barbara were married in a simple ceremony in the living room of their ranch house. He wore tennis shoes, jeans and a long-sleeved shirt. Barbara wore a white trouser suit. The only others present were Steve's flying instructor, Sammy Mason, and his wife.

Steve returned to Cedars-Sinai in February for further tests. X-rays revealed the cancer was spreading and he was given little more than two months to live. He remained determined to fight on.

A couple of weeks later Steve went into the café at the Santa Paula airport, where a young man engaged him in conversation. Steve invited the young man to see his planes and motorcycle collection at the hangar, where they were met by Barbara. The young man asked if he could take photos for his art class in college, and Steve being Steve, happily gave him permission.

A few weeks later, in March 1980, those photos appeared in the *National Enquirer* along with a story, 'STEVE MCQUEEN'S HEROIC BATTLE AGAINST CANCER'. The young photographer had been a plant. It turned out that one of the nurse's aides at Cedars-Sinai and her boyfriend broke the news of his cancer to the *National Enquirer*.

The article revealed that McQueen had 'a vicious and inoperable lung cancer' that was killing him. It stated, 'The end could come within two months,' and added that 'the steely-eyed screen hero is battling back bravely'.

The article stunned friends who had no idea Steve had cancer, but he continued to deny the reports, even to Bud Ekins.

At the premiere of *Tom Horn* on 28 March at Grauman's Chinese Theater in Los Angeles, Steve and Barbara arrived in his pickup truck just minutes before the show. Hundreds of people lined the streets. This was McQueen's chance to show he was alive and well. To reporters who asked if he had lung cancer, he replied, 'Whatever you've heard is ridiculous, just rumours. Do I look like I have lung cancer?'

There were still hundreds of fans waiting when the film ended. Steve and Barbara came out of the theatre, barely making it to the truck as the crowd surged forward. He put his foot down on the throttle and almost ran down one dogged photographer determined to get a head-on photograph. They made it back to the ranch, where, exhausted, Steve remained in solitude for the next week.

Much of his time was taken up with browsing through health magazines, searching for any kind of cure. He contacted an unlicensed doctor who had advertised his cure for cancer: several weeks of intravenous feeding, large quantities of vitamins and a special diet. Steve received his treatment in a mobile home because the doctor could not carry out his treatment legally in his office. When Steve returned to Cedars-Sinai he was told his cancer was still advancing. He gave up on that treatment.

Then he came across an article in the *Journal of the Nutritional Academy* about Dr William Donald Kelley, who treated cancer with a programme, devised on a computer, that worked out a diet, nutritional supplements and detoxification which, the doctor claimed, built up a patient's immune system and overall health.

Dr Kelley claimed to have been struck by cancer of the liver and pancreas in 1965, had experimented with large doses of nutritional liver and pancreatic enzymes, as well as coffee enemas, and thus cured himself. He even wrote a book, *One Answer to Cancer*, in 1969, which detailed his cure.

In 1976 he had his dentistry licence suspended for five years after a number of his patients complained that he was more interested in their general health than their teeth. Also that year a court injunction temporarily stopped publication of his book. He was investigated by at least 15 government agencies, including the FBI, the Internal Revenue Service, and the Food and Drug Administration.

This man was an outsider, a maverick, and he hadn't given up practising what he believed. He was Steve's kind of man. Besides, McQueen was desperate to try anything. He met with Kelley at the doctor's organic farm in Winthrop, Washington, and was impressed enough to promise that he would begin the programme that Dr Kelley outlined for him with a 'body-cleansing diet', but no more than that – not until he felt more confident about the rest of the programme.

Knowing it was time to build bridges, Steve began contacting people he had fallen out with, including Mario Iscovich, by then a successful screenwriter (and later a successful producer), who was invited for lunch at the Santa Paula ranch. McQueen admitted that he was probably going to die, and asked, 'Is everything all right between you and me?'

Iscovich replied, 'I was mad only for a little bit.'

They hugged each other – Steve never usually hugged anyone – and Iscovich left, never to see Steve again.

McQueen also did something I only discovered because Yul Brynner told me when I interviewed him a couple of times when he was in London in 1980. Steve telephoned Brynner in London and said, 'Yul, I want to thank you.'

'Never mind the thanks,' replied Brynner. 'What's this about you having cancer?'

'It's gonna get me, Yul. But let me thank you.'

'What did I do?'

'You let me be by your side in the *Seven* movie, and you coulda had me kicked off when I rattled you, but you let me stay and that picture made me, so thanks.'

When I was at Brynner's house one Sunday towards the end of Steve's life, I spoke to Steve on Brynner's phone, and he told me, 'Yeah, I had to make it up with Yul coz without him I wouldn't have been in that picture.'

During Steve's phone call to Brynner, they talked and laughed about their fights, about Steve's constant attempts to upstage Brynner, and how Yul had always tried to have the biggest and best of everything. Yul told Steve, as he told me, 'When you begin your career playing kings, you never stop. I played the part until I *was* the king of wherever I was. I *am* the king.' To Steve he added, 'I am the king . . . and you are the rebel prince . . . every bit as royal . . . and dangerous to cross.'

Steve had liked that.

Brynner told Steve, 'Don't give in. Don't let it beat you.'

Just five years later, Brynner, after being diagnosed with lung cancer in 1983 and given months to live, gave up his own battle.

Steve also called Pat Johnson, whom he hadn't seen since their bust-up when making *Le Mans*. People who hadn't heard from him in years were getting messages suddenly. He didn't let all of them know he had terminal cancer. The people who had been his friends for years, like Don Gordon and James Coburn, were kept from the truth.

Richard Attenborough was another old friend who was invited to meet him. 'I was in Hollywood for a few days,' Attenborough told me, 'and he found out I was there and we agreed to meet at the Brown Derby. It's a place with this long corridor leading to the bar, and when I got there, I looked down the corridor to the bar and there was just one guy in there, and he had this heavy beard.'

I thought, "Typical McQueen, always late." Five minutes went by, then 10, then 15. So I went into the bar to ask the bartender if Steve might have left a message, and this guy with the beard said to me, "Hi, stranger," and, my God! It was Steve! He greeted me with a big bear hug, which he'd never done before. That was his way of saying goodbye.

'We didn't talk about his cancer. He didn't mention it. I wasn't going to ask. We just talked about old times, and we laughed. I was very moved, because I had heard the rumours, but he didn't say anything about it.'

Other friends were contacted for private farewells. Stuntman Loren Janes, one of the few friends McQueen had told about his cancer, met him for lunch under the wing of McQueen's plane at Sand Airport. They talked until the sun set, then said goodbye, and Steve got in his plane and flew away.

Don Gordon was invited for dinner at the ranch. 'After we ate, I walked with Steve to his hangar – just the two of us,' Gordon told me when I met him in London in 1980. At that time, Gordon didn't know Steve had cancer and so he was just telling me about their friendship and about the way they parted before Gordon left for London. 'He's a wonderful friend,' he said. 'I told him when I get back we'll go flying.'

A few months later, after Steve died, Don Gordon again recalled that farewell, but this time with the knowledge that he never saw Steve again after that. 'Before I left for London, we had time – just the two of us, and then he hugged me. I had no idea he was so sick. He never said he was dying to me. I don't know why he never told me. But he was saying goodbye to me.'

James Coburn didn't hear from Steve but had read the story in the *National Enquirer*. He contacted Neile. 'She was sworn to secrecy and kept her word to Steve,' Coburn said. 'She told me he was fine, but I knew she'd cover up for him if he'd asked her to, so I did some checking up of my own – asking around, talking to other friends, speaking to a few people I knew who worked for some of the trade press. Ask the right questions in the right places and you can get answers, and sure enough, I found out he had terminal lung cancer. When you learn something like that about a friend, you feel like you have to do *something*, but there was nothing I could do. I tried calling Steve but he wasn't taking calls. I talked to some of our other buddies, like Jim Garner, but nobody was getting through.'

Suddenly Steve was cutting himself off from everyone. He had made peace with those he had fallen out with. He was pushing away those who had remained friends for many years because he couldn't bear them to see him deteriorating. Now he prepared himself for whatever was to come.

CHAPTER 21

A Fight to the End

Steve and Barbara had not had a honeymoon, so they finally set off on one – a cruise on the *Pacific Princess* to Acapulco in April 1980. He was so short of breath that for most of the voyage he remained in his cabin. As they were disembarking, a photographer snapped a picture of him which turned up in the tabloids; he looked thin and exhausted.

They were driven to a private villa at a luxurious hotel and remained in seclusion for their stay. The honeymoon was an ordeal for Steve, and when he got back home he called Dr Kelley and made plans to be treated in the doctor's new clinic at the Plaza Santa Maria in Mexico.

Before McQueen left for Mexico, he arranged for a special lunch in a room at Ma Maison. Suzanne Pleshette was among the guests, which even included one or two reporters. 'I asked him how he was,' she told me, 'and he gave me the thumbs-up sign, so I said, "Really, how are you?" and he smiled that same smile and gave me two thumbs up. He was putting on a brave show but I didn't know it, and neither did anyone else. He was putting on the performance of his career, showing everyone that he was well. He gave the impression he would be making a new movie. When I got to talk to him, he only asked me how I was, and if Tommy [her new husband] was treating me right, and he was still my big brother and I was his kid sister, and he was taking care of me.'

Hilly Elkins, who hadn't heard from Steve in years, was also at that lunch, but a few days later he met privately with Steve. Elkins knew he was dying when it came time for them to say goodbye, because Steve hugged him.

As his condition deteriorated, Steve requested that Sammy Mason take him flying one last time, but Steve didn't show up at the hangar, too weak even to make the attempt.

The Hunter premiered on 28 July 1980 to an underwhelming response from the critics. Most of them laid into Steve's physical deterioration. The *Los Angeles Herald Examiner* noted McQueen's 'once crisp physical reflexes look shot', while the *Village Voice* called him 'a tired daredevil' who was 'all used up'. Rona Barrett on the *Good Morning America* show, however, called the picture 'a riveting new film' and a 'smashing adventure-yarn coloured with marvellously quirky humour'.

When viewed 30 years later alongside *The Great Escape* and *Bullitt*, it now seems a better film than in 1980, mainly because it's hugely enjoyable to watch Steve McQueen doing a spoof of Steve McQueen, who, in the picture, is unable to drive a car properly, unable to fight and unable to run fast and far.

Variety wasn't at all impressed with the Steve McQueen spoofing, saying that his characterisation 'has made for an annoyingly unrealised and childish onscreen character. Steve McQueen may have felt that the time had come to revise his persona a bit, but what's involved here is decoration.'

And the public were having none of that. They stayed away from McQueen's final movie.

On 30 July 1980, Steve checked into Cedars-Sinai with shortness of breath, chronic headaches, searing back pain and a virtual loss of appetite. X-rays revealed that his cancer was getting worse. Doctors told Barbara that it was inoperable and she should take him home and keep him sedated. She was to return him to the hospital when the pain became too much so they could keep him as comfortable as possible with morphine until, hopefully, he simply died in his sleep.

But McQueen refused to give up. 'I don't believe that bullshit,' he told Barbara. He called Dr Kelley and made final plans to be admitted to his clinic, and on 31 July 1980, Steve drove himself and Barbara into Mexico, to the seaside town of Rosarito, and into the Plaza Santa Maria, a health spa leased by Dr Kelley, who had set up his practice there in April that year.

He was introduced by Dr Kelly to his associates Dr Dwight McKee, hospital director Bill Evans and Steve's metabolic technician, Teena Valentino. After a full check-up by Dr McKee, a needle was inserted and attached to a tap which drew off 1,100 cc of fluid, which almost filled Steve's lungs and abdominal cavity, and he was given Demerol to ease his back pain.

About a week after Steve arrived in Mexico, Dr Kelley called a press conference and announced that McQueen was his patient. He revealed that his 'non-specific metabolic therapy' involved a computerised diet, nutritional supplements and 'detoxification' by coffee enemas and fasting.

'There are no recoveries from Steve's form of cancer in the medical literature,' Dr Kelley announced. 'If he recovers, we'll be breaking new ground.'

Steve stuck to the strict regimen for a month but then began calling on friends to sneak in some of his favourite foods, like cakes, pies, pork chops, sweets and ice cream. He only took a single bite from each, just to enjoy the flavour, telling his metabolic technician, Teena Valentino, that this was about the only pleasure he had left in life.

He also had brought to him some items from home to lift his spirits – a flying helmet and goggles, a pair of binoculars, and photos of his planes. By this time Steve was so weak that he could only manage to sit up in bed for about 20 minutes. His doctors advised that Steve not return to Santa Paula – if he lived – because the pesticides used there would affect him. Barbara suggested they move to Ketchum, Idaho.

On 26 September, Neile, Chad and Terry visited him. Steve told Neile he wanted to hold a press conference to promote Dr Kelley and the Plaza Santa Maria. Ever his confidante and adviser, she begged him to hold off on the press conference until he was well, and not to allow anyone to take photographs of him; he had become thin with a bloated belly. Neile felt that the whole set-up was a farce and the clinic was trying to cash in on Steve's name, but she didn't tell him that. After just 35 minutes, he was so exhausted that she and the children had to leave.

The next day, 27 September, Steve's lawyer, Ken Ziffren, and business manager, Bill Maher, arrived so he could make his last will and testament. Two days after that, Steve called press agent Warren Cowan to release a statement to the press announcing he had cancer. Part of the statement read, 'The reason why I denied that I had cancer was to save my family and friends from personal hurt and to retain my sense of dignity, as, for sure, I thought I was going to die.'

On 2 October, there was good news from the doctors, who announced to Steve that his tumours were shrinking. The following day his press statement hit the headlines. Dr Kelley then issued his own press statement: 'We have been able to prolong the patient's life beyond earlier doctors' expectations. I believe that Mr McQueen can fully recover and return to a normal lifestyle.'

Two days later, on 5 October, Steve gave permission to a Mexican news station to interview him. The next day, Barbara released her own statement from Mexico to the press:

> Steve's great wish is that the United States would allow the medical treatment he is undergoing in this country so we could go home and Steve could continue his program among the people and surroundings he loves. He has asked me to tell you, 'My body may be broken but my heart and spirit are not.' He wants to thank the thousands of people who have sent their good thoughts and prayers, and hopes they will keep them coming.

The same day an audio-taped message was released to the press, radio and television:

> To the President of Mexico, and to the people of Mexico. Congratulations to your wonderful country on the magnificent

work that the Mexican doctors, assisted by the American doctors, are doing at the Plaza Santa Maria hospital in helping my recovery from cancer. Mexico is showing the world this new way of fighting cancer through non-specific metabolic therapy. Again, congratulations – and thank you for saving my life. God bless you all. Steve McQueen.

To his fans and friends, Steve said, 'Keep your fingers crossed and keep the good thoughts coming. All my love, and God bless you.'

Scores of reporters converged on the Plaza Santa Maria hospital, while photographers tried to get pictures of Steve with telephoto lenses from the nearby hills. Steve had managed to sneak out with Barbara, Teena Valentino and her husband, Jack, and retreated for a short stay in Tijuana on 10 October. They stayed just a few days while X-rays were done – there were no X-ray facilities at Dr Kelley's clinic – and then returned to the Plaza Santa Maria, where Steve was overwhelmed to find thousands of letters and messages from fans and well-wishers.

Don Gordon, in London to film the *Omen III: The Final Conflict*, read in the newspapers that Steve had cancer and was being treated in Mexico. Horrified and alarmed, he called Neile and suggested they get him out of Mexico and away from 'the quack doctors', as he called them. He even suggested kidnapping him. 'I was serious,' he told me. 'I wanted to get in there with a pal of mine who has a helicopter. But Neile wouldn't have it. I would have done it too. He needed a better chance than they gave him. Coffee enemas? Fuck them!'

Some friends, like James Coburn, approved of Steve's choice. He told me, 'Who is to say Steve made the wrong choice? The doctors and the American Medical Association say he made the wrong choice. They don't believe in alternative therapy, but I believe they make a profit out of disease and suffering, and the alternative therapies are something the American Medical Association can't make money from.' Later, Coburn would suffer from extremely painful rheumatoid arthritis, and he found relief in his last years from alternative therapy.

'If you believe in something hard enough, you can overcome all kinds of things,' said Coburn. 'The doctors in LA gave him two months. The doctors in Mexico gave him a lot more. Maybe their treatment didn't do anything, but Steve's *belief* in it did. When you are told you are going to die, you have only two options. You either lie down and die, or you fight it. Steve fought to the end.'

While Don Gordon felt helpless and distanced, Steve's spirits and hopes were high. He made plans to move with Barbara to Ketchum; he wanted to open a museum there for all his antique possessions where he would sit around a pot-bellied stove and talk to the old-timers. He was ready for real retirement.

Steve was in terrible pain, but presumably because it went against the regimen that had been prescribed for him, he was denied pain relief. His pain was often so unbearable that he took it out on Barbara, who, patient and understanding, allowed him to rant, after which he always apologised. Finally, unable to bear the pain any longer, he had a friend smuggle in strong painkillers and took three in one go.

Despite the doctors' optimism, the pain got even worse and Steve grew weaker. It was obvious to his few friends allowed to visit that he was declining. He told the doctors he wanted to go home and, against their recommendations, he drove himself and Barbara back to Cedars-Sinai on 24 October for X-rays, which revealed he had a massive tumour in the lining of his stomach. It wasn't shrinking but growing. He asked if they would cut it out, and they told him that, in his weakened condition, if they did that, his heart would give out and he would die. Then he and Barbara returned home to Santa Paula.

Steve had lost more weight, his abdomen was extended and he was in constant pain. His .45 automatic remained at his bedside, ready to use on himself if he could bear it no longer. He had told me, 'I thought about using my .45. And flying my plane and crashing it.'

He had a visit from Neile, Chad and Terry on 2 November. Barbara took Chad and Terry to town to allow Neile some private time with Steve, who talked about her and the kids joining him and Barbara for Christmas. Then he told her, 'Sorry I couldn't keep my pecker in my pants, baby.' Then he fell asleep. It was the last time she saw him.

Steve was informed by his doctors in Mexico that he could undergo an operation to remove the tumour at the Santa Rosa Clinic in Juarez, Mexico. Dr Kelley and his associates believed the operation would give him a 50 per cent chance of surviving the surgery. The doctors at Cedars-Sinai had given him virtually no chance at all.

The Reverend Billy Graham had heard about Steve's conversion and, while Steve was at Plaza Santa Maria, had expressed a wish to meet him. McQueen now requested Dr Graham to visit, and he arrived on 3 November. Steve was unable to get out of bed. Dr Graham read several passages from the Bible and prayed with him. They were interrupted only when a nurse came to give Steve his shots to try and relieve the unending and wearying pain. Steve asked about the afterlife, and Dr Graham reassured him about everlasting life in heaven.

At the end of the meeting, Steve told Dr Graham that he was going straight to Mexico for his operation. He was wheelchaired to a van waiting to take him to Ventura Airport where a private jet would fly him to El Paso, Texas, before crossing the border into Mexico. Dr Graham went with him in the van and gave him his Bible and inscribed it for him. When they got to the waiting jet, Steve said to Dr Graham, 'I'll see you in heaven.'

Accompanied by Barbara, Chad and Terry, as well as Teena Valentino, now a trusted friend, Steve was flown to El Paso, where, at the Eastwood Medical Center, he had a CAT scan, which revealed multiple masses in his thorax, lungs, abdomen and pelvis. The main tumour in his stomach was so big that it gave him the appearance of being six months pregnant. If that tumour was removed, he hoped he would have a chance at life, and a nice flat stomach once more.

On 5 November, Steve and Barbara crossed the border and arrived at the Santa Rosa Clinic in Juarez. His blood levels were tested and it was decided by his surgeon, Dr Santos Vargas, that the operation should take place the next day.

On 6 November Steve was prepped, bathed and given an enema, then put on a gurney and taken to theatre. En route, he handed his Bible and watch to Teena. Then he was wheeled into the operating room. Barbara had come from the Las Fuentes Motel, where she was staying with Chad and Terry, hoping to see Steve before the operation, but she arrived too late.

The operation took six hours. When he woke up at around three in the afternoon, his first words were, 'Is my stomach flat now?' He was assured it was.

He was kept heavily sedated and was watched over by Dr Dwight McKee. When he woke again he found Barbara at his side and, although he was very groggy, they talked about their future, convinced he had beaten cancer. His doctors and nurses were so optimistic about his vital signs and his chance of recovery that they had the heart monitor removed from the room.

That evening Chad and Terry were able to visit him along with Barbara, although he was only barely conscious. When they decided they should let him rest, Teena Valentino stirred Steve to tell him, 'Barbara and the kids want to say goodnight.' He waved to them as they left his room. Then he asked Teena for ice cubes. He had been asking for them all day. Teena had heard patients ask for ice cubes at the Plaza, usually before they died.

While Steve slept under heavy sedation, a blood clot slipped into his heart at 3.45am on 7 November 1980. Five minutes later he was dead. There was nothing the doctors could do to save him from the embolism that caused his fatal cardiac arrest.

Dr McKee called Barbara at the motel and broke the sad news. When Terry, in the next room, saw Barbara's face, she knew immediately her father had died. Chad refused to believe it and, insisting he see his father, was allowed to stay alone in Steve's room for a while. The Bible which Dr Billy Graham had given to him was on his chest, opened at Steve's favourite verse, John 3:16: 'For God so loved the world, that he gave his only begotten Son, that whosoever believes in him shall not perish, but have everlasting life.'

Chad later recalled that his dad's eyes, which had become grey in recent weeks, had returned to being blue in death, and there was a smile on his face. Chad closed his dad's eyes, kissed his forehead and said, 'So long, Pop. I love you.'

Steve's body was moved to the Prado Funeral Home in Juarez and prepared. Somehow a photographer from *Paris Match* magazine managed to get in and take a photo of him. It appeared on the front cover of the magazine, and also on the front page of the *New York Post*. Ali MacGraw publicly expressed her anger over the photograph on the TV show *Entertainment Tonight*. She said, 'The hurt is monumental, to be raped that way.'

From the Prado Funeral Home, Steve's casket was flown back to Ventura in a private Learjet, from where it was driven to a mortuary for a cremation.

A private memorial service was held at Steve's Santa Paula home on 9 November, by the pond at the back of the ranch. Barbara and Neile invited just a few friends, including Ali MacGraw. Young actor LeVar Burton, who co-starred in *The Hunter*, was among the guests, as was Sammy Mason the pilot, and Steve's long-time motorcycle-riding buddy Bud Ekins. And of course, Chad and Terry.

Pastor Leonard DeWitt conducted the service, reading John 3:16 and giving a closing prayer. Then seven planes flew over in the 'missing man' formation, one of them carrying Steve's ashes to be scattered over the Pacific Ocean.

Steve, who had once been a kid starving on the streets and turning to crime to survive, died leaving an estate worth around $12 million. He left $3 million to each of his children. Barbara received $1 million. The Boys Republic received $200,000. The ranch was left to Chad, and Bud Ekins was allowed to pick out the best bikes from Steve's collection. Sammy Mason was left a classic Pitcairn Mailwing plane.

All of Steve's other possessions – the huge collection of motorbikes, 55 cars and everything from toys to telephones – were left to Terry and Chad, who eventually decided to auction off everything because of the constant care needed as well as the insurance. In November 1984 it was all sold at auction at the

Imperial Palace Hotel, netting over $2 million for Terry and Chad.

It almost sounds too corny to say that Steve McQueen died in peace when he had, in fact, spent months in agonising pain, but he was certainly *at* peace – with himself, with his God, and, I think, with his past, which he had been trying to run from all his life. He had run long and hard and far, always on the edge, pushing himself and all around him to go to the precipice. He was someone who charmed people and infuriated them, frustrating friends and colleagues, and yet usually winning them over with what was so often called a childlike charm.

Steve wanted to be rich – he achieved that. But he was still the last person to pick up the bill, even though he spent vast amounts on his much-prized possessions, which he always intended to be displayed in a museum. He wanted to be considered a film-maker and not just an actor – he achieved that, although, to be frank, he was never a *successful* film-maker. His best movies were the ones he was not in control of. And yet Steve was somehow always in control of what he did in those movies. He knew how to move, how to give a subtle look that could express more than three pages of dialogue, and nearly always how to steal the attention of the audience from any other actor on screen with him.

Steve was a really fine screen actor. I think, in the end, that's the best that can and should be said about him.

For a long time after he died, Steve's friends debated whether or not he would have survived had it not been for the embolism. Some say he died from cardiac arrest and not from cancer. But all that matters is that he died when he was ready to die. Which leads to another debate: whether he really was a Christian or just someone in need of something to help him believe that there has to be more to death than just a hole in the ground, or ashes washed away in the ocean. For some years Steve had, he told me, been seeking something to give him peace and a kind of spirituality in his life. He insisted he didn't turn to God only because he knew he was ill, but whether he did or didn't, his belief in God was with him when he needed it, and that's all that matters, especially to a man who almost dared fate by taking himself to the limits of danger, morality and even sanity.

Steve McQueen did live close to the edge and plummeted into the abyss in 1970, but he survived, climbed back up and changed his life. That's how it was for him, living on the edge – and, hopefully, dying in grace.

Filmography

Somebody Up There Likes Me (MGM) *d* Robert Wise, *p* Charles Schnee, *s* Ernest Lehman (from the autobiography of Rocky Graziano), *ph* Joseph Ruttenberg, *lp* Paul Newman, Pier Angeli, Everett Sloane, Eileen Heckart, Sal Mineo, Harold J. Stone (Steve McQueen unbilled as Fido). 1956

Never Love a Stranger (Allied Artists) *d* Robert Stevens, *p* Harold Robbins and Richard Day, *s* Harold Robbins and Richard Day, *ph* Lee Garmes, *lp* John Drew Barrymore, Lita Milan, Robert Bray, Steve McQueen, Salem Ludwig, R. G. Armstrong. 1958

The Blob (Paramount/Tonylyn) *d* Irvin S. Yeaworth, *p* Jack H. Harris, *s* Theodore Simonson and Kate Phillips, *ph* Thomas Spalding, *lp* Steve McQueen, Aneta Corsaut, Earl Rowe, Olin Howlin, Steven Chase, John Benson. 1958

The Great St. Louis Bank Robbery (United Artists) *d* Charles Guggenheim and John Stix, *p* Charles Guggenheim, *s* Richard T. Heffron, *ph* Victor Duncan, *lp* Steve McQueen, David Clarke, Crahan Denton, Molly McCarthy, James Dukas. 1959

Never So Few (MGM/Canterbury Productions) *d* John Sturges, *p*

Edmund Grainger, *s* Millard Kaufman (from the novel by Tom T. Chamales), *ph* William H. Daniels, *lp* Frank Sinatra, Gina Lollobrigida, Peter Lawford, Steve McQueen, Richard Johnson, Paul Henreid. 1959

The Magnificent Seven (United Artists/Mirisch/Alpha) *d* John Sturges, *p* Walter Mirisch, *s* William Roberts (from the original screenplay for *The Seven Samurai*), *ph* Charles Lang Jr, *lp* Yul Brynner, Eli Wallach, Steve McQueen, James Coburn, Charles Bronson, Robert Vaughn, Brad Dexter, Horst Buchholz. 1960

The Honeymoon Machine (MGM/Avon) *d* Richard Thorpe, *p* Lawrence Weingarten, *s* George Wells (from the play *The Golden Fleecing* by Lorenzo Semple Jr), *ph* Joseph LaSahelle, *lp* Steve McQueen, Brigid Bazlen, Jim Hutton, Paula Prentiss, Dean Jagger, Jack Weston. 1961

Hell Is for Heroes (Paramount) *d* Don Siegel, *p* Henry Blanke, *s* Robert Pirosh and Richard Carr, *ph* Harold Lipstein, *lp* Steve McQueen, Bobby Darin, Fess Parker, Nick Adams, Bob Newhart, Harry Guardino, James Coburn. 1962

The War Lover (Columbia) *d* Philip Leacock, *p* Arthur Hornblower Jr, *s* Howard Koch (from the novel by John Hersey), *ph* Bob Huke, *lp* Steve McQueen, Robert Wagner, Shirley Anne Field, Gary Cockrell, Michael Crawford. 1962

The Great Escape (United Artists/Mirisch/Alpha/British Company) *d* & *p* John Sturges, *s* James Clavell and W.R. Burnett (from the book by Paul Brickhill), *ph* Daniel L. Fapp, *lp* Steve McQueen, James Garner, Richard Attenborough, James Donald, Charles Bronson, Donald Pleasence, James Coburn, John Leyton, Gordon Jackson, David McCallum. 1963

Soldier in the Rain (Allied Artists) *d* Ralph Nelson, *p* Martin Jurow, *s* Maurice Richlin and Blake Edwards (from the novel by William Goldman), *ph* Philip Lathrop, *lp* Jackie Gleason, Steve

McQueen, Tuesday Weld, Tony Bill, Tom Poston, Ed Nelson. 1963

Love with the Proper Stranger (Paramount/Boardwalk/Rona) *d* Robert Mulligan, *p* Alan J. Pakula, *s* Arnold Schulman, *ph* Milton Krasner, *lp* Natalie Wood, Steve McQueen, Edie Adams, Herschel Bernardi, Tom Bosley, Harvey Lembeck. 1963

Baby, the Rain Must Fall (Columbia/Park Place/Solar) *d* Robert Mulligan, *p* Alan J. Pakula, *s* Horton Foote (from his play *The Travelling Lady*), *ph* Ernest Laszlo, *lp* Lee Remick, Steve McQueen, Don Murray, Paul Fix, Josephine Hutchinson, Ruth White. 1965

The Cincinnati Kid (MGM/Filmways/Solar) *d* Norman Jewison, *p* Martin Ransohoff, *s* Ring Lardner Jr and Terry Southern (from the novel by Richard Jessup), *ph* Philip Lathrop, *lp* Steve McQueen, Edward G. Robinson, Ann-Margret, Karl Malden, Tuesday Weld, Joan Blondell, Rip Torn, Jack Weston. 1965

Nevada Smith (Paramount/Solar) *d* & *p* Henry Hathaway, *s* John Michael Hayes (based on the character Nevada Smith from the novel *The Carpetbaggers* by Harold Robbins), *ph* Lucien Ballard, *lp* Steve McQueen, Karl Malden, Brian Keith, Suzanne Pleshette, Arthur Kennedy, Janet Margolin, Howard Da Silva, Raf Vallone, Pat Hingle, Martin Landau, Paul Fix. 1966

The Sand Pebbles (20th Century-Fox/Argyle/Solar) *d* & *p* Robert Wise, *s* Richard Anderson (from the novel by Richard McKenna), *ph* Joseph MacDonald, *lp* Steve McQueen, Richard Attenborough, Richard Crenna, Candice Bergen, Marayat Andriane, Mako, Larry Gates. 1966

The Thomas Crown Affair (United Artists/Mirisch/Simkoe/Solar) *d* & *p* Norman Jewison, *s* Alan R. Trustman, *ph* Haskell Wexler, *lp* Steve McQueen, Faye Dunaway, Paul Burke, Jack Weston, Yaphet Kotto. 1968

Bullitt (Warner Brothers/Solar) *d* Peter Yates, *p* Philip D'Antoni, *s* Alan R. Trustman and Harry Kleiner (from the novel *Mute Witness* by Robert L. Pike), *lp* Steve McQueen, Robert Vaughn, Jacqueline Bisset, Don Gordon, Robert Duvall, Simon Oakland, Norman Fell. 1968

The Reivers (National General/Solar/Cinema Center) *d* Mark Rydell, *p* Irving Ravetch, *s* Irving Ravetch and Harriet Frank Jr (from the novel by William Faulkner), *ph* Richard Moore, *lp* Steve McQueen, Sharon Farrell, Will Geer, Rupert Crosse, Mitch Vogel, Clifton James, narrated by Burgess Meredith. 1969

Le Mans (National General/Solar/Cinema Center) *d* & *s* Lee H. Katzin, *p* Jack N. Reddish, *ph* Robert B. Hauser and René Guissart Jr, *lp* Steve McQueen, Siegfried Rauch, Elga Andersen, Ronald Leigh-Hunt, Fred Haltincer, Luc Merenda and 45 Le Mans drivers. 1971

On Any Sunday (Cinema 5/Solar) *d* & *p* Bruce Brown, *ph* Bob Bagley, *lp* Steve McQueen, Mert Lawwill, Malcolm Smith, Gene Romero, Jim Rice, Dick Mann, Whitey Martino. 1971

Junior Bonner (ABC/Cinerama/Solar) *d* Sam Peckinpah, *p* Joe Wizan, *s* Jeb Rosebrook, *ph* Lucien Ballard, *lp* Steve McQueen, Robert Preston, Ida Lupino, Joe Don Baker, Barbara Leigh, Mary Roan, Ben Johnson, Matthew Peckinpah. 1972

The Getaway (National General/First Artists/Solar/Cinerama) *d* Sam Peckinpah, *p* David Foster and Mitchell Brower, *s* Walter Hill (from the novel by Jim Thompson), *ph* Lucien Ballard, *lp* Steve McQueen, Ali MacGraw, Ben Johnson, Sally Struthers, Al Lettieri, Slim Pickens, Richard Bright, Jack Dodson, Dub Taylor, Bo Hopkins. 1972

Papillon (Allied Artists/Columbia/Corona/General Production Company) *d* Franklin J. Schaffner, *p* Robert Dorfmann and Franklin J. Schaffner, *s* Dalton Trumbo and Lorenzo Semple Jr (from the book by Henri Charrière), *lp* Steve McQueen, Dustin Hoffman, Victor Jory, Don Gordon, Anthony Zerbe, Robert Deman, Woodrow Parfrey, Bill Mumy. 1973

The Towering Inferno (20th Century-Fox/Warner Brothers) *d* John Guillermin and Irwin Allen, *p* Irwin Allen, *s* Stirling Silliphant (from the novels *The Tower* by Richard Martin Stern and *The Glass Inferno* by Thomas N. Scortia and Frank Robinson), *ph* Fred Koenekamp, *lp* Steve McQueen, Paul Newman, Faye Dunaway, William Holden, Fred Astaire, Susan Blakely, Richard Chamberlain, Jennifer Jones, O. J. Simpson, Robert Vaughn, Robert Wagner. 1974

An Enemy of the People (Warner Brothers/First Artists/Solar) *d* & *p* George Schaefer (associate producer Steve McQueen), *s* Alexander Jacobs (from the Arthur Miller translation of the Henrik Ibsen play), *ph* Paul Lohmann, *lp* Steve McQueen, Charles Durning, Bibi Andersson, Eric Christmas, Michael Cristofer, Richard Dysart. 1978

Tom Horn (Warner Brothers/Solar/First Artists) *d* William Wiard, *p* Fred Weintraub (executive producer Steve McQueen), *s* Thomas McGuane and Bud Shrake (from *Life of Tom Horn, Government Scout and Interpreter, Written by Himself*), *ph* John Alonzo, *lp* Steve McQueen, Linda Evans, Richard Farnsworth, Billy Green Bush, Slim Pickens, Peter Canon, Elisha Cook Jr. 1980

The Hunter (Paramount/Rastar/Mort Engleberg) *d* Buzz Kulik, *p* Mort Engleberg, *s* Ted Leighton and Peter Hyams (from the book by Christopher Keane), *ph* Fred Koenekamp, *lp* Steve McQueen, Eli Wallach, Kathryn Harrold, LeVar Burton, Ben Johnson, Richard Venture, Tracey Walter, Ralph 'Papa' Thorson (as the bartender). 1980

TV-ography

Girl on the Run (uncredited), 1953

Goodyear Television Playhouse, episode *The Chivington Road*, 1955

The United States Steel Hour, episode *Bring Me a Dream*, 1956

Studio One, episode *The Defender Part 1*, 1957

Studio One, episode *The Defender Part 2*, 1957

West Point, episode *Ambush*, 1957

The 20th Century-Fox Hour, episode *Deep Water*, 1957

Climax!, episode *Four Hours in White*, 1958

Tales of Wells Fargo, episode *Bill Longley* (in title role), 1958

Trackdown, episode *The Brothers & The Bounty Hunter* (as Josh Randall), 1958

Wanted: Dead or Alive (as John Randall in 94 episodes), 1958–61.

Alfred Hitchcock Presents, episode *Human Interest Story*, 1959

Alfred Hitchcock Presents, episode *Man from the South*, 1960

Bibliography

Fine, Marshall, *Bloody Sam: The Life and Films of Sam Peckinpah*, Miramax Books (US), 2005

Finstead, Suzanne, *The Biography of Natalie Wood*, Century (UK), 2001

Lambert, Gavin, *Natalie Wood: A Life*, Faber and Faber (UK), 2004

Lovell, Glenn, *Escape Artist: The Life and Films of John Sturges*, University of Wisconsin Press (US), 2008

MacGraw, Ali, *Moving Pictures*, Bantam Books (US), 1991

Norman, Barry, *The Film Greats*, Futura Publications (UK), 1986

St. Carnez, Casey, *The Complete Films of Steve McQueen*, Citadel Press (US), 1984

Sandford, Christopher, *McQueen*, HarperCollins (UK) 2001

Terrill, Marshall, *Steve McQueen: Portrait of an American Rebel*, Donald I. Fine (US), 1993

Toffel, Neile McQueen, *My Husband, My Friend*, Atheneum (US), 1986

Van Doren, Mamie, *Playing the Field*, Berkley Publishing (US), 1987

Wagner, Robert, *Pieces of My Heart*, Hutchinson (UK), 2009

Index